Computational Lir

LANGUAGE AND COMPUTERS: STUDIES IN PRACTICAL LINGUISTICS

No 37

edited by Jan Aarts and Willem Meijs

Computational Linguistics in the Netherlands 2000

Selected Papers from the Eleventh CLIN Meeting

Edited by

Walter Daelemans
Khalil Sima'an
Jorn Veenstra
Jakub Zavrel

Amsterdam – New York, NY 2001

The paper on which this book is printed meets the requirements of "ISO 9706:1994, Information and documentation - Paper for documents - Requirements for permanence".

ISBN: 90-420-1257-9 (bound)

Printed in The Netherlands

Preface

It was our pleasure to organize the millennium version of the yearly Dutch-Flemish Computational Linguistics in the Netherlands workshop (CLIN 2000) at Tilburg University on November 3, 2000. As in previous years, the interest was overwhelming (with about 35 accepted presentations), and the number of "international" i.e. non-benelux submissions still seems to be growing (reaching almost 50% now). For the proceedings, for which there was a separate call for papers, we received twenty full paper submissions. Thirteen papers passed a reviewing panel consisting of the editors and Paola Monachesi, Michael Moortgat, Gertjan Vannoord, Marc Swerts, Frank Van Eynde, Emiel Krahmer, Steven Gillis, Kristiina Jokinen, Franciska de Jong, Remko Scha, Antal van den Bosch, and Gert Durieux. Many thanks to all authors and reviewers for the hard work they put in to keep the CLIN proceedings a high-quality publication.

Gregory Grefenstette, of the Xerox Research Centre Europe in Grenoble, presented the keynote lecture on *Very Large Lexicons*. We are very grateful to Greg for providing a written version of his inspiring talk for this book.

Unlike previous years, the topics of the accepted papers are widely varying and could not be clustered easily. We therefore chose an alphabetical ordering. We have a historical-philosophical paper (ten Hacken); two papers related to the Spoken Dutch Corpus project (Moortgat and Moot; Hoekstra, Moortgat, Schuurman, and van der Wouden); a few papers using machine learning (Tjong Kim Sang, Van den Bosch, Krahmer, and Swerts); a few on tagging and parsing (Borin and Prütz; Bouma, Vannoord, and Malouf; Kempe); two on applications (Kraaij and Pohlmann, Poibeau and Kosseim); one on generation (Van der Sluis and Krahmer); one on computational phonology (Carson-Berdsen, Joue, and Walsh); and one on formal language theory (Marcus, Martín-Vide, Mitrana, and Păun). Everyone will find something of interest in this book!

Finally, thanks to everyone who helped with the local organization, to our publisher RODOPI and the Language and Computers series editor Jan Aarts, for the smooth cooperation and encouragement, to CLIF (Computational Linguistics in Flanders) for sponsoring the keynote lecture, and to Tilburg University for providing a venue.

Tilburg, July 2001

Walter Daelemans
Khalil Sima'an
Jorn Veenstra
Jakub Zavrel

For more information about the CLIN series of workshops, see
`http://odur.let.rug.nl/ vannoord/clin/clin.html`

Contents

Very Large Lexicons

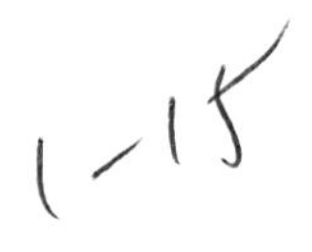

Gregory Grefenstette

Clairvoyance Corp., Pittsburgh, USA

Abstract

Three independent phenomena have appeared over the last fifteen years that make it possible to think about linguistics in a different way. The first is the appearance of the World Wide Web; the second is the development of robust and rapid, though shallow, linguistic analyzers, and the third is the availability of cheap memory. In this chapter, we show how these three phenomena come together in the creation of a new linguistic resource: the Very Large Lexicon.

1 Introduction

Linguists are used to building models of language by hand. But the presence of a large amount of freely available text, coupled with robust parsers for treating it, gives us a new way of looking at language models. We can now consider things on a massive scale. Just as the four-color problem (Tymoczko 1990) was solved using a battery of computers, and as computer scientists are looking once again at brute force methods (Nievergelt, Gasser, Maeser and Wirth 1995), we can imagine treating linguistics problems in the same way. As a tool for such an approach, in this chapter, we sketch the idea of a Very Large Lexicon.

First we describe the existing natural language processing tools that allow a computer to work with text by abstracting away surface differences. Then we discuss how big the Web is and what language model we can extract from it. We examine whether we could store such a model. Finally we outline what would be included in a Very Large Lexicon and describe one possible application of it.

2 Phenomenon One – Natural Language Processing

The computer is a very simple tool. Essentially, it can only test for equality between two sequences of bits. (To be fair, it can also tell if one number is greater or less than another number. But this is really all a computer can do.) In order to exploit the power of the computer for the tasks we want it to perform, we must reduce things to some format that can be exactly compared. We, as humans, have innate abilities to see similarities: given two photos of the same tree from slightly different angles, we could still tell it was the same because we can abstract away differences. In the same way, with respect to text, we can see the three statements in Figure 1 as instances of some concept like "steal painting" although the surface forms of the expressions are different.

In order to make make two different pieces of text look exactly alike to the computer, Computational Linguistics has created a number of models of language that map different strings of text or phonemes into identical forms.

...three paintings were stolen ...

... accused of stealing three paintings

... paintings they were about to steal...

Figure 1: We can abstract away the surface of details to see each of these text segments of variants of "steal a painting"

There are many important applications of this action of abstracting away details. Classification systems (Yang and Pedersen 1997) ignore most of a document in order to reduce it to one of a number of predetermined classes (e.g., medical, financial, etc.). Information retrieval systems (Frakes and Baeza-Yates 1992) abstract away many aspects of a document by indexing words and phrases, reducing the document to a normalized list, so that the computer can match it to a query, reduced to a similar list. Information extraction systems (Robert Gaizauskas 1997) use models of events (such as company mergers) in which things irrelevant to the event are ignored and from which patterns corresponding to the event are recognized. Terminology recognition and control (Jacquemin 1999) uses a model of correct and incorrect terminology and the variations that they can undergo, so that technical text can be more precisely written. Text mining (Ghani, Jones, Mladenic, Nigam and Slattery n.d.) converts running text into abstracted lists and patterns in order to discover recurring patterns and combinations over a number of texts. Translating programs (Hutchins and Somers 1992) use models of grammar that map grammatical structures from one language to another, and models of the lexicon that use limited context to perform proper word choice in the target language.

In order to perform these abstractions, Natural Language Processing (NLP) uses a number of remapping models, either built by hand or derived from statistical analysis that allow the computer to see two different sequences as being the same. Examples of these models are:

- Speech language models (Placeway, Schwartz, Fung and Nguyen 1993): use models of real words in order to map phonetic strings into readings of words.
- Lexicons (Chanod and Tapanainen 1995): map different word forms to the same normalized form. For example *thinks, thinking* and *thought* are mapped to *think (verb).* Stemming (Porter 1980) is sometimes used as a quick-and-dirty lexical normalization.
- Part-of-Speech taggers (Church 1988): use models of known sequences of grammatical categories (given by the lexicons) to choose between possible readings of sentences. Applying these models allows the computer to see abstract categories such as nouns, verbs, and adjectives in the place of real, different words.
- Grammars (Pereira and Warren 1980): use models of part-of-speech groupings that are mapped into higher-level structure, such noun phrases an verb

```
[ ]:LEFTCONTEXT
            token
                [ ]:MIDDLE
                        token
                           relation:[ ]
                                [ ]:RIGHTCONTEXT
```

Figure 2: Shallow parsers sometimes use regular expressions for modeling context and for transducing this recognized context to the empty string (written here as *[]*), while retaining in the output the tokens, and introducing in the output the recognized relation (written here as relation matching the empty string on input *relation:[]*).

phrases, that allow the computer to recognize two different sentences as, for example, being transitive uses of the verb *steal*.

2.1 Robust, Shallow Parsing

Shallow parsers (Grefenstette 1999a) can extract a syntactic dependency between two words by modeling, for example using regular expressions (Karttunen, Chanod, Grefenstette and Schiller 1996), the structure of the syntactic context to the left of the first word (with, for example as seen in Figure 2, a regular expression `LEFTCONTEXT`), between the words (with a regular expression `MIDDLE`), and to the right of the last word (with a regular expression `RIGHTCONTEXT`). None of this context is output (it removed by mapping it to the empty string, `[ ]`) by the transducing filter as the context is recognized. The only items that are output by the filtering transducer are the tokens (the tagged words) that are found surrounded by the contexts, and a relation label inserted after the last token. Schematically this gives the structure in Figure 2.

These models, when applied to text, along with other models of lexical normalization and part of speech tagging, will produce abstracted versions of the syntactic relations that are found. Figure 3 shows how an input sentence is abstracted to a collection of dependency relations between the words in the sentence.

The last twenty years has seen the creation of a large number of shallow, robust parsers (Voutilainen, Heikkila and Anttila 1992, Hindle 1993, Debili 1982, Abney 1991, Ejerhed and Church 1983, Jensen, Heidorn and Richardson 1993, Ait-Mokhtar and Chanod 1997) able to extract syntactic relations quickly from large quantities of texts. Nuria Gala (Pavia 2000) is working on producing a shallow parser whose results can be assured to have a high precision.

3 Phenomenon Two – The World Wide Web

Natural Language Processing now provides us with tools (lexicons, part-of-speech taggers, grammars, parsers) from which we can derive an abstracted model of how language is used. The World Wide Web provides us with the text from which to

36 Helmantel paintings were stolen at this burglary.

[SC [NP 36 Helmantel paintings NP]/SUBJ :v were stolen SC] [PP at this burglary PP] .

ADJ(36,painting)

SUBJPASS(painting,steal)

NN(Helmantel,painting)

VMODOBJ(steal,at,burglary)

Figure 3: Shallow parsers sometimes produce a list of syntactic relations sing their models of these relations. A first pass on part-of-speech tagged text *(part-of-speech tags not shown here)* introduces more structure that is used by the syntactic relations models. Here a model of adjective modifiers produces ADJ, a syntactic relation between *36* and *painting*; Others models: a passive subject model (SUBJPASS), a noun modifier model (NN) and a verb modifier model (VMODOBJ) produce other abstracted versions of the sentence.

extract the models.

Everyone knows that the World Wide Web is huge. In order to give some idea of its size, Figure 4 gives the frequency of some random phrases on the Web and in the largest constructed corpus of English, the British National Corpus (see the URL info.ox.ac.uk/bnc/ for more information on this corpus). For example, we see that the ordinary phrase "deep breath" appears 374 times per 100 million words in the British National Corpus, but appeared in texts indexed by Altavista more than 79,000 times in June of 2001. These numbers show that the WWW is orders of magnitudes larger than this large corpus, and growing.

Lawrence and Giles estimated (Lawrence and Giles 1999) that the publicly indexable web contained about 800 million pages as of February 1999, or about 6 terabytes of text after removing the HTML. In June of 2001, Google's homepage invited its users to search among its 1,346,966,000 web pages.

Using techniques described in (Grefenstette and Nioche 2000), we estimated that Altavista allows access to over 75 billion words of English in March, 2001, and many billions of words of other languages, The complete estimates are shown in Figure 5. Lawrence and Giles calculated that Altavista only indexes about 15% of the web, so the numbers given in Figure 5 must be considered as lower bounds on the amount of text available on the WWW.

The WWW is clearly big, but is it a good place to derive a language model from. It is not as clean as the corpora of newspaper texts that computational linguists are used to working with. Erros can arise from a number of sources: the people using the Internet may be writing their texts in a non-native language; they may be using incorrect speech; they will be making grammatical and spelling errors. How can we propose to derive a model of how language is used from the Web?

To allay these fears, we can make some anecdotal observations. Figures 6 and

sample phrases	BNC 100 M Words	WWW 1999	WWW 2001
medical treatment	202	46064	342155
prostate cancer	28	40772	473210
deep breath	374	54550	79440
acrylic paint	20	7208	22288
perfect balance	28	9735	30077
electromagnetic radiation	24	17297	57421
powerful force	54	17391	32663
concrete pipe	8	3360	16737
upholstery fabric	5	3157	7008

Figure 4: Comparison of the frequency of some random English noun phrases in the British National Corpus and in Altavista in 1999 and in Altavista in 2001

7 show some common grammatical errors in Spanish and Dutch. The Spanish errors are called *dequeismos*, which means to place a spurious *de* between a verb and its following relative clause. The Dutch examples show improper choice of prepositions. Examples are easy to generate for English, also. For example, in June 2001, there were 1692 "I beleave", 41617 "I beleive" but 3,800,810 "I believe." In all these cases the number of correct forms is much greater than the number of erroneous forms. This seems to indicate that the WWW can be a source for modeling language if thresholds are applied. The Web is so big that the signal (correct forms and correct usage) is so strong and noise can be ignored.

4 Phenomenon Three – Disk Space

In the last two sections we have talked about two phenomema: Natural Language Processing and robust parsing, and the WWW and its size. Their conjunction offers promise that we can build a large model of how language is used, and build this for many written languages. But how large will this model be, and will we be able to store it?

First we can begin by deciding which words to model. With the NLP tools we have, we can generate all the surface forms for a language (up to a given character length). WWW browsers (e.g. Altavista, Alltheweb) allows us to rank these surface forms by frequency. So, we can consider the 200,000 most frequent surface forms for a language. Suppose that we want to build a very simple language model consisting of a two dimensional matrix of the relative collocation frequency of one word to another. Suppose that we store this frequency in 4 bytes. This means we need 200,000 by 200,000 by 4 bytes, or 160 gigabytes. (We would actually need much less, since the matrix would be very sparse, and could be stored using a more efficient representation.)

Though such a size for a model may still seem daunting, disk drives are getter bigger and cheaper. In June, 2001, disk space cost about $ 3 per gigabyte. By Moore's Law (Schaller 1997) of computer power doubling every 18 months, and

	Word count estimate
Welsh	14,993,000
Albanian	10,332,000
Breton	12,705,000
Lithuanian	35,426,000
Latvian	39,679,000
Esperanto	57,154,000
Basque	55,340,000
Latin	55,943,000
Estonian	98,066,000
Irish	88,283,000
Icelandic	53,941,000
Roumanian	86,392,000
Croation	136,073,000
Slovenian	119,153,000
Turkish	187,356,000
Malay	157,241,000
Catalan	203,592,000
Slovakian	216,595,000
Finnish	326,379,000
Danish	346,945,000
Polish	322,283,000
Hungarian	457,522,000
Czech	520,181,000
Norwegian	609,934,000
Dutch	1,063,012,000
Swedish	1,003,075,000
Portuguese	1,333,664,000
Italian	1,845,026,000
Spanish	2,658,631,000
French	3,836,874,000
German	7,035,850,000
English	76,598,718,000

Figure 5: Estimates of number of words of text available for some languages on the WWW through Altavista in March, 2001.

	www.alltheweb.com (June 2001)
"pienso de que"	171 times
"pienso que"	83966 times
"piensas de que"	89 times
"piensas que"	11485 times
"piense de que"	9 times
"piense que"	12867 times
"pensar de que"	716 times
"pensar que"	188508 times

Figure 6: Frequency of pages containing 'dequeismos errors' (placing a spurious 'de' between the verb and the relative) on the Web. The correct cases appear two orders of magnitude more often.

	www.alltheweb.com (October 2000)
"hun hebben het"	10 times
"ze hebben het"	2459 times
"groter als"	1079 times
"groter dan"	20421 times
"betreffende hen"	12 times
"betreffende hun"	329 times
"behalve hen"	12 times
"behalve hun"	310 times

Figure 7: Frequency of some Dutch preposition choice errors on the Web: the erroneous cases appear much less often than the correct cases.

TREC cross-language query: Welke mogelijkheden zijn er voor hergebruik van afval?

afval	40494
mogelijkheden	198060
van	30169524
hergebruik	12397
welke	388139
er	2313010
zijn	5041618
voor	7958353

Welke mogelijkheden zijn er voor **hergebruik** van afval?

Figure 8: Word counts of Dutch words from the Web can be used to weight words in an informational retrieval system. In the example above, the original query about recycling garbage is represented with word size corresponding roughly to the weights derivable from inverse WWW frequency.

growing tenfold every five years, we can predict that a terabyte (1000 gigabytes), which cost $ 3000 in 2001, will cost $ 300 in 2006 and $ 30 in 2011. The whole storage market is being driven by the demand for cheap video and music. Storage of text models will always be very small compared to these media, and very soon we should be able to effectively store such large models cheaply.

5 The Very Large Lexicon

The convergence of these three phenomena (storage, NLP and the WWW) means that we can consider building a new linguistic resource. This resource, massive, but automatically derivable, is not what we are used to dealing with in NLP. What we propose is more than a simple lexicon containing all the forms of words, more than a list of idiomatic expressions, more than a large model of word pairs, more than a grammar, more than a dictionary made for humans. We propose storing an abstracted expression, derived from shallow parsing and other current NLP tools, of how lexical items are really used. In this section we will consider what this Very Large Lexicon should contain. As a minimum, we think it should store:

- relative frequencies of words
- co-occurrence patterns, and their frequencies
- dependency relations between words

5.1 Relative frequency of words

Many web portals give word and page counts for the queries users send. By generating queries consisting of all the word forms of a language, we can easily gather the word frequencies of the basic lexical items of a language. (There is one caveat: web portals do not distinguish between languages in these counts so that, for example, English and German 'die' counts are conflated. There are ways to overcome these effects by referring to expected frequencies from smaller known-language corpora.)

Knowing the relative frequencies of words is useful for many NLP tasks: i.e. information retrieval system suppose that the word frequency is an indication of the importance of words, see Figure 8. These web frequencies can be used just as real corpus frequencies are used in closed-corpus information retrieval systems.

5.2 Collocation frequencies

If we know the frequencies of each word, and if we know the co-occurrence frequencies of the words, we can build into the Very Large Lexicons the list of the words with highest mutual information for each word. As an example, we took the words 'thief' and 'piano' and for each word we generated co-occurrence queries with all the other words in an English full-form lexicon using the NEAR operator of the Altavista advanced search option. Calculating mutual information (Church and Hanks 1990), we get the associated word lists shown in Figure 9. These groups

thief: *accused adventure alarm arch armor arrest assassination attack attempt beggar bicycle blessed break brothers burglary capture car catch chances character chase cheats clerical climbing come con conviction cook cop crack crime criminal cry cryptographic dagger damn dangerous dark destroy detection devil disappeared discovery doctors dragon dream druid dwarf elf enemy escape evil excite faith fight fled fool gentleman grab guard guild guilty guns guy hack hang happy hash healing heaven hero hidden honest honors horse hunting intrusion jewelry kill knight liability likelihood locked magic master merchant monk murder mystery newspaper night overtake ...*

piano: *accompanied accordion acoustic allegro alto arrangements artist ballad ballet band banjo bar baritone bass bassoon beginning bench brass brothers cello chamber choir choral chords chorus clarinet classic composed composition concert conduct conservatory dance disc dive drum duet duo ear electric ensemble evening fiddle fireplace flat flute folk forte grand guild guitar guy hammer happy harmonic harmony harp harper harpsichord hobbies horn improvisation inspired instrumentation instruments jazz key keyboard lesson listen lounge lyrics mandolin melody mezzo minor minority mood music musicians nocturnal oboe occasion opera opus orchestra organ overture pedagogy pedal percussion ...*

Figure 9: The hundred words with the highest mutual information with 'thief' and 'piano' on the WWW, in alphabetic order. These associations might be useful for OCR, or speech recognition.

of words, discovered automatically from WWW text, give an idea of what is associated with the given word. Such information might prove useful in deciding between possible readings of words in speech recognition or in optical character recognition.

5.3 Dependency relations and a sample entry

We have mentioned that NLP parsing tools can extract dependency relations between words. We think that the Very Large Lexicon should have (in addition to entries for individual words containing frequency, grammatical, normalization and collocation information) entries for each dependency relation. Associated with each normalized dependency relation, is a frequency within the documents treated. There is also a link to other forms of the dependency relation involving other derivational forms of the words and other syntactic relations between them (e.g. between "...presidential election..." and "...elect...president...").

An example of such an entry is given in Figure 10. In this example, we imagine that the Very Large Lexicon is derived from domain classified documents (Doyle 1965, Chakrabarti, Dom, Agrawal and Raghavan 1998). In the example, the entire lexicon has been derived from documents categorized as "political." In addition, to variant forms of the dependency relation, the entry should contain both common words and other dependency relations found within some window around instance of the entry. Any recognized entities (Donaldson 1993) are also to be stored. The last part of the example, though other items might be included in the entry, is a set of pointers to dependency relations involving the words in the entry. These

LEXICON:	Politics	
ENTRY:	ADJ(presidential election)	
FREQUENCY:	27,486/100,000,000	
VARIANTS:	DOBJ(elect president)	SUBJPASS (president was elected)
	NNPREP(election of president)	NPDOBJ(elected president)
CONTEXT:	*50 words (frequency > 5) before/after*	
	other entries found more than once in window, e.g. NN(acceptance speech)	
ENTITIES:	*other recognized people, places, things*	
	pointers to lexical class members	
NETWORK:	ADJ(presidential, *)	presidential things
	ADJ(*, election)	types of elections

Figure 10: Sample entry. An entry in the Very Large Lexicon for politics.

other entries form a sort of automatically generatable network (Grefenstette 1997) of concepts related to the entry.

6 Example of using a Very Large Lexicon

We can simulate the presence of a Very Large Lexicon containing information sketched in the previous section by using existing web browsers. Consider the following task, you must translate "groupe de travail" from French to English. The dictionary gives the following translations for "groupe": *cluster, group, grouping, concern, collective.* For "travail" we have *work, labor, labour.* Suppose, in addition, that we know that French structures such as *A de B* are likely to be translated as *B A* in English. In an already constructed Very Large Lexicon you could just look up the most likely combination. In the meantime, we can use a web portal, such as Altavista. If we look up all the possible combinations and note their frequencies, we get: *labour cluster: 2; labor cluster: 6; labor grouping: 7; labour grouping: 17; work grouping: 31; work cluster: 107; labour group: 439; labor group: 724; work group: 66593.* Here the most common combination gives the best translation.

In (Grefenstette 1999b) we tested this method on an entire German-English and Spanish-English dictionary. For all ambiguous compositional translations in both language pairs, the most frequent combinations on Web pages gives the right translations 86% and 87% of the time. Figure 11 and 12 show some examples of the generated ambiguous translation candidates and their frequencies on the Web.

This type of question, here lexical choice in translation, could be answered by a Very Large Lexicon. The same type of problems arises in other language applications such speech recognition and optical character recognition. Many other NLP applications could benefit from having a large abstracted model what structures and word combinations are commonly used, and with what frequencies.

compound	*candidate*	*Altavista frequency*	** if gold standard*	*MAX if most frequent*
Angebotspreis	offer price	9767	*	MAX
Angebotspreis	offer prize	206	-	
Apfelkraut	apple herb	167	-	MAX
Apfelkraut	apple syrup	159	*	
Apfelsaft	apple juice	13841	*	MAX
Apfelsaft	apple sap	25	-	
Appartementhaus	apartment chop	0	-	
Appartementhaus	apartment cut	127	-	
Appartementhaus	apartment house	8356	*	MAX
Appartementhaus	apartment rampage	0	-	
Appartementhaus	flat chop	10	-	
Appartementhaus	flat cut	621	-	
Appartementhaus	flat house	882	-	
Appartementhaus	flat rampage	0	-	
Bogenbrücke	arch bridge	2304	*	MAX
Bogenbrücke	bow bridge	224	-	

Figure 11: Ambiguous German term translations, using the translations of parts of compounds words The Altavista count corresponds to the number of times the English candidate was found there and the next two columns show whether the given English translation was the one given by the dictionary for the entire compound, and whether it was the most frequent on the Web. 86% of the ambiguous German compounds had both a * and MAX in the last two columns, showing that the most common combination was the translation given by the dictionary.

compound	*candidate*	*Altavista frequency*	** if gold standard*	*MAX if most frequent*
agregado-de-prensa	press-attaché	403	*	MAX
agregado-de-prensa	squeezer-attaché	0	-	
agua-corriente	common-water	2815	-	
agua-corriente	current-water	5213	-	
agua-corriente	draft-water	1438	-	
agua-corriente	draught-water	11	-	
agua-corriente	flowing-water	13264	-	
agua-corriente	going-water	343	-	
agua-corriente	ordinary-water	2040	-	
agua-corriente	power-water	12695	-	
agua-corriente	running-water	49358	*	MAX
agua-corriente	stream-water	9264	-	
agua-corriente	usual-water	1252	-	
agua-mineral	mineral-water	33058	*	MAX
agua-mineral	ore-water	178	-	
agua-salada	pickle-water	284	-	
agua-salada	salt-water	98690	*	MAX
águila-real	actual-eagle	60	-	
águila-real	essential-eagle	11	-	
águila-real	real-eagle	176	-	
águila-real	royal-eagle	431	*	MAX
ahorro-de-energa	decisiveness-saving	0	-	
ahorro-de-energa	energy-saving	140148	*	MAX

Figure 12: Ambiguous Spanish term translations, using the translations of parts of compounds words. The Altavista count corresponds to the number of times the English candidate was found there and the next two columns show whether the given English translation was the one given by the dictionary for the entire compound, and whether it was the most frequent on the Web. 87% of the ambiguous Spanish terms had both a * and MAX in the last two columns, showing that the most common combination was the translation given by the dictionary.

7 Conclusion

As a summary of this chapter, we have said that computers are useful, but only when we can reduce the problems we want to treat to their level. Language Models allow us to remove detail from text and make different things look similar so that a computer can treat them. The World Wide Web presents us now with a tremendous amount of text from which we can extract models of how language is used. Current Natural Language Processing tools can deal with the large amounts of text that the Web provides. With these tools, we can classify texts and extract abstracted models of how words interact. We can store these large models in a new structure, Very Large Lexicons. These models are huge but computer memory is cheap and becoming cheaper. With such Very Large Lexicons, automatically extracted from the WWW, we can solve many natural language processing problems, and imagine newer and more powerful natural language processing applications.

References

Abney, S.(1991), Parsing by chunks, *in* S. A. Robert Berwick and C. Tenny (eds), *Principle-Based Parsing*, Kluwer Academic Publishers, Dordrecht.

Ait-Mokhtar, S. and Chanod, J.-P.(1997), Incremental finite-state parsing, *ANLP'97*, Washington, pp. 72–79.

Chakrabarti, S., Dom, B., Agrawal, R. and Raghavan, P.(1998), Scalable feature selection, classification and signature generation for organizing large text databases into hierarchical topic taxonomies, *VLDB Journal: Very Large Data Bases* **7**(3), 163–178.

Chanod, J. and Tapanainen, P.(1995), Creating a tagset, lexicon and guesser for a french tagger, *Proceedings of the ACL SIGDAT Workshop*, Dublin, Ireland.

Church, K.(1988), A stochastic parts program and noun phrase parser for unrestricted text, *Proceedings of the 2nd Conference on Applied Natural Language Processing* pp. 136–143.

Church, K. W. and Hanks, P.(1990), Word association norms, mutual information, and lexicography, *Computational Linguistics* **16**(1), 22–29.

Debili, F.(1982), *Analyse Syntaxico-Semantique Fondee sur une Acquisition Automatique de Relations Lexicales-Semantiques*, PhD thesis, University of Paris XI, France.

Donaldson, D. D.(1993), Internal and external evidence in the identification and semantic categorization of proper names, *in* B. Boguraev and J. Pustejovsky (eds), *Proceedings of the SIGLEX Workshop on Acquisition of Lexical Knowledge from Text*, Columbus, OH, pp. 32–43.

Doyle, L. B.(1965), Is automatic classification a reasonable application of statistical analysis of text?, *Journal of the ACM* **12**(4), 473–489.

Ejerhed, E. and Church, K.(1983), Finite state parsing, *in* F. Karlsson (ed.), *Papers from the Seventh Scandinavian Conference of Linguistics*, University of Helsinki, Department of General Linguistics, pp. 410–432.

Frakes, W. B. and Baeza-Yates, R. (eds)(1992), *Information Retrieval: Data Structures and Algorithms*, Prentice Hall, New Jersey.

Ghani, R., Jones, R., Mladenic, D., Nigam, K. and Slattery, S.(n.d.), Data mining on symbolic knowledge extracted from the web, *Proceedings of the Sixth International Conference on Knowledge Discovery and Data Mining*.

Grefenstette, G.(1997), Sqlet : Short query linguistic expansion techniques: Palliating one or two-word queries by providing intermediate structure to text, *RIAO'97, Computer-Assisted Information Searching on the Internet*, Montreal, Canada.

Grefenstette, G.(1999a), Light parsing as finite-state filtering, *in* A. Kornai (ed.), *Extended Finite State Models of Language*, number 0-521-63198-x, Cambridge University Press.

Grefenstette, G.(1999b), The world wide web as a resource for example-based machine translation tasks, Vol. 21 of *Translating and the Computer*, London.

Grefenstette, G. and Nioche, J.(2000), Estimation of english and non-english language use on the www, *Proceedings of RIAO'2000, Content-Based Multimedia Information Access*, Paris, pp. 237–246. http://arXiv.org/find/cs/1/au:+nioche/0/1/0/past/0/1.

Hindle, D.(1993), A parser for text corpora, *in* B. Atkins and A. Zampolli (eds), *Computational Approaches to the Lexicon*, Clarendon Press.

Hutchins, W. J. and Somers, H. L.(1992), *An Introduction to Machine Translation*, Academic Press, New York.

Jacquemin, C.(1999), Syntagmatic and paradigmatic representations of term variation, *Proc. of 37th Annual Meeting of the Association for Computational Linguistics*.

Jensen, K., Heidorn, G. E. and Richardson, S. D. (eds)(1993), *Natural Language Processing: The PLNLP Approach*.

Karttunen, L., Chanod, J., Grefenstette, G. and Schiller, A.(1996), Regular expression for language engineering, *Natural Language Engineering*.

Lawrence, S. and Giles, C. L.(1999), Accessibility of information on the web, *Nature* **400**, 107–109.

Nievergelt, J., Gasser, R., Maeser, F. and Wirth, C.(1995), All the needles in a haystack: Can exhaustive search overcome combinatorial chaos?, *Lecture Notes in Computer Science* **1000**, 254–276.

Pavia, N. G.(2000), Heterogeneite des corpus: vers un parseur robuste reconfigurable et adaptable, *RECITAL (student session of TALN conference)*.

Pereira, F. C. N. and Warren, D. H. D.(1980), Definite clause grammars for language analysis—A survey of the formalism and a comparison with augmented transition networks, *Artificial Intelligence* **13**(3), 231–278.

Placeway, P., Schwartz, R., Fung, P. and Nguyen, L.(1993), The estimation of powerful language models from small and large corpora, *Proceedings of the IEEE Conference on Acoustics, Speech, and Signal Processing II*, pp. 33–36.

Porter, M. F.(1980), An algorithm for suffix stripping, *Program* **14**(3), 130–137.

Robert Gaizauskas, A. M. R.(1997), Coupling information retrieval and information extraction: A new text technology for gathering information from the web, *RIAO'97, Computer-Assisted Information Searching on the Internet*, Montreal, Canada, pp. 356–376.

Schaller, R.(1997), Moore's law: past, present and future, *IEEE Spectrum*.

Tymoczko, T.(1990), The four-color problem and its philosophical significance, *in* J. L. Garfield (ed.), *Foundations of cognitive science: the essential readings*, Paragon House.

Voutilainen, A., Heikkila, J. and Anttila, A.(1992), A lexicon and constraint grammar of English, *Proceedings of the Fourteenth International Conference on Computational Linguistics*, COLING'92, Nantes, France.

Yang, Y. and Pedersen, J. O.(1997), A comparative study on feature selection in text categorization, *Proc. 14th International Conference on Machine Learning*, Morgan Kaufmann, pp. 412–420.

Phonotactic Constraint Ranking for Speech Recognition

Julie Carson-Berndsen, Gina Joue and Michael Walsh

University College Dublin

Abstract

The aim of this paper is to highlight areas in which a computational linguistic model of phonology can contribute to robustness in speech technology applications. We discuss a computational linguistic model which uses finite state methodology and an event logic to demonstrate how declarative descriptions of phonological constraints can play a role in speech recognition. The model employs statistics derived from a cognitive phonological analysis of speech corpora. These statistics are used in ranking feature-based phonotactic constraints for the purposes of constraint relaxation and output extrapolation in syllable recognition. We present the model using a generic framework which we have developed specifically for constructing and evaluating phonotactic constraint descriptions. We demonstrate how new phonotactic constraint descriptions can be developed for the model and how the ranking of these constraints is used to cater for underspecified representations thus making the model more robust.

1 Introduction

While the success of commercial speech recognition applications has led to a more widespread acceptance of spoken language interfaces, there still seems to be a need for further investigation into the interactions between purely stochastic approaches and more linguistic-symbolic approaches to improve the robustness of multilingual speech systems. The starting point for discussion in this paper is a formally-specified computational linguistic model which has been enhanced by statistical information from various sources to improve the robustness of the model in dealing with the variability of speech and with 'noisy' input data. Although this paper will concentrate primarily on the extensions to the computational model, we assume also that the fine-grained knowledge representations which are used by the model can be applied to fine-tune stochastic models by providing important underlying structural information (cf. also Jusek et al. (1994)) .

The computational linguistic model is the *Time Map* model (Carson-Berndsen 1998) which uses a description of the constraints on the permissible combinations of sounds in a language (phonotactic constraints) to recognise well-formed syllable structures. The phonotactic constraints describe not only those words in the system lexicon but can make predictions as to which words would be considered well-formed by a native speaker of a language. In contrast to stochastic approaches to speech recognition, the *Time Map* model interprets the speech signal in terms of overlap and precedence relations between properties. This allows variability of speech utterances to be modelled by avoiding a segmentation of the speech signal into strictly non-overlapping units. In order to be robust, the model must also cater for imperfect or 'noisy' input representations and therefore requires a mechanism by which the phonotactic constraints may be relaxed under certain conditions. This paper discusses a methodology for constraint ranking which provides a principled basis for constraint relaxation in the model, based not only on domain knowledge, but also on cognitive factors which influence human production and interpretation. When enhanced by such motivated constraint relaxation procedures, the computational linguistic model will be able to offer insights into how robustness can be addressed in spoken language interface design.

In what follows, we will firstly sketch the *Time Map* model within a generic development environment which facilitates the extension of the technology to other languages (in particular languages which have received little attention thus far) and feature systems. Secondly, we will introduce the notions of constraint relaxation and output extrapolation as assumed by the model and discuss how these mechanisms are employed using a ranking of the constraints. We then discuss how the constraint ranking is achieved based on a functional cognitive analysis of phonological data. The paper concludes with some references to further developments with respect to the extension of the language functionality.

2 LIPS and the Time Map Model

The *Time Map* model was proposed as a computational linguistic model for speech recognition by Carson-Berndsen (1998) and has been tested within a speech recognition architecture for German. The model has recently been extended to English and has been provided with an interface which allows users to define and evaluate phonotactic descriptions for other languages and sublanguages. This generic development environment is known as the Language Independent Phonotactic System (Carson-Berndsen and Walsh 2000a). LIPS aims to provide a diagnostic evaluation of the phonotactic descriptions in the context of speech recognition. That is to say, rather than just providing recognition results, partial analyses can be output indicating which constraints have or have not been satisfied and where the parsing breaks down. This, together with the constraint relaxation and output extrapolation procedures to be discussed below, allows adequate parameters to be chosen that define a compromise between maximal recognition rates and minimal analysis overhead.

The *Time Map* model uses a finite-state network representation of the phonotactic constraints in a language, known as a phonotactic automaton, together with axioms of event logic to interpret multilinear representations of speech utterances. A subsection of a phonotactic automaton for CC- combinations in English syllable onsets can be seen in figure 1 and an example multilinear representation of a simple single word utterance in figure 2. The transitions in the phonotactic automaton define constraints on overlap relations which hold between features in a particular phonotactic context (i.e. the structural position within the syllable domain). [1]

[1]The monadic symbols written on the arcs in figure 1 are purely mnemonic for the feature overlap constraints they represent.

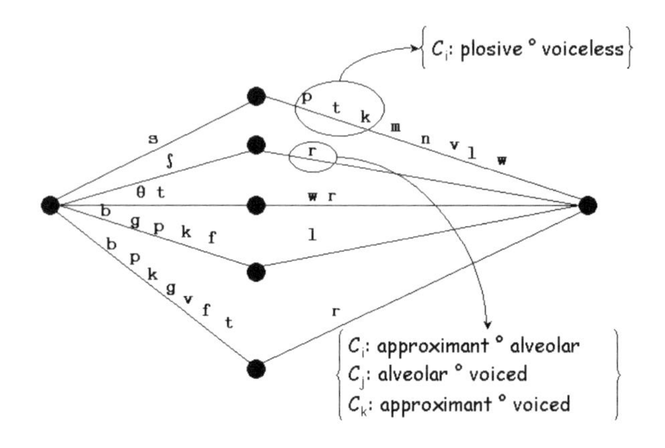

Figure 1: Subsection of phonotactic automaton for English CC- onsets

The multilinear representation consists of phonological features which have been constructed based on acoustic features extracted from the speech signal; each feature has a start and end point in terms of signal time in milliseconds.

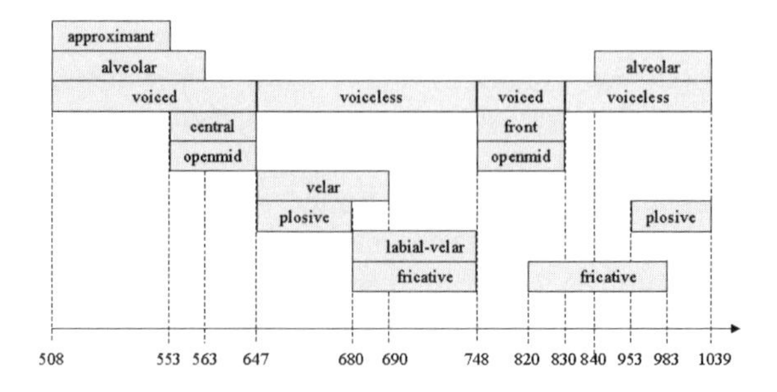

Figure 2: A multilinear representation of the utterance *request*

Phonological parsing in LIPS is guided by the phonotactic automaton which provides top-down constraints on the interpretation of the multilinear representation, specifying which overlap and precedence relations are expected by the phonotactics. If the constraints are satisfied, the parser moves on to the next state in the automaton. Each time a final state of the automaton is reached, a well-formed syllable has been found which is then passed to a corpus lexicon. The lexicon distinguishes between actual and potential syllables (cf. figure 3).

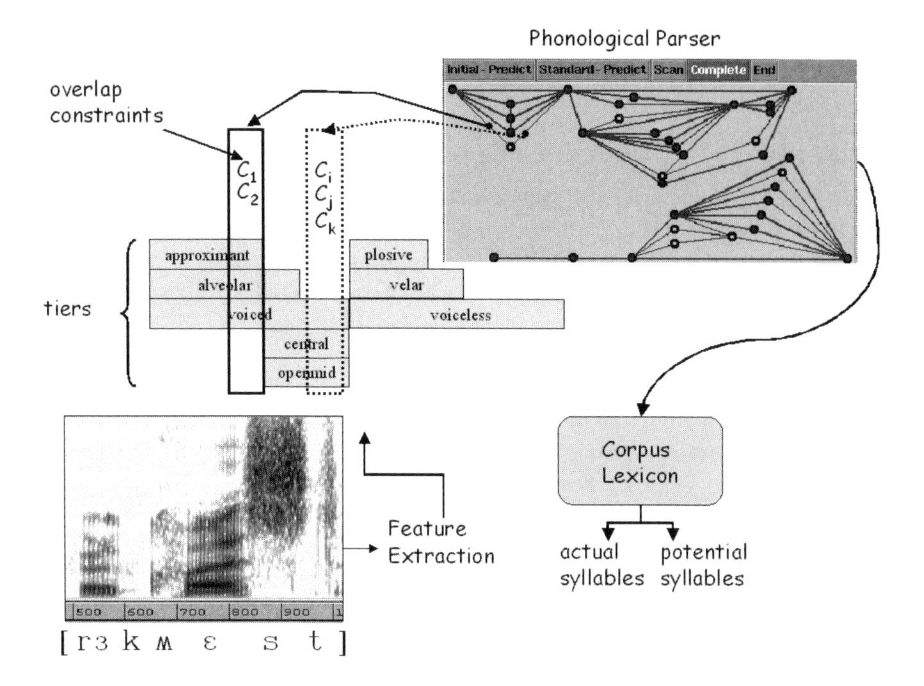

Figure 3: Architecture of the *Time Map* model

Since input to the phonological parser is, in general underspecified due to noise, the *Time Map* model must provide a means of minimising the discrepancy between the expectations defined in the top-down constraints and the actual data by allowing constraint relaxation and output extrapolation. These issues are the topic of the next section.

3 Constraint Relaxation and Output Extrapolation

Carson-Berndsen (2000) identified areas in which statistical information can play a role at different levels of granularity within the *Time Map* model and discussed these with respect to the overall architecture (cf. figure 3). The first area of integration concerns *constraint ranking* which is the lowest level of granularity in that the constraints refer to individual temporal relations. The second integration area is in connection with the *transition weighting* of the phonotactic automaton. Transition weighting is a higher level of granularity in that the whole transition is weighted rather than individual constraints. The third integration area for statistics is the lexicon that refers to a yet higher level of granularity, namely the syllable. This paper goes a step further in that the first two levels of granularity, namely constraint ranking and transition weighting, are addressed more fully and a means of incorporating them into the model is proposed. We do not comment any further on lexicon issues here, however.

The notion of constraint ranking plays an important role in constraint relaxation and output extrapolation. Constraint ranking can be based on a number of factors: linguistic-preferential, cognitive and statistical. Linguistic-preferential refers to issues of markedness and defaults, cognitive refers to human processing issues and statistical refers to data-oriented issues. Carson-Berndsen (2000) concentrated primarily on corpus-based ranking, but did state that it is more likely that a combination of these factors will be most appropriate for constraint ranking, and for this reason LIPS allows parameters to be chosen and manipulated in order to find the optimal balance between maximal recognition rates and minimal analysis overhead (Carson-Berndsen and Walsh 2000b).

Constraint relaxation should be performed in the model if only *some* of the constraints specified by the phonotactic automaton can be satisfied. As it stands, this is a very arbitrary statement. However, when coupled with a constraint ranking, it becomes a method for dealing with variability and underspecification in the input representation. Constraint ranking is a data-oriented ordering of constraints in particular phonotactic contexts. For example, constraints may be ranked with respect to frequency, duration and percentage overlap of features in specific structural contexts. This information can either be specific to a single corpus or may be based on data from several different corpora. Based on this ranking, constraint relaxation can be applied when an infrequent feature is encountered or a duration is outside a given standard deviation. Furthermore, it is possible to combine this type of ranking with cognitive factors in order to go beyond a corpus-dependent ordering (Carson-Berndsen and Joue 2000). This approach will be discussed further in section 5 below. Constraint relaxation can then be regarded as a means by which particular constraints on an input representation can be ignored. Output extrapolation, on the other hand, is performed to further specify the output representation if the constraints specify expectations that do not conflict with information found in the input. The application of output extrapolation does not guarantee that the output syllable structures are fully specified, however, only that they are well-formed. Here again, a ranking of the constraints, which can participate in output extrapolation, is required.

In LIPS, we distinguish between online processing where speech utterances are interpreted using the constraints and constraint rankings, and offline processing, which is concerned with finding the optimal parameters and constraint rankings for the system (cf. figure 4). In what follows, the integration of constraint rankings into the model are discussed. While the constraint rankings refer to the lowest level of granularity, i.e. individually ranked constraints on temporal overlap relations between features, taken collectively these rankings also provide the basis for the weighting in the phonotactic automaton through the use of transition thresholds, i.e. the next level of granularity.

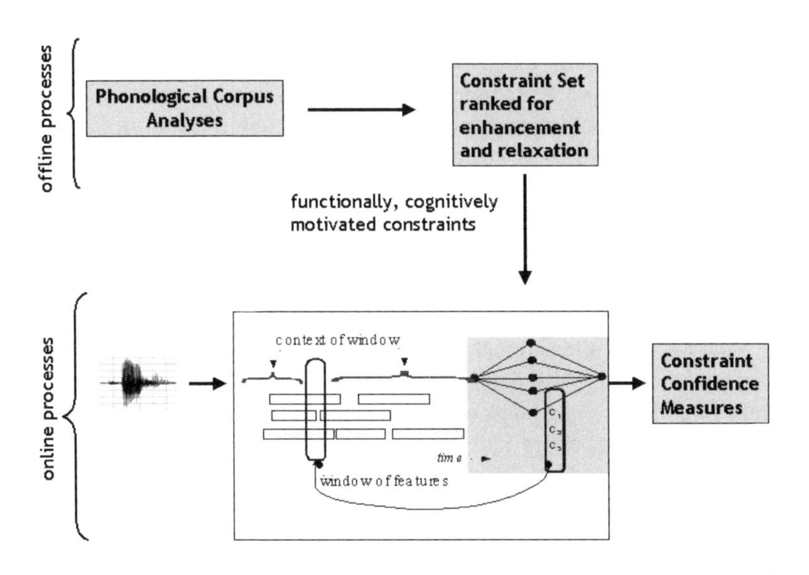

Figure 4: Online and Offline Processing with LIPS

4 Incorporating Constraint Ranking into LIPS

Constraint ranking is incorporated into the phonotactic automaton during the offline processing stage. A transition in the phonotactic automaton may have a number of constraints c_1, c_2, c_3, ... Each of these are constraints on overlap and precedence relations between features that are to be satisfied. For example, c_1 can specify that feature f_1 overlaps feature f_2 ; this is represented as follows: [2]

(1) $c_1 = f_1 \circ f_2$.

Each constraint has a ranking value i.e. c_1 has a ranking value v_{c_1}. Thus, a transition that involves constraints on overlap relations representing a /g/ may look like this:

$$\left\{ \begin{array}{ll} C_1\text{: velar} \circ \text{voiced} & V_{C1} = 5 \\ C_2\text{: voiced} \circ \text{plosive} & V_{C2} = 6 \\ C_3\text{: plosive} \circ \text{velar} & V_{C3} = 3 \end{array} \right\} = /\,g\,/$$

(0) ⟶ (1)

[2]The ∘ symbol indicates the overlap relation

Here the second constraint is ranked highest (i.e. largest v) and the third constraint ranked lowest. Rankings of constraints reflect influence of constraints on previous transitions (left-context dependencies) and other effects such as syllable position. In order for a transition to be traversed, the total values of constraints satisfied by the speech input must exceed the threshold on the transition. If a threshold of 9 is assigned to this transition, for example, then c_2 is strengthened which has the effect of enhancing the constraint: it must now be satisfied in order for the transition to be taken. If the threshold is low, it allows for relaxation of one or more of the constraints on the speech input representation. Adjusting the threshold values so that not all constraints need be satisfied in order to traverse the transition, copes with underspecification in the input representation. The threshold is a parameter of the automaton transition that can depend on speech variables such as rate or register. Ultimately the phonotactic automaton may be able to learn to adjust rankings of constraints and thresholds through training.

The notion of constraint ranking and constraint satisfaction proposed here is not unrelated to that used in Optimality Theory (Prince and Smolensky 1993). The main difference is reflected in the interpretation of constraint violation. Although a certain constraint may not be satisfied in a specific input representation, the model does not automatically assume that this constraint has been violated but if other required constraints are satisfied and the threshold is exceeded then this may be regarded as an acceptable input. Thus, unlike Optimality Theory, this approach allows for the acceptability of inputs even when dominant conditions are violated. Output extrapolation, on the other hand, allows the output representation to be augmented as if the constraint had been satisfied and there is nothing in the input representation which contradicts this assumption. Output extrapolation would fail if the constraint had been violated in the optimality theoretic sense. The approach described here allows a more flexible representation of the process of speech and language, which we believe to be a more plausible account (see, for example, Bybee, 2000) .

4.1 Resolving Ambiguities

Given the input representation of the speech utterance and phonotactic automaton, there may potentially be no best transition from the current node in the automaton. This ambiguity may arise because the input speech does not satisfy enough constraints on all possible transitions from the current node to provide enough weight to traverse any of the transitions. If the speech input does not satisfy *any* constraints on the possible current transitions, then although parsing fails, the diagnostic evaluation procedure of LIPS allows partial analyses which indicate whether output extrapolation at the level of the transition should be undertaken . If some constraints are satisfied, a further constraint relaxation is done by considering right context constraints.

Right-context information can either contribute as immediate *transition resolvers* or to *diagnostically rank* the hypothesis space of the phonotactic automaton. In either case, right-context dependency in the proposed model requires a set of *constraint variation tendencies* between the sets of constraints on each possible transition pair.[3] In a sense, these tendencies indicate what could be missing in underspecified speech input or what processes could have occurred in the speech input to cause a change from the intended speech and are used for output extrapolation. Weights associated with each constraint variation tendency allows different constraints to be relaxed to different degrees. Although the weights on these tendencies can also be used collectively to adjust the threshold of the transitions in question, we favour adjusting values on individual constraints as it provides finer tuning and finer distinctions of the influence of different constraints.

Each constraint variation tendency has the basic form

(2) $pot(C_i) \prec pot(C_j) \Rightarrow C_k \prec C_l, w$

where

- $pot(C_i)$ is a potential constraint (or set of constraints) on a given transition,
- $pot(C_j)$ is a potential constraint (or set of constraints) on a following transition,
- C_k is a constraint or a set of constraints on the given transition that was actually satisfied by the speech input,
- C_l is a constraint or a set of constraints on a following transition that is satisfied by the speech input, and
- w is the probability that the given constraint variation tendency holds.

The tendency can be read in several ways: when the satisfied constraints C_k on transition t_1 precede the satisfied constraints C_l on a following transition t_2, then there is a w probability that constraints $pot(C_i)$ on t_1 and constraints $pot(C_j)$ should be relaxed. Similarly, it can be read as: When the language specifies that feature overlap relations of $pot(C_i)$ should precede $pot(C_j)$, there is a likelihood of w that only the feature events C_k preceding C_l will be seen in the real speech input.

In order for a precedence relation to apply, the speech input must satisfy the implication of the relation ($C_k \prec C_l$) and the condition ($pot(C_i) \prec pot(C_j)$) must include constraints that exist on the transitions of the phonotactic automaton in question. If such is the case, the constraints in the condition of the relations are hypothesised to be potentially present in the speech input and extrapolated in the output, but its ranking value on the transition in the automaton is scaled by the percentage indicated by w. In other words, if there is a value w for a given sequence of satisfied constraints $C_k \prec C_l$ and a sequence of possibly satisfied constraints $pot(C_i) \prec pot(C_j)$, then w scales the ranking value(s) of C_i to account for the possibility that a subset of constraints in C_i does not occur because of constraints

[3]For now, right context is considered as the next possible single transition from the current transition. Thus the constraint variation tendencies relate the constraints on pairs of transitions.

C_l. Not all constraints on transition pairs need to be involved in precedence relations, and such a relation can exist for any combination of sequences of constraints.

Once all constraint ranking adjustments are completed using relevant precedence relations, the adjusted constraint rankings are totaled for each transition. The best transition is the one with the greatest scaled positive total distance from the threshold:

(3) $d_t = (\Sigma v_t - \theta_t)/\theta_t$

If d for each candidate transition is the same, then the transition with the highest scaled total of actually satisfied constraints will be considered the better transition. That is, the best transition would have the highest $d_{t_{act}} = (\Sigma v_{t_{act}} - \theta_t)/\theta_t$, where each $v_{t_{act}}$ is only a value of constraints explicitly satisfied by the speech input with no adjustments from the constraint variation tendencies list.

4.2 An Example

To illustrate this constraint ranking method for relaxation and enhancement, suppose we have a multilinear speech input representation as in figure 5, a phonotactic automaton as in figure 6, and a set of constraint variation tendencies:

(4) labial ∘ nasal ≺ apical ∘ plosive ⇒ apical ∘ nasal ≺ apical ∘ plosive, w =20%

(5) velar ∘ voiced ≺ apical ∘ voiced ⇒ apical ∘ voiced ≺ apical ∘ voiced, w =10%

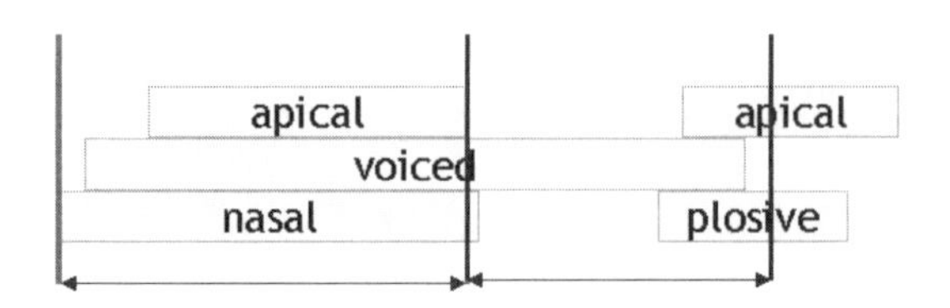

Figure 5: Example multilinear input representation

As shown in figure 6, the rankings of constraints on transition t_3 depend on the constraints on transition t_1 i.e. $v_{t_1 \frown t_3}$ (likewise for transition t_4 on t_2), so even though the exact constraints on t_3 occur also on t_4, the different respective preceding constraints (on t_1 and t_2) lead to different ranking values of the constraints.

The threshold on transition t_1 is θ_{t_1} = 8 (to enhance constraints $c_{t_1,1}$, or $c_{t_1,3}$ in conjunction with at least another constraint) and the threshold on transition t_2 is θ_{t_2} = 9, but our input speech stream satisfies only $c_{t_1,2}$ and $c_{t_2,2}$. Since the speech stream is too ambiguous, the model looks ahead to the next possible transitions (t_3 and t_4) for possibilities of constraint relaxation on transitions t_1 or t_2. It checks which constraints on t_3 and t_4 are satisfied and compares all the satisfied

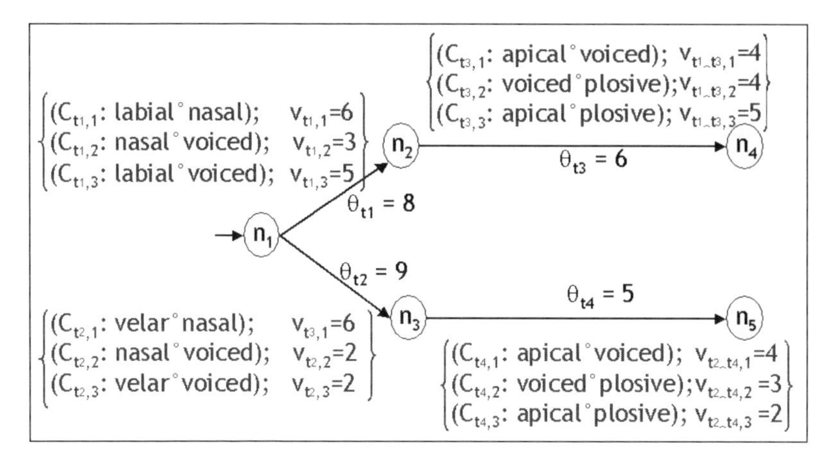

Figure 6: Example transitions of phonotactic automaton

constraints to a list of constraint variation tendencies (in our example, there are only two tendencies as given in variation 4 and variation 5).

A constraint variation tendency can only be applied if the constraints to the right of the implication are satisfied by the speech input and if the conditions of the tendency are constraints that actually occur in the phonotactic automaton. Although the the implication of variation 5 (apical $\circ$ voiced $\prec$ apical $\circ$ voiced) occurs as constraints on transition t_3 and are constraints satisfied by the speech input in Figure 5, the first part of the condition of variation 5 (velar $\circ$ voiced) does not occur as constraints on transition t_1. Thus, constraint variation tendency 5 does not apply at all. Constraint variation tendency 4, however, applies to the transition pair $t_1 \frown t_3$ as the implication of variation 4 is satisfied by the speech input in the current and next windows and its condition covers constraints which occur on transitions t_1 and t_3 of the automaton.

The tendency formulated in variation 4 informs us that we can relax constraints $c_{t_1,1}$ and $c_{t_1,3}$. To indicate that these constraints were relaxed, the ranking values of these constraints can either be scaled by w of variation 4, or the threshold of the transition (t_1) be scaled. We chose to adjust ranking values instead as this allows finer tuning of constraint ranking. Thus, the new value for $c_{t_1,1}$ is 1.2 ($= w * v_{t_1,1} =$ 0.2 * 6) and for $c_{t_1,3}$ is 1.0 (= 0.2 * 5). With these new values, the total value from satisfied and possibly satisfied constraints is 5.2 (=1.2+3+1), which does not clear the threshold of 8 on transition t_1. If variation 4 were applicable to the transition pair $t_2 \frown t_4$, adjusting ranking values should also be done.

Transition t_1 is a better transition than t_2, as its scaled distance from the threshold is closer. The path ultimately traversed from t_1 onwards might not lead to the best syllable hypothesis, however. The sum of scaled distances from the transition threshold (Equation (3)), provides a method of ranking transitions, and ultimately paths, through the automaton. It offers a diagnostic evaluation of the automaton's hypotheses. As a diagnostic tool, it does not force a decision within n-arcs time, but the decision is made based on comparison of the confidence values for the hypotheses for the entire path through the automaton.

5 A Functional Cognitive Basis for Constraint Rankings

So far this paper has generally discussed how constraint relaxation and output extrapolation can be incorporated into the *Time Map* model to improve robustness. However, we have avoided to specify the exact nature of how ranking of the constraints is achieved. There are doubtless many strategies, but we argue for a functional cognitive paradigm for ranking constraints. This paradigm is based on Phonology as Human Behavior (PHB), a combinatorial phonological analysis which argues that the skewed distribution of speech sounds are structured because of a collaborative relationship between human articulatory constraints and perceptual constraints for efficient communication (Tobin 1997, Diver 1995). The importance of either perceptual ease or articulatory ease, and even the balanced interaction of the two, has been noted by various researchers in different fields (Zipf 1949, Lindblom 1990, ten Bosch 1991, Kawasaki-Fukumori 1992, Nearey 1997). PHB makes the additional claim that not only is this interaction important, but that the interaction influences the actual sounds which occur in any language's sound inventory or frequency in a language's lexical inventory. Thus, to explain the nonrandom structure in speech sounds, PHB focuses on identifying the constraints and the interactions among them, and identifying the features of speech sounds which are involved in these interactions.

Any sound pattern that can be found can be explained by this interaction. Since perceptual and articulatory constraints are physiological, and thus common among speakers and listeners, the same constraints are involved regardless of language or context (such as social environment). However, how different constraints interact or what constraints dominate are context-dependent linguistically and nonlinguistically. In this view, then, constraint ranking becomes the evidence of what processing and production factors are involved and how they interact. The combination of constraint ranking, precedence relations and the threshold capture the contextual effects governing speech, such as social factors (such as familiarity). For example, rate of speech can be taken into account by adjusting thresholds of transitions so that, overall, not as many constraints need be relaxed compared to carefully enunciated speech. Alternatively, constraint variation tendencies and their influence on constraint rankings can account for the physiological constraints which become more obvious during fast speech.

PHB posits features which are indicative of gestural control and coordination including, for example, active articulators (*apex*, *velum*, *larynx*), the type of gestural movement (*mobile*, *stable*), or number of articulators involved in the production of a given speech sound. The theory describes the interdependency of these features with perceptual constraints for the goal of communication in terms of interacting disfavourings or tendencies. For example, PHB posits the disfavouring for the same active articulator to be used in adjacent sounds, as in *tl*, and the favouring of vowels (easy to articulate) but the disfavouring of too many vowels (difficult to make perceptual distinctions).

Understanding these direct factors that shape speech sounds and the interactions of such factors, leads to motivated predictions of the dynamic structural tendencies or changes in speech. Moreover, since in speech the constraints are based on human physiological considerations, the set of constraints should be similar across languages. The interaction of constraints with each other (the ranking of constraints) is then language-specific and even speaker- and context-specific.

The ranking value v of each constraint in our model is based on corpus analyses of pairwise distributions of temporal relations between features, i.e., how likely the sequence of a given set of overlap relations preceding another set occurs. The higher the value of v, the more frequently sounds with these features occur, and satisfying the constraints of these events have greater relative weight and are less likely to be relaxed. The lower the value of v, the less frequent the sequence of events occurs and thus the more frequent these constraints should be relaxed.

The ranking value for a constraint can also be dependent on any number of constraints in the preceding transition. For example, the ranking value of $c_{t_2,1}$ may depend on the fact that it follows $c_{t_1,1} \circ c_{t_1,3}$. The ranking value is not the actual distribution of the relevant feature relations in the corpus, but is scaled by the total percentage of all the constraints on the transition pairs. So if according to the corpus the distribution of $c_{t_1,1} \circ c_{t_1,3} \prec c_{t_2,1}$ is 20% then the ranking value for $c_{t_2,1}$ is 20/(20 + $v_{c_{t_2},2}$ + $v_{c_{t_2},3}$ + ...). This allows a scaled evaluation of how likely transition t_2 is to be traversed.

In this cognitive approach, the constraint variation tendency list is compiled according to favourings/disfavourings that constrain the development and production of speech as defined by PHB. The constraint variation tendencies then indicate the type of variations on the automaton constraints that may occur due to human physiological and behavioural factors.

6 Conclusion

This paper has been concerned with constraint relaxation and output extrapolation procedures in a computational linguistic model for speech recognition. In this model, a constraint ranking provides the basis for initiating these procedures for robust interpretation of multilinear representations of speech utterances. The generic development environment for the computational linguistic model has both an online and an offline functionality which allows optimum incorporation of statistical information to be further investigated. The development environment has been specifically designed to extend to phonotactic descriptions of other languages allowing, on the one hand, specific constraint rankings to be integrated and, on the other hand, facilitating the investigation of more language independent constraints based on cognitive factors such as those suggested by Phonology as Human Behavior. Recognition results on German data (Carson-Berndsen 1998) gathered from the original purely knowledge-based model without constraint rankings produced a phoneme recognition rate of 72.5% and syllable recognition rate of 37%.

However, a closer look at the evaluation revealed that the relatively low syllable recognition rate was due to one or two features being unreliable, leading to a complete syllable not being recognised. Furthermore, since phoneme recognition was not a task of the phonological parser, the phoneme rate was calculated on the basis of the recognised syllables. The treatment of overlap which is an inherent feature of our model also caused problems for standard string aligment evaluation procedures. For example, our model does not arbitrarily segment the nasal /m/ in *im Moment* 'at the moment' into two phonemes in a connected word graph unless there is evidence of a pause or change of feature, but outputs two overlapping syllable hypotheses. The model delays segmentation into connected units until word level information allows disambiguation. Subsequent diagnostic evaluation tests using our current model have highlighted the fact that the initial figures can be improved significantly through constraint relaxation and output extrapolation based on constraint rankings. A full scale evaluation using constraint ranking together with a new feature extraction component has now to be undertaken. Future work involves diagnostically evaluating phonotactic descriptions of other languages in the context of speech recognition and it is anticipated that this will provide insights into the choice of feature sets which are optimal to the task.

References

Bybee, J.(2000), The phonology of the lexicon: evidence from lexical diffusion, *in* M. Barlow and S. Kemmer (eds), *Usage-based models of Language*, CSLI, Stanford, California, pp. 65–85.

Carson-Berndsen, J.(1998), *Time–Map Phonology: Finite State Models and Event Logics in Speech Recognition*, Kluwer Academic Publishers.

Carson-Berndsen, J.(2000), Finite state models, event logics and statistics in speech recognition, *Philosophical Transactions of the Royal Society Series A* **358**(1769), 1255–1266.

Carson-Berndsen, J. and Joue, G.(2000), Cognitive constraints in a computational linguistic model for speech recognition, *Proceedings of AICS*, Galway, pp. 15–24.

Carson-Berndsen, J. and Walsh, M.(2000a), Generic techniques for multilingual speech applications, *Proceedings of TALN 2000*, Lausanne, pp. 61–70.

Carson-Berndsen, J. and Walsh, M.(2000b), Interpreting multilinear representations of speech, *in* M. Barlow (ed.), *Proceedings of the Eighth Australian International Conference on Speech Science and Technology*, Canberra, pp. 472–477.

Diver, W.(1995), The theory, *in* E. Contini-Morava and B. Goldberg (eds), *Meaning as Explanation: Advances in Sign-Oriented Linguistic Theory*, Mouton de Gruyter, Berlin and New York, pp. 45–113.

Jusek, A. et al.(1994), Detektion unbekannter Wörter mit Hilfe phonotaktischer Modelle, *Mustererkennung 94, 16. DAGM-Symposium Wien*, pp. 238–245.

Kawasaki-Fukumori, H.(1992), An acoustical basis for universal phonotactic constraints, *Language and Speech* **35**(1–2), 73–86.

Lindblom, B.(1990), Explaining phonetic variation: A sketch of the h&h theory, *in* W. Hardcastle and A. Marchal (eds), *Speech Production and Speech Modeling*, Kluwer, Dordrecht.

Nearey, T.(1997), Speech perception as pattern recognition, *Journal of Acoustical Society of America* **101**, 3241–3254.

Prince, A. and Smolensky, P.(1993), *Optimailty Theory: Constraint Interaction in Generative Grammar*, TR-2, Center for Cognitive Science, Rutgers University.

ten Bosch, L.(1991), Modelling vowel systems by effort and contrast, *Proceedings XIIth International Congress of the Phonetic Sciences, Aix-en-Provence*, Vol. 4, pp. 406–409.

Tobin, Y.(1997), *Phonology as Human Behavior: Theoretical Implications and Clinical Applications*, Duke University Press, Durham and London.

Zipf, G.(1949), *Human Behaviour and the Principle of Least Effort*, Addison-Wesley, Cambridge, Massachusetts.

Through a glass darkly

Part-of-speech distribution in original and translated text

Lars Borin and Klas Prütz

Department of Linguistics, Uppsala University

Abstract

In the past, so-called *translationese* has been investigated mainly as a lexical phenomenon, despite suggestions that it also must have a syntactic dimension. In this article, we explore the use of part-of-speech- (POS) -tagged parallel and comparable corpora as one means of investigating translation effects in the syntactic domain. We suggest a method for isolating putative translation effects in the form of over- and underused POS n-grams, which relies upon the existence of tagged comparable corpora for all the investigated languages, and not only for the target language, as in previous investigations. We discuss some of the patterns of overuse which we have found using this method, and some ways in which the method could be used for other investigations.

1 Introduction

Translationese has been characterized as "deviance in translated texts induced by the source language" (Johansson and Hofland 1994, 26). The kind of deviance referred to here is not to be equated with errors in the normal sense, however. Rather, it should reveal itself in 'odd' choices of lexical items and syntactic constructions, which conceivably could be the result of both assimilation and dissimilation with respect to the source language or the source text. Intuitively, the idea that the source language could influence the target language in this way seems plausible to anybody who has struggled to convey his message in a recalcitrant foreign language.[1]

Intuition is a good servant but a bad master, and should be backed up by principled empirical investigation. Translationese could be argued to fall under the more general heading of language contact phenomena, which have been the subject of linguistic research for a long time (e.g. Weinreich 1953; Thomason and Kaufman 1988; Saxena 1997). On the other hand, language contact researchers investigate above all fairly obvious and eminently noticeable changes in the linguistic system or a subsystem of a language. Translationese, on the other hand, should, by its nature, manifest itself by more subtle means than the methodology of language contact research normally is equipped to handle. It ought to be seen, above all, in deviant patterns of usage, i.e. it should be eminently suited for investigation by the methods of corpus linguistics.

No surprise, then, that it is among corpus linguists that we find many students of the linguistic correlates of translationese. However, their studies mostly confine themselves to lexical phenomena (e.g. Gellerstam 1985; Ebeling 1998; Johansson

[1] This is only an analogy, of course, since translators normally translate into their native language.

forthcoming), but translation effects should be noticeable in other linguistic domains as well, e.g. in syntax. Gellerstam (1985, 94) in his mainly lexical study states that "no doubt there are also syntactic fingerprints in translations", but does not elaborate on the matter beyond giving a single example from his corpus.

The reason for the predominance of lexical studies of translationese is in all probability that the tools are readily available for carrying out lexical investigations on languages with none or insignificant morphology (to draw a somewhat arbitrary line: those where most inflected parts of speech have less than 10 forms in their inflectional paradigms). These tools are concordancers, possibly with some statistical processing capabilities, and sentence aligners. Using them, you simply create monolingual and bilingual concordances for the lexical items that you are interested in, and then analyze this data in time-honored linguistic fashion. In a somewhat more exploratory manner, you can produce frequency lists of word types, word bigrams, trigrams, etc., and compare, e.g., vocabulary size and spread between translated and original texts of the same general type, as well as collocational patterns. This is done on the level of text words, however, i.e. inflected forms, and not that of lemmas or lexemes, which is what you normally would be interested in in a study of this type.

In order to investigate syntactic phenomena, we need texts which have been provided with some kind of syntactic markup, or tagging. At the very least, they should be tagged for part-of-speech (POS), which actually is something of a misnomer, because POS tags are often actually fairly detailed morphological descriptions. POS-tagged corpora are still hard to find, except for a few languages and a few text types, and taggers that you can use yourself are still much less common than concordancers, and for obvious reasons much more language-dependent. Even more useful for syntactic studies of translation phenomena would be parsed text material, of course, but this is harder still to come by.

In stylometric studies, such as authorship attribution, tagged corpora have been used for quite some time (e.g. Kjetsaa et al. 1984). In the study of second and foreign language learning, more specifically the study of interlanguage (see Selinker 1992), there have recently been studies in which learner corpora (see Granger 1998) have served as basis for investigations of POS n-gram differences between native and learner English (Aarts and Granger 1998; Berglund and Prütz 1999), with a method which is very similar to the one proposed here, but with the very important difference that tagged L1[2] texts are not used.

The present work represents an attempt to move studies of translation effects into the syntactic arena. It benefits from the corpus collection and tagging work done as part of the ETAP project,[3] and will benefit also from the work with sen-

[2]I.e., the language learners' native language, Dutch, Finnish and French in Aarts and Granger's (1998) investigation.

[3]ETAP is the acronym of the project title "Etablering och annotering av parallellkorpus för igenkänning av översättningsekvivalenter" (in English: "Creating and annotating a parallel corpus for the recognition of translation equivalents"). This project is a part of a joint research programme between the universities in Stockholm and Uppsala, "Translation and Interpreting – A Meeting between Languages and Cultures" financed by the Bank of Sweden Tercentenary Foundation (Riksbankens Jubileumsfond); see <http://www.translation.su.se>.

tence and word alignment done in the same project.

We will investigate whether differences in POS n-gram occurrences are indicative of translation effects. For our investigation, we have used two ETAP corpora, representing news text translated into English from Swedish, together with the parallel Swedish original, and two publicly available corpora of original English, the Flob and Frown corpora. The corpora are described in more detail in the next section. In section 3, we describe how the tagging of the corpora was done, as well as the tagsets used. Section 4 is devoted to finding the differences between original and translated English text with regard to POS n-grams, using a method where both L1 and L2 POS-tagged corpora are used. Section 5 contains a discussion of our findings, and in section 6, we sum up and look ahead.

2 The corpora

For this investigation, four corpora were used, all representing the text type news text. The corpora are

(1-2) The Flob corpus is a corpus of British English compiled in the 1990's at Freiburg University with the same composition as the well-known Lancaster–Oslo–Bergen (LOB) corpus of British English. We used the parts of the corpus marked as "press, reportage", being the category which we deemed most similar in content and style to the IVT1 corpus (see below).[4]

Similarly, the Frown corpus is a more recent version of the Brown corpus of American English, also compiled at Freiburg University. Here, too, we used the press/reportage parts of the corpus.

(3-4) The Swedish and English portions of the parallel newspaper text corpus IVT1 of the ETAP project. *Invandrartidningen* (IVT) is a periodical for immigrants in Sweden, appearing in 40 issues annually, in 8 language versions, Arabic, Bosnian–Serbian–Croatian, English, Finnish, Persian, Polish, Spanish, and simplified Swedish. The IVT1 corpus is made up of about half a year's worth of issues of IVT in five languages: the Swedish original (which is not published as such, but only used for translation into the other languages, including 'translation' into simplified Swedish),[5] Bosnian–Serbian–Croatian, English, Polish, and Spanish.

In Table 1, we give some statistics for the four corpora.

[4]The Flob and Frown corpora also have two other "press" categories, viz. "editorial" and "review", but as *Invandrartidningen* is a fairly pure news publication, we deemed it better to leave these out. Furthermore, the "reportage" category in Flob and Frown turned out to contain almost exactly the same amount of text as IVT1 (see Table 1).

[5]We are grateful to the *Invandrartidningen Foundation* and the editor-in-chief of *Invandrartidningen*, Dag Zotterman, who graciously made electronic and paper copies of the periodical available to us, as well as the Swedish original manuscript material from which all translations were made.

Table 1: Word and POS statistics for the four corpora

	Flob	Frown	IVT/EN	IVT/SE
tokens	98855	101319	119779	97339
word 1-grams (= types)	14625	14741	12702	15890
word 2-grams	62828	63941	62988	60343
word 3-grams	90578	92276	101843	87763
POS tag 1-grams	30	30	30	36
POS tag 2-grams	584	618	608	835
POS tag 3-grams	4679	5163	5241	6359
POS tag 4-grams	18471	20281	20939	22756
POS tag 5-grams	42871	46474	48930	48540

3 Tagging the corpora

All four corpora were tagged with a Brill tagger (Brill 1992). The Swedish tagger was trained on another ETAP subcorpus, the SGP corpus of political texts, on newspaper texts (from the local daily *Upsala Nya Tidning*, graciously made available for our use by the SCARRIE project), and on fiction texts from the Stockholm Umeå Corpus (Ejerhed and Källgren 1997), using a tagset devised to be compatible with the morphological descriptions in SVE.UCP (Prütz forthcoming; Sågvall Hein 1988; Sågvall Hein and Sjögreen 1991). The English tagger was trained on the written part of the BNC Sampler (Burnard 1999), using the BNC tagset (Leech and Smith 1998). See the Appendix for a listing of the two tagsets.

The Swedish Brill tagger has been tested on a held-out subset of the SGP corpus and the accuracy is estimated to 95.7 per cent correct tags. The tagger trained on the BNC Sampler text was tested using text from the Uppsala Student English corpus (USE; Axelsson 2000; Axelsson and Berglund forthcoming), giving an estimated accuracy of 96.7 per cent correct tags.

For the purposes of this investigation, both tagsets were reduced after the texts were tagged, the English set from 145 to 30 tags and the Swedish one from 151 to 36 tags (the reduced tagsets are listed and compared in the appendix). This was done for two reasons.

First, earlier work has indicated that training and tagging with a large tagset, and then reducing it, not only improves tagging performance, but also gives better results than training and tagging only with the reduced set. Prütz's (forthcoming) experiment with the Swedish Brill tagger and the same full and reduced tagsets as those used here gave an increased accuracy across the board of about two percentage points from tagging with the large tagset and then reducing it, compared to tagging with the full set. Tagging directly with the reduced set resulted in a lower accuracy, by a half to one percentage point, depending on the lexicon used.

Second, coarse-grained tagsets are more easily comparable than fine-grained ones even for such closely related languages as Swedish and English (Borin 2000, forthcoming).

4 POS n-gram differences between original and translated English text

The main hypothesis which inspired the work reported here is that 'translationese' is not confined to the lexical level, which has been the one normally investigated in works on translationese (see above in section 1). Further, we believe that distributional differences in POS n-grams (with n ranging from 1 to 5 in our investigation) may turn out to be indicative of translation effects in the syntactic domain.

First, we will look at the simplest case, that of POS unigram (n=1) frequencies. In Table 2, POS unigram frequencies for the four corpora are shown, excluding tags for punctuation. On the surface of it, POS unigrams do not seem very promising for illustrating translation effects. On the contrary, the three English corpora are very similar in their POS distribution, and different from the Swedish text in roughly the same ways. The differences include a significantly[6] greater number of NN (common noun) tags for all English texts compared to the Swedish corpus. We really do expect this to be the case, due to the way the orthographies of the languages work; in English, (noun–noun) compounds are normally written as two (or more, if one of the parts is in itself a compound) orthographic words, while in Swedish—just as in German—the parts are written together as one orthographic word (examples from IVT/SE – IVT/EN):

vapenexport	—	nattåg	—	polisrazzia
arms exports	—	night trains	—	police raid

For the same reason, we expect—and find as well—significantly more T (determiners, including articles) tags in English than in Swedish, because of the definite article being written separately in English but as part of the noun (an inflectional suffix) in Swedish.

But there are also more intriguing differences, less easily explained by differences in language structure or orthographic conventions. One such difference concerns the POS tag R (adverb), where Swedish has significantly more R tag instances than any of the three English corpora, among which IVT/EN has the highest number of R tags (although not significantly more than Flob or Frown). Even though we have not looked at the details of this case (are there many more adverb lemmas, or simply more of the same ones?), we are reminded of the following observation on the differences between English and Kalam, a language of the New Guinea Highlands:

> The special features of Kalam event-reports first surfaced as a language-learning difficulty. I had been living in the Upper Kaironk for a couple of months and had learnt to converse, hesitantly, about a range of familiar subjects. I noticed that bystanders, who were fond of repeating to others nearby what I said (even if the others could hear

[6]Significance testing was done using the Mann-Whitney test, following Kilgarriff's (to appear) suggestion that this is a more suitable test for determining which units are used most differently in two text corpora than, e.g., the χ^2 test. The significance level used throughout was $p \leq 0.025$. See further section 4 below.

Table 2: POS unigram frequencies in the four corpora (excluding punctuation)

Flob		Frown		IVT/EN		IVT/SE		rank
NN	21933	NN	21919	NN	22020	NN	20196	1
I	10467	I	9703	I	9726	V	11799	2
V	8536	V	8462	V	8722	I	10675	3
T	8126	T	7737	T	7601	P	7219	4
NC	6553	A	6898	A	6576	R	6750	5
A	6444	NC	6604	P	6567	A	5911	6
P	5646	P	5451	R	4839	C	4672	7
R	4582	R	4308	C	4238	NC	4063	8
C	4116	C	4262	NC	3895	VI	3877	9
VI	2888	VI	2808	VI	3443	T	3355	10
K2	2706	M	2369	K2	2525	F	1369	11
M	2263	K2	2088	M	2302	E	1319	12
E	1676	E	1586	E	1680	VS	1239	13
K1	1629	K1	1550	K1	1429	Q	1172	14
P$	1257	P$	1118	P$	1241	M	1150	15
$	184	$	593	$	565	P$	844	16
O	53	O	91	O	82	NN$	686	17
S	29	S	52	S	77	K2	565	18
X	25	X	21	X	27	NC$	224	19
						G	187	20
						L	162	21
						K1	124	22
						O	54	23
						S	48	24
						X	24	25
						VK	18	26

> perfectly well), often added details to my utterances. For instance, if someone asked, “Where’s Kiyas?” (the young man who was my chief informant) and I answered, “He’s in his garden”, a bystander might say, “He said ‘Kiyas has gone to Matpay to work in his garden. He’ll be back later’, he said”.
>
> After a while it dawned on me that these elaborations were not just imaginative creations of individuals but followed a consistent pattern. People were editing my utterances, supplying information that I should have given in the first place to make my utterance complete. (Pawley 1993, 109)

It could well be that Swedish newswriters feel a greater need to supply where, when and how events took place than their English counterparts would.[7] It is a

[7] It could also be that in English, the preference is for adverbials in the form of e.g. prepositional phrases, rather than simple adverbs. We would need at least a syntactically parsed corpus in order to

different question whether this tendency in news text reflects a deeper difference in the genius of the two languages, as Pawley claims for English and Kalam in the passage just quoted, or whether it points to a difference in preferred news text style in the two languages, Swedish preferring a more colloquial (or concrete) style and English a more formal (or abstract) language.

Similarly to the adverbs, there is a significantly higher incidence of infinitives (VI) and pronouns (P) in the IVT/EN text, compared to Flob and Frown, corresponding to even higher figures for the IVT/SE text. These differences could reflect translation effects, as follows.

In the case of the infinitives, there is a readily available structural factor which could account for the effect: Linguistic system constraints force you to use the infinitive in most dependent non-finite clauses in Swedish, whereas in English there is also the present participle/gerund (K1 in the reduced tagset used here) available as an alternative, depending on the main clause. The translation effect in this case would be seen as a tendency in the translator to translate (obligatory) infinitives with (optional) infinitives, choosing an appropriate main clause form for this to be possible.

As for the pronouns, however, there is no such structural explanation that leaps to mind. If the Swedish news style is more colloquial than its English counterpart, as conjectured above, the higher incidence of pronouns could be a mark of this. In spoken English, pronouns are much more frequent than in the written variety. Thus, in the London-Lund Corpus of spoken English, pronouns are actually more frequent than nouns (Altenberg 1990, 185). In academic writing by Swedish university students, i.e. advanced learners of English, there is also an overuse of pronouns (Axelsson and Berglund forthcoming; Berglund and Prütz 1999). This fact should be seen in the light of observations about how well Swedish university students of English master the colloquial registers of the language, but have less training in the more formal registers, and consequently display an excessively colloquial style in their formal written production (Ohlander 1995).

We now turn to an investigation of n-grams where n>1. There are many more 2-, 3-, etc. grams than 1-grams (see Table 1), and it is not feasible to do this investigation manually. Instead, we followed the procedure described below, which is logically divided into a (computationally less demanding) *hypothesis generation* stage and a *hypothesis testing* stage. The intention is to identify n-grams evidencing putative translation effects in the hypothesis generation stage, and then subject these to significance testing. Thus, hypothesis generation was done as follows.

1. First all texts were tagged as described in section 3 above.

2. POS n-grams were extracted from the texts, and sorted in order of decreasing frequency. All frequencies were normalized; figures shown in Table 3 are frequency/100000 tokens. The rank of the n-grams was defined to be in-

investigate this hypothesis (see section 6). Against this conjecture we may adduce the fact that the frequency of prepositions is roughly the same in all our corpora; in fact, of the four corpora, IVT/SE has both the most adverbs and the greatest number of prepositions (see Table 2).

versely related to their frequency, so that the item with the highest frequency gets rank 1, etc.[8]

3. The Flob n-gram ranking was then compared to the others. We used Flob as the standard against which the other texts were compared because the IVT/EN texts follow British English most closely in their orthography, vocabulary, etc. Thus, for each of the text pairs Flob–Frown, Flob–IVT/EN, and Flob–IVT/SE, we produced a thresholded rank difference list, using a (heuristically chosen) threshold of 30, i.e. the rank difference must be 30 or greater for it to count as a difference. In the rank comparisons, a positive number means that the n-gram in question has a lower frequency in the other text, and a negative number that it has a higher frequency.

4. The difference lists were then processed as follows. First, we ran the comparisons of Flob with IVT/EN and IVT/SE through a small program which kept only rank differences which IVT/EN and IVT/SE had in common in comparison with Flob, i.e. differences with the same sign, hence both denoting either higher or lower rank.

5. After this, we did the exact opposite, but with Frown as the comparison, i.e. we discarded from the result all rank differences common to the comparisons of Flob with Frown and with IVT/EN. Thus, Frown was used as a control, as it were, helping us avoid ascribing rank differences to translation effects, when they are in fact simply an effect of the normal variation found in the investigated text type. In this way, 2 2-grams (of 29), 36 3-grams (of 98), 14 4-grams (of 72), and 1 5-gram (of 9) were eliminated.

6. Finally, certain n-grams were removed from the resulting lists. All n-grams containing the tag NC (proper noun) were discarded, since we believe that a higher or lower relative propensity of proper nouns is not a distinguishing trait in translationese. We also discarded all n-grams containing punctuation, except those having a full-stop as their first or last tag (but no punctuation tags elsewhere in the sequence). The motivation for this is is less well-founded, but let us simply say that we wish to limit ourselves, at least for the time being, to looking at clause-internal syntax darkly mirrored in a POS tagging of a text.[9] The elimination of punctuation tags resulted in a further

[8]Ties get the same rank, and there are no unfilled positions in the ranking. Thus, the frequency distribution 8, 7, 6, 6, 6, 2, 2, 1, 1, 1, 1, 1 would result in 5 ranks, numbered 1–5, and having 1, 1, 3, 2, and 5 members, respectively. The highest-numbered ranks in the corpora—i.e., for the n- grams with frequency 1—were as follows.

	Flob	Frown	IVT/EN	IVT/SE
2-grams	211	219	221	223
3-grams	242	255	254	229
4-grams	157	156	169	149
5-grams	99	94	97	83

[9]Of course, at the same time we eliminate e.g. commas functioning as coordination conjunctions,

reduction of the number of n-grams. A total of 20 2-grams, 39 3-grams, 36 4-grams, and 6 5-grams were eliminated in this step.

In the following stage of the investigation, the hypothesis testing was done using the Mann-Whitney (or U) test for each of the surviving n-grams (see Kilgarriff to appear), and we kept only those n-grams simultaneously showing a significant difference between the two corpus pairs Flob–IVT/EN and Flob–IVT/SE above the 97.5% level ($p \leq 0.025$) for a directional test (since we did know the expected direction of the difference). In Table 3, we see the n-grams remaining after removal of non-significant (in the sense just described) differences (6 3-grams and 5 4-grams were eliminated by the test).

5 Discussion

In this preliminary study, we will limit ourselves to discussing a small number of representative cases. Translation effects should in principle manifest themselves as both overuse and underuse of syntactic constructions, just as the case is in foreign language learners' interlanguage (Aarts and Granger 1998). Here, we will only discuss cases of overuse in our material—i.e. those where the rank difference ($\Delta rank$) is a negative number in Table 3—but we hope to be able to return to the equally interesting cases of underuse at a later time.

There are some n-grams indicating that there are more verb-initial sentences in IVT/EN than in the two original English corpora (the 2-gram ". V" and the 3-gram ". V P"). This is probably not due primarily to a translation effect, however. Rather, it reveals a difference in text type composition among the corpora. The IVT corpora contain a fair amount of text from the section "Letters from the readers" in the periodical. The language of this section differs from that of the rest of the corpus, e.g. in containing a large amount of direct questions. Hence the many verb-initial sentences, characteristic of Swedish yes-no questions:

Examples from the "Readers' letters" section of IVT, issue 20, 1997 (sentence-initial V underlined)

IVT/SE:	IVT/EN:
Måste djuren sitta i karantän? Jag har en liten hund kvar i USA, kan jag ta hit den? Måste den sitta i karantän?	Must our animals be kept in quarantine? I have a small dog in the United States. Can I bring it here? Must it be kept in quarantine?

On the other hand, an example of what seems to be a real instance of translationese syntax is the overuse of preposition-initial sentences in IVT/EN, as seen in the 2-gram ". I" (full-stop–preposition). There is no difference in preposition (1-gram) frequency among the four texts (see Table 2), however. Thus, we seem to be

i.e. clause-internally. We also do not wish to claim that rules of orthography, such as the use of punctuation, cannot be subject to translation effects. We are simply more interested in syntax more narrowly construed. The reason for keeping leading and trailing full-stops is that a full-stop is an unambiguous sentence (and clause) boundary marker, thus permitting us to look at POS distribution at sentence (and some clause) boundaries.

Table 3: Remaining significantly different n-grams ($p \leq 0.025$) after filtering through Frown and removal of sequences containing NC and punctuation tags

Flob freq	Δrank	2-gram	Flob freq	Δrank	5-gram
366	71	T M	60	36	NN I T M NN
267	-38	. I	25	-30	NN I P$ NN .
176	-58	. R			
64	47	P$ M			
62	-65	P VI			
60	-52	C VI			
21	-95	. V			
Flob freq	**Δrank**	**3-gram**	**Flob freq**	**Δrank**	**4-gram**
209	93	T M NN	116	78	I T M NN
204	105	I T M	103	60	NN E VI T
189	49	NN A NN	102	44	A NN E VI
162	-42	I P NN	101	74	NN I T M
161	92	V P V	101	-36	I A NN .
142	-38	P NN V	94	65	A NN NN NN
114	53	A NN E	88	57	NN NN NN I
109	-44	. T A	84	62	K1 T NN I
106	-43	P$ NN .	82	-51	. P V R
95	50	M NN C	78	43	I T A A
87	-50	P NN .	64	43	P V P V
57	-54	. P NN	63	-37	I P$ NN .
51	39	T M A	60	49	V T NN V
31	-60	NN C VI	50	37	K2 I NN NN
20	-53	. I P	39	-50	. P V VI
17	-121	V P VI	39	-38	NN V R A
2	-69	. V P	29	-32	. P NN V

confronted with a difference between Flob and IVT/EN which mirrors a difference between Flob and IVT/SE, i.e. a putative translation effect.

We know that Swedish is more liberal than (written standard) English when it comes to allowing constitutents other than the subject in the sentence-initial position of declarative sentences. Frequently, you will find quite heavy adverbials—which are often prepositional phrases—or prepositional objects in this position, while in English, although certainly possible, this construction is less preferred than in Swedish:

Examples from IVT, issue 19, 1997 (sentence-initial prepositions underlined)

IVT/SE:
För att bli svensk folkmusiker tog Ale en ovanlig omväg. I Malmö, där han bodde, blev han bekant med en invandrad grekisk musiker som satte en bouzouki i händerna på Ale.

IVT/EN:
In becoming a Swedish folk musician, Ale Möller took a strange path. He lived in Malmö and got to know an immigrant Greek musician who placed a bouzouki in his hands.

Possibly the same feature of Swedish syntax lies behind the overuse of sentence-initial adverbs (the 2-gram ". R") in IVT/EN, as compared to Flob. We have already seen that adverbs by themselves are overused in IVT/EN, and now it seems that quite a few of those extra adverbs end up in sentence-initial position.

The overuse of pronouns noted earlier is further reflected in the 4-grams ". P V R" (full-stop–pronoun–finite verb–adverb) and ". P V VI" (full-stop–pronoun–finite verb–infinitive), where—as revealed by an inspection of the actual text word sequences—the P corresponds in all instances to pronominal subjects (in the form of personal, demonstrative, or expletive pronouns). In the same way, the P in the (clause-internal) 3-gram "V P VI" (finite verb–pronoun–infinitive) corresponds in practically all cases to a pronominal subject or object in the text.

Finally, the higher use of the 2-gram "C VI" (conjunction–infinitive) and the 3-gram "NN C VI" (common noun–conjunction–infinitive) could be seen as further confirmation of the conjecture made in section 4 above, that the translator of IVT tends to carry over Swedish infinitive clauses, even when an English verb form in *-ing* perhaps should have been the preferred choice.

6 Conclusions and outlook

Our results, although of a preliminary nature, are encouraging. It seems that we are able to tease out some interesting syntactical traits of so-called translationese, using POS tagged corpora and the method described in section 4 above.

To be more precise, we have shown that there are significant differences in the distribution of POS n-grams that IVT/EN and IVT/SE share when contrasted against Flob, that could be indicative of a translation effect in IVT/EN.

Here, we have to put in a caveat: We cannot be absolutely certain that we have, in fact, produced firm evidence for translationese in IVT/EN, as the differences that we have seen could, in principle, be due to non-linguistic differences between the corpora, e.g. differences in content or topic. We could be dealing with different sublanguages, as it were, with slightly different syntactic profiles. One such difference has turned up already, namely the "Letters from the readers" material present in IVT, but not in Flob (discussed in section 5 above). We believe that the IVT and Flob corpora are otherwise comparable as to content and topic, but only further more detailed examination can show whether this belief is justified or not.

The method naturally lends itself to a working mode where we go from linguistic abstractions, i.e. POS n-grams, to increasingly concrete cases, i.e. via more specific—or longer—n-grams, to sequences of text words corresponding to particular POS n-grams. It is important to note that hypotheses are formulated on the basis of the abstractions, but checked out with the help of increasingly less abstract representations. Thus, the ability to create—manually or partly or fully automatically—linguistic abstractions of texts is a necessary prerequisite for any linguistic investigation. Corpus linguistics brings to this process the possibility of making automatic such abstractions of large amounts of text, thus enabling us to discern subtle patterns of usage in a more 'objective' way than previously (cf. Grefenstette forthcoming).

If we compare our method to that used by Aarts and Granger (1998) in their investigation of interlanguage in language learning, we may note that we use an L1 POS tagged corpus (IVT/SE), in order to correlate the differences between L2 and L1 English to those between L1 English and L1 Swedish, while Aarts and Granger use only L2 learner English texts, comparing them with L1 English texts, but not with texts in the learners' native languages (Dutch, Finnish and French). No doubt, there were practical reasons for working only with the target language, but there is also a school of thought in second and foreign language learning research which holds that interlanguage goes through more or less the same stages, regardless of the learner's native language (see Lightbown and Spada 1993), so that there would, strictly speaking, be no need to look at anything but the target language. We still believe, however, that contrastive factors are important both in the case of translators and second language learners.

An obvious further development of the investigation reported here would be to look at parts-of-speech in certain positions, i.e. to look at more abstract 'meta-patterns', defined e.g. by regular expressions over POS sequences. Thus, it would be interesting, for instance, to investigate 3-grams with sentence punctuation[10] in the first position and finite verbs in third position, to see whether the obligatory V2 structure of Swedish influences English translations from Swedish. We have seen that one aspect of V2 structure—viz. that there is a greater tendency for other constituents than the subject to occupy the first sentence position—seems to be a feature of Swedish–English translationese, but by abstracting even more away from the text in the way sketched here, we could possibly see whether this influence goes further.

Of course, we know that the "2" in V2 refers to a constituent position, and not to a word position, but with a POS-tagged corpus, word positions are all that we have. The hypotheses which must be assumed in order for the procedure just outlined to yield valid results are (1) that phrases consisting of single words—e.g. NP's consisting of single nouns—are frequent, and (2), that their relative frequency is approximately the same in both original and translated text.

This is not, on the whole, a good assumption—at least not the second part of it—which brings us to another natural continuation of the work reported here. Even though POS-tagged texts allow us to make interesting observations about the differences between original and translated language, parsed text would be even more useful, but such texts and publicly available parsers for a range of languages are much harder to come by than POS taggers.

[10] Sentence punctuation being represented also by other tags in addition to the full-stop tag (see the Appendix) seen in the n-grams discussed in sections 4 and 5.

Finally, we would like to try out the method described here (or a refinement of it) on learner language as well, comparing the results we would get with those achieved by Aarts and Granger (1998) and Berglund and Prütz (1999). This would be a first step toward creating error tagged learner corpora (cf. Dagneaux et al. 1998) for at least English and Swedish, with the ultimate aim of using these resources in intelligent computer-assisted language learning (ICALL) applications.

Acknowledgements

We wish to thank the participants of the joint Stockholm–Uppsala Translation Programme Summer Seminar 2000 and two anonymous reviewers for their insightful and constructive comments on successive versions of this text.

References

Aarts, J. and Granger, S.(1998), Tag sequences in learner corpora: a key to interlanguage grammar and discourse, *in* S. Granger (ed.), *Learner English on Computer*, Longman, London, pp. 132–141.

Altenberg, B.(1990), Spoken English and the dictionary, *in* J. Svartvik (ed.), *The London–Lund Corpus of Spoken English. Description and Research*, Lund University Press, Lund, pp. 177–191.

Axelsson, M. W.(2000), USE – the Uppsala Student English corpus: an instrument for needs analysis, *ICAME Journal* **24**, 155–157.

Axelsson, M. W. and Berglund, Y.(forthcoming), The Uppsala Student English corpus (USE): a multi-faceted resource for research and course development, *in* L. Borin (ed.), *Parallel Corpora, Parallel Worlds*.

Berglund, Y. and Prütz, K.(1999), Tagging a learner corpus – a starting point for quantitative comparative analyses, Presentation at the KORFU '99 Symposium, Växjö University, Sweden.

Borin, L.(2000), Something borrowed, something blue: Rule-based combination of POS taggers, *Second International Conference on Language Resources and Evaluation, Proceedings, Vol. 1*, ELRA, Athens, pp. 21–26.

Borin, L.(forthcoming), Alignment and tagging, *in* L. Borin (ed.), *Parallel Corpora, Parallel Worlds*.

Brill, E.(1992), A simple rule-based part-of-speech tagger, *Proceedings of the Third Conference on Applied Natural Language Processing*, Trento.

Burnard, L. (ed.)(1999), *Users Reference Guide for the BNC Sampler*, Published for the British National Corpus Consortium by the Humanities Computing Unit at Oxford University Computing Services, February 1999. Available on the BNC Sampler CD. See <http://info.ox.ac.uk/bnc/>.

Dagneaux, E., Denness, S. and Granger, S.(1998), Computer-aided error analysis, *System* **26**, 163–174.

Ebeling, J.(1998), Contrastive linguistics, translation, and parallel corpora, *META*.

Ejerhed, E. and Källgren, G.(1997), *Stockholm Umeå Corpus version 1.0, SUC 1.0*, Department of Linguistics, Umeå University.

Gellerstam, M.(1985), Translationese in Swedish novels translated from English, *in* L. Wollin and H. Lindquist (eds), *Translation Studies in Scandinavia. Proceeedings from the Scandinavian Symposium on Translation Theory (SSOTT) II, Lund 14–15 June, 1985*, pp. 88–95.

Granger, S. (ed.)(1998), *Learner English on Computer*, Longman, London.

Grefenstette, G.(forthcoming), Multilingual corpus-based extraction and the Very Large Lexicon, *in* L. Borin (ed.), *Parallel Corpora, Parallel Worlds.*

Johansson, S.(forthcoming), Towards a multilingual corpus for contrastive analysis and translation studies, *in* L. Borin (ed.), *Parallel Corpora, Parallel Worlds.*

Johansson, S. and Hofland, K.(1994), Towards an English–Norwegian parallel corpus, *in* U. Fries, G. Tottie and P. Schneider (eds), *Creating and Using English Language Corpora*, Rodopi, Amsterdam, pp. 25–37.

Kilgarriff, A.(to appear), Comparing corpora, *International Journal of Corpus Linguistics.* References here are to ms available on the WWW: <http://www.itri.bton.ac.uk/~Adam.Kilgarriff/ijcl.pdf>.

Kjetsaa, G., Gustavsson, S. and Beckman, B.(1984), *The Authorship of The Quiet Don*, Solum, Oslo.

Leech, G. and Smith, N.(1998), *The Automatic Tagging of the British National Corpus (Information to be used with the BNC Sampler Corpus)*, UCREL, Lancaster University.

Lightbown, P. M. and Spada, N.(1993), *How Languages are Learned*, Oxford University Press, Oxford.

Ohlander, S.(1995), Variation och standard inom universitetsundervisningen i engelsk grammatik, *in* L.-G. Andersson and F. Börjeson (eds), *Språkundervisning på universitetet. Rapport från ASLA:s höstsymposium, Göteborg, 11–13 november 1993*, ASLA, Uppsala, pp. 117–133.

Pawley, A.(1993), A language which defies description by ordinary means, *in* W. A. Foley (ed.), *The Role of Theory in Language Description*, Mouton de Gruyter, Berlin, pp. 87–129.

Prütz, K.(forthcoming), Part-of-speech tagging for Swedish, *in* L. Borin (ed.), *Parallel Corpora, Parallel Worlds.*

Sågvall Hein, A.(1988), Towards a comprehensive Swedish parsing dictionary, *Studies in Computer-Aided Lexicology*, Almqvist & Wiksell International, Stockholm, pp. 268–298.

Sågvall Hein, A. and Sjögreen, C.(1991), Ett svenskt stamlexikon för datamaskinell morfologisk analys, *in* M. Thelander et al (eds.), *Svenskans beskrivning 18*, Lund University Press, Lund.

Saxena, A.(1997), Internal and external factors in language change. aspect in Tibeto-Kinnauri, *Technical Report 32*, Department of Linguistics, Uppsala University.

Selinker, L.(1992), *Rediscovering Interlanguage*, Longman, London.

Thomason, S. G. and Kaufman, T.(1988), *Language Contact, Creolization, and Genetic Linguistics*, University of California Press, Berkeley.

Weinreich, U.(1953), *Languages in Contact*, Mouton, The Hague.

Appendix: Reduced English and Swedish tagsets

SE-R	EN-R	description	examples
–	–	dash	–
!	!	exclamation mark	!
"	"	quotes	”
(	(	left bracket	(
)	)	right bracket	(
,	,	comma	,
.	.	full-stop	.
	...	ellipsis	...
:	:	colon	:
;	;	semicolon	;
?	?	question mark	?
	$	genitive clitic	’
A	A	adjective	röd, red
C	C	conjunction	och, that
E	E	infinitive mark	att, to
F		numeric expression	16
G		abbreviation	d.v.s.
I	I	preposition	på, on
K1	K1	present participle	seende, eating
K2	K2	past participle	sedd, eaten
L		compound part	hög-
M	M	numeral	två, two
NC	NC	proper noun	Eva, Evelyn
NC$		proper noun, genitive	Åsas
NN	NN	noun	häst, goat
NN$		noun, genitive	tjuvs
O	O	interjection	bu, um
P	P	pronoun	vi, we
P$	P$	pronoun, possessive or genitive	vår, our
Q		pronoun, relative	som
R	R	adverb	fort, fast
S	S	symbol or letter	G
T	T	determiner	en, the
V	V	verb, finite	såg, ate
VI	VI	verb, infinitive	se, eat
VK		verb, subjunctive	såge
VS		verb, supine	sett
X	X	unknown or foreign word	

Alpino: Wide-coverage Computational Analysis of Dutch

Gosse Bouma, Gertjan van Noord, and Robert Malouf

Alfa-informatica
Rijksuniversiteit Groningen

Abstract

Alpino is a wide-coverage computational analyzer of Dutch which aims at accurate, full, parsing of unrestricted text. We describe the head-driven lexicalized grammar and the lexical component, which has been derived from existing resources. The grammar produces dependency structures, thus providing a reasonably abstract and theory-neutral level of linguistic representation. An important aspect of wide-coverage parsing is robustness and disambiguation. The dependency relations encoded in the dependency structures have been used to develop and evaluate both hand-coded and statistical disambiguation methods.

1 Introduction

For English, tremendous progress has been made in the area of wide-coverage parsing of unrestricted text. Many of the proposed systems are statistical parsers, but systems based on a hand-written grammar exist as well. The aim of Alpino[1] is to provide computational analysis of Dutch with coverage and accuracy comparable to state-of-the-art parsers for English.

The Alpino grammar (described in more detail below) is a lexicalized grammar in the tradition of constructionalist Head-driven Phrase Structure Grammar (Pollard and Sag 1994, Sag 1997). The grammar consists of hand-written, linguistically motivated rules and lexical types. To evaluate the coverage and disambiguation component of the system, a testbench of syntactically annotated material is absolutely crucial. Given the current lack of such material for Dutch, we have started to annotate corpora with dependency structures. Dependency structures provide a convenient level of representation for annotation, and a fairly neutral representation for further processing. The annotation format is taken from the project *Corpus Gesproken Nederlands* (*Corpus of Spoken Dutch*) (Oostdijk 2000). The construction of dependency structures in the grammar and our treebanking efforts are described in section 4. Both the lexicalist nature of the Alpino grammar and the use of dependency structures imply that lexical items must be associated with detailed valency information. For the Alpino lexicon we have extracted this information from the Celex and Parole lexical databases (section 3).

In section 5 we describe Alpino's parsing architecture. Section 6 describes a variety of disambiguation strategies which have been integrated in Alpino. In addition, we report on a number of preliminary disambiguation experiments. We conclude with some remarks on future work.

[1]Alpino is being developed as part of the NWO PIONIER project *Algorithms for Linguistic Processing*, `www.let.rug.nl/~vannoord/alp`

2 Grammar

The Alpino grammar is an extension of the successful OVIS grammar (van Noord, Bouma, Koeling and Nederhof 1999, Veldhuijzen van Zanten, Bouma, Sima'an, van Noord and Bonnema 1999), a lexicalized grammar in the tradition of Head-driven Phrase Structure Grammar (Pollard and Sag 1994). The grammar formalism is carefully designed to allow linguistically sophisticated analyses as well as efficient and robust processing.

In contrast to earlier work on HPSG grammar rules in Alpino are relativey detailed. However, as pointed out in Sag (1997), by organizing rules in an inheritance hierarchy, the relevant linguistic generalizations can still be captured. The Alpino grammar currently contains over 100 rules, defined in terms of a few general rule structures and principles. The grammar covers the basic constructions of Dutch (including main and subordinate clauses, (indirect) questions, imperatives, (free) relative clauses, a wide range of verbal and nominal complementation and modification patterns, and coordination) as well as a wide variety of more idiosyncratic constructions (appositions, verb-particle constructions, PP's including a particle, NP's modified by an adverb, punctuation, etc.). The lexicon contains definitions for various nominal types (nouns with various complementation patterns, proper names, pronouns, temporal nouns, deverbalized nouns), various complementizer, determiner, and adverb types, adjectives, and 36 verbal subcategorization types.

The formalism supports the use of recursive constraints over feature-structures (using delayed evaluation, van Noord and Bouma (1994)). This allowed us to incorporate an analysis of cross-serial dependencies based on argument-inheritance (Bouma and van Noord 1998) and a trace-less account of extraction along the lines of Bouma, Malouf and Sag (2001).

3 Lexical Resources

Accurate, wide-coverage parsing of unrestricted text requires a lexical component with detailed subcategorization frames. For lexicalist grammar formalisms, the availability of lexical resources which specify subcategorization frames is even more crucial. In HPSG, for instance, phrase structure rules rely on the fact that each head contains a specification of the elements it subcategorizes for. If such specifications are missing, the grammar will wildly overgenerate.

We have used two existing lexical databases (Celex and Parole) to create a wide-coverage lexicon with detailed subcategorization frames enriched with dependency relations. Celex (Baayen, Piepenbrock and van Rijn 1993) is a large lexical database for Dutch, with rich phonological and morphological information. For use within the CGN project, this database has been extended with dependency frames (Groot 2000). This version of the lexicon contains 11,800 verbal stems, with a total of 21,800 dependency frames. By far the most frequent frames are those for intransitive (4,100) and transitive (6,500) verbs. A fair number of frames occurs more than 100 times, but 300 of the 650 different dependency frame *types* in the database occur only once.

Dependency Frame	Overlap	Celex only	Parole only	Total
[SU:NP][OBJ1:NP]	1810	1211	240	3261
[SU:NP]	257	1697	42	1996
[SU:NP][PC:PP⟨*pform*⟩]	337	541	273	1151
[SU:NP][OBJ1:NP][PC:PP⟨*pform*⟩]	129	375	308	812
[SU:NP][VC:S⟨subordinate⟩]	103	136	103	342
[SUP:NP⟨het⟩][OBJ1:NP][SU:CP]	7	247	5	259
[SU:NP][OBJ2:NP][OBJ1:NP]	65	171	28	264
[SU:NP][SE:NP][PC:PP⟨*pform*⟩]	65	62	102	229
[SU:NP][SE:NP]	49	137	65	251
[SU:NP][VC:VP]	10	16	37	63

Table 1: Dependency Frames and the number of stems occurring with this frame in both resources, in CGN/Celex only, in Parole only, and the total number of stems with this dependency frame in the Alpino Lexicon.

The Dutch Parole lexicon[2] comes with detailed subcategorization information, including dependency relations. The Parole lexicon is smaller than Celex, with 3,200 verbal stems and a total of 5000 dependency frames. There are 320 different dependency frame types, 190 of which occur only once.

Dependency frames for the Alpino lexicon have been constructed using the dependency information provided by CGN/Celex, Parole, and by entering definitions by hand. The latter has been done mostly for auxiliary and modal verbs: a small class of high-frequent elements which are exceptional in a number of ways. The CGN/Celex dictionary is very large. As the Celex database comes with frequency information, we currently only include those lexical items whose frequency is above a certain threshold. For verbal stems, this means that roughly 50% of the stems in Celex is included in the Alpino lexicon. All verbal stems from the Parole lexicon with a dependency frame covered by the grammar are included.

Currently, for 28 different CGN/Celex dependency frames a definition in the grammar has been provided. This covers over 80% of the verbal dependency frames in the CGN/Celex database, 10,400 of which are sufficiently frequent to be included in the Alpino lexicon. For 15 different dependency frames in the Parole lexicon a definition in Alpino is present. Using these, we extract over 4,100 dependency frames (82% of the total number of dependency frames in the Parole database). An overview of overlap and non-overlap for the most frequent frames extractable from both sources is given in table 1. For transitive and intransitive verbs, we see that over 85% of the stems in Parole are present in CGN/Celex as well. For most other dependency frames, however, the overlap is generally much smaller, and a significant portion of the stems present in Parole is not present in

[2] `http://www.inl.nl/corp/parole.htm`

Celex. This suggests that, for more specific subcategorization frames, both resources are only partially complete, and that not even the union of both provides exhaustive coverage.[3]

4 Dependency Structures

Within the CGN-project (Oostdijk 2000), guidelines have been developed for syntactic annotation of spoken Dutch (Moortgat, Schuurman and van der Wouden 2000), using dependency structures similar to those used for the German Negra corpus (Skut, Krenn and Uszkoreit 1997).

Dependency structures make explicit the dependency relations between constituents in a sentence. Each non-terminal node in a dependency structure consists of a head-daughter and a list of non-head daughters, whose dependency relation to the head is marked. A dependency structure for (1) is given in figure 1. Control relations are encoded by means of co-indexing (i.e. the subject of *hebben* is the dependent with index **1**). Note that a dependency structure does not necessarily reflect (surface) syntactic constituency. The dependent *haar nieuwe model gisteren aangekondigd*, for instance, does not correspond to a (surface) syntactic constituent in (1).

(1) Mercedes zou haar nieuwe model gisteren hebben aangekondigd
Mercedes should her new model yesterday have announced
Mercedes should have announced her new model yesterday

The Alpino grammar produces dependency structures compatible with the CGN-guidelines. We believe this is a useful output format for a number of reasons. First of all, annotating a text with dependency structures is relatively straightforward and independent of the particular grammatical framework assumed. Thus, a dependency treebank can be used to debug and test various versions of the Alpino grammar. Second, as we adopt the CGN-guidelines, a considerable amount of annotated material will be available within the near future which can be used for development and testing. Third, it has been suggested that dependency relations provide a convenient level of representation for evaluation of computational grammars based on radically different grammatical theories (Carroll, Briscoe and Sanfilippo 1998). Finally, statistics for dependency relations between head words can be used to develop accurate models for parse-selection (Collins 1999); preliminary experiments are described in section 6.

Grammatical Construction of Dependency Structures. To produce dependency structures with the Alpino grammar, a new level of representation has been added to the grammar. The attribute DT dominates a dependency structure, with attributes for the lexical head (HD) and the various dependents. The value of a dependent attribute can be a dependency structure or a leaf node consisting of a

[3]The less frequent verb stems in Celex (currently not included in Alpino) are almost exclusively assigned the intransitive or transitive dependency frame.

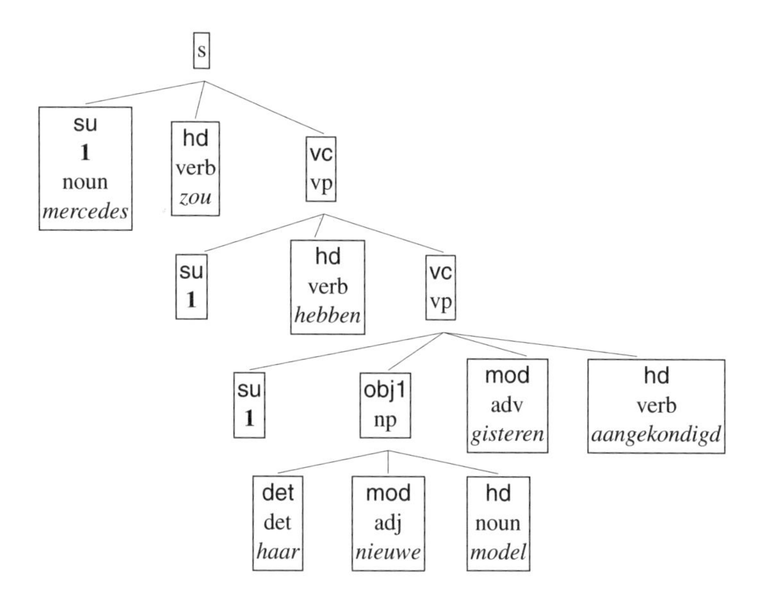

Figure 1: Dependency structure for example (1).

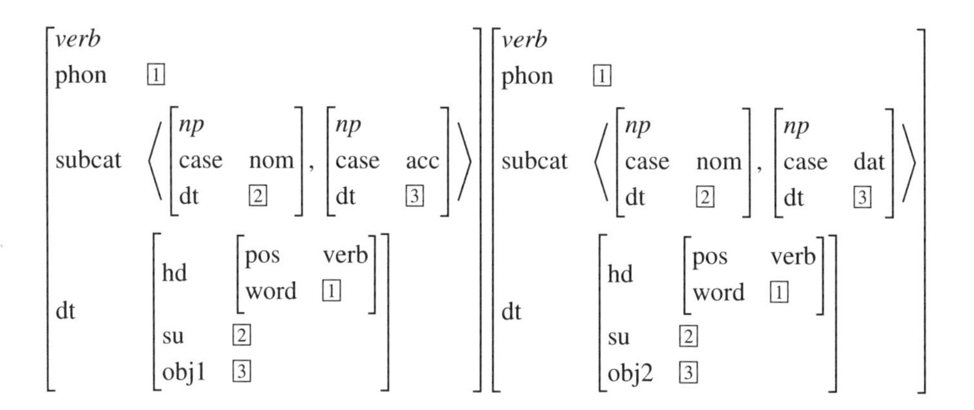

Figure 2: Schematic lexical entry for transitive verbs taking a direct object (OBJ1), and for transitive verbs taking an indirect object (OBJ2).

POS-tag and word only.

The construction of dependency structures is driven by the lexicon. For each subcategorization type recognized in the lexical hierarchy a mapping between elements on the list-valued feature which specifies basic subcategorization properties (SUBCAT) and attributes of DT is defined. Two examples are given in figure 2. The leftmost feature structure exemplifies a finite, transitive verb. The value of DT of the nominative NP on subcat is identical to the value of the SU dependent. Similarly, the value of DT of the accusative NP on subcat is identical to the value of the OBJ1 dependent. The rightmost feature structure exemplifies a finite, transitive verb for which the object is assigned to the OBJ2 (secondary object) dependency relation. In some cases, the addition of dependency structures leads to more fine-grained distinctions. For instance, PP-arguments can be linked to PC (*prepositional complement*) or LD (*locative or directional complement*), where the distinction between these two is primarily semantic in nature. Therefore, verbs taking a prepositional complement are assigned a subcategorization frame that differs from the frame assigned to verbs taking such a LD complement.

In HEAD-COMPLEMENT structures, the DT attribute can simply be shared between head daughter and mother. In HEAD-MODIFIER structures, the dependency structure of the modifier is added to the list-valued MOD dependent of the head.

Dependency Treebanks. For development and evaluation purposes, we have started to annotate various sample text fragments with dependency structures.

The annotation process typically starts by parsing a sentence with the Alpino grammar. This produces a (often large) number of possible analyses. The annotator picks the analysis which best matches the correct analysis. To facilitate selection of the best parse among a large number of possibilities, the HDRUG environment has been extended with a graphical tool based on the SRI TreeBanker (Carter 1997) which displays all fragments of the input which are a source of ambiguity. By disambiguating these items (usually a much smaller number than the number of readings), the annotator can quickly pick the most accurate parse.

For example, the sentence *Jan zag het meisje* 'Jan saw the girl' has (in principle) two readings corresponding to the dependency structures in figure 3. The readings of a sentence are represented as a set of sets of dependency paths, as in figure 4. From these sets of paths, the parse selection tool computes a set of *maximal discriminants* which can be used to select among different analyses. In this case, the path 's:hd = v *zag*' is shared by all the analyses and so is not a useful discriminant. On the other hand, the path 's:obj1:hd = n *meisje*' does distinguish between the readings but it is not maximal, since it is subsumed by the path 's:obj1 = np *het meisje*' which is shorter and makes exactly the same distinctions. The maximal discriminants are presented to the annotator, who may mark any of them as either good (the correct parse must include it) or bad (the correct parse may not include it). In this simple example, marking any one of the maximal discriminants as good or bad is sufficient to uniquely identify the correct parse. For more complex sentences, several choices will have to be made to select a single best parse. To help the annotator, when a discriminant is marked as bad or good, the following

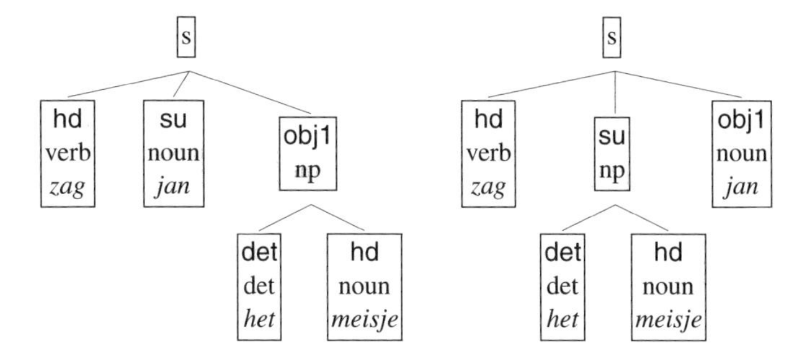

Figure 3: Dependency structures for two readings of *Jan zag het meisje*.

s:hd = v *zag*	s:hd = v *zag*
*s:su = np *jan*	*s:su = np *het meisje*
*s:obj1 = np *het meisje*	s:su:det = det *het*
s:obj1:det = det *het*	s:su:hd = n *meisje*
s:obj1:hd = n *meisje*	*s:obj1 = np *jan*

Figure 4: Dependency paths for *Jan zag het meisje* (* indicates a maximal discriminant).

inference rules are applied to further narrow the possibilities (Carter 1997):

- If a discriminant is bad, any parse which includes it is bad.
- If a discriminant is good, any parse which does not include it is bad.
- If a discriminant is only included in bad parses, it must be bad.
- If a discriminant is included in all the undecided parses, it must be good.

This allows users to focus their attention on discriminants about which they have clear intuitions. Their decisions about these discriminants combined with the rules of inference can then be used to automatically make decisions about less obvious discriminants.

If the parse selected by the annotator is fully correct, the dependency structure for that parse is stored as XML in the treebank. If the best parse produced by the grammar is not the correct parse as it should be included in the treebank, the dependency structure for this parse is sent to the Thistle editor.[4] The annotator can now produce the correct parse manually.

We have started to annotate various smaller fragments using the annotation tools described above. The largest fragments consist of two sets of sentences ex-

[4]LT Thistle (Calder 2000), `www.ltg.ed.ac.uk/software/thistle/`, is an editor and display engine for linguistic data-structures which supports XML.

tracted from the Eindhoven corpus (Uit den Boogaart 1975). The CDBL10 treebank currently consists of the first 519 sentences of ten words or less from section CDBL (newspaper text). The CDBL20 treebank consists of the first 252 sentences with more than 10 but no more than 20 words.

Evaluation. Evaluation of coverage and accuracy of a computational grammar usually is based on some metric which compares tree structures (such as recall and precision of (labelled) brackets or bracketing inconsistencies (crossing brackets) between test item and parser output). As is well-known, such metrics have a number of drawbacks. Therefore, Carroll et al. (1998) propose to annotate sentences with triples of the form ⟨*head-word, dependency relation, dependent head-word*⟩. For instance, for the example in (1) we might obtain:

⟨zou, su, mercedes⟩
⟨zou, vc, hebben⟩
⟨hebben, su, mercedes⟩
⟨hebben, vc, aangekondigd⟩
⟨aangekondigd, su, mercedes⟩
⟨aangekondigd, obj1, model⟩
⟨aangekondigd, mod, gisteren⟩
⟨model, det, haar⟩
⟨model, mod, nieuwe⟩

Dependency relations between head-words can be extracted easily from the dependency structures in our treebank, as well as from the dependency structures constructed by the parser. It is thus straightforward to compute precision, recall, and f-score on the set of dependency triples.

5 Robust Parsing

The initial design and implementation of the Alpino parser is inherited from the system described in van Noord (1997), van Noord et al. (1999) and van Noord (2001). However, a number of improvements have been implemented which are described below.

The construction of a dependency structure on the basis of some input proceeds in a number of steps, described below. The first step consists of lexical analysis. In the second step a parse forest is constructed. The third step consists of the selection of the best parse from the parse forest.

Lexical Analysis. The lexicon associates a word or a sequence of words with one or more *tags*. Such tags contain information such as part-of-speech, inflection as well as a subcategorization frame. For verbs, the lexicon typically hypothesizes many different tags, differing mainly in the subcategorization frame. For sentence (1), the lexicon produces 83 tags. Some of those tags are obviously wrong. For example, one of the tags for the word `hebben` is `verb(hebben,pl,part_sbar_transitive(door))`. The tag indicates a finite plural verb which requires a separable prefix `door`, and which subcategorizes for an SBAR complement. Since `door` does not occur anywhere in sentence (1), this tag will not be useful for this sentence. A filter containing a number of hand-written rules has been implemented which checks that such simple conditions hold. For sentence (1), the filter removes 56 tags. After the filter has applied, feature structures are associated with each of these tags. Often, a single tag is mapped to multiple feature structures. The remaining 27 filtered tags give rise to 89 feature structures.

An important aspect of lexical analysis is the treatment of unknown words. The system applies a number of heuristics for unknown words. Currently, these heuristics attempt to deal with numbers and number-like expressions, capitalized words, words with missing diacritics, words with 'too many' diacritics, compounds, and proper names.

If such heuristics still fail to provide an analysis, then the system guesses a tag by inspecting the suffix of the word. A list of suffixes is maintained which predict the tag of a given word. If this still does not provide an analysis, then it is assumed that the word is a noun.

In addition to the treatment of unknown words, the robustness of the system is enhanced by the possibility to skip tokens of the input. Currently this possibility is employed only for certain punctuation marks. Even though punctuation is treated both in the lexicon and the grammar, the syntax of punctuation is irregular enough to warrant the possibility to ignore punctuation. For instance, quotation marks may appear almost anywhere in the input. The corpus contains:

(2) De z.g. " speelstraat , die hier en daar al bestaat ?
The so-called " play-street , that here and there already exists ?

Apparently, the author intended to place `speelstraat` within quotes, but the second quote is not present. During lexical analysis, tags are optionally extended to include neighbouring words which are classified as 'skipable'.

Creating Parse Forests. The Alpino parser takes the result of lexical analysis as its input, and produces a *parse forest*: a compact representation of all parse trees. The Alpino parser is a left-corner parser with selective memoization and goal-weaking. It is a variant of the parsers described in van Noord (1997). We generalized some of the techniques described there to take into account relational constraints, which are delayed until sufficiently instantiated (van Noord and Bouma 1994).

As described in van Noord et al. (1999) and van Noord (2001), the parser can be instructed to find all occurrences of the start category *anywhere in the input*. This feature is added to enhance robustness as well. In case the parser cannot find an instance of the start category from the beginning of the sentence to the end, then the parser produces parse trees for large chunks of the input. A best-first search procedure then picks out the best sequence of such chunks. Depending on the application, such chunks might be very useful. In the past, we successfully employed this strategy in a spoken dialogue system (Veldhuijzen van Zanten et al. 1999).

beam	cdbl10		cdbl20	
	accuracy (%)	speed (msec)	accuracy (%)	speed (msec)
1	79.99	190	73.63	740
2	80.66	270	74.59	1470
4	81.11	350	75.07	2350
8	81.22	530	75.35	3630
16	81.36	590	75.31	5460
32	81.36	790	74.98	7880
∞	81.36	640	-	-

Table 2: Effect of beam-size on accuracy and efficiency of parse selection

Unpacking and Parse Selection. The motivation to construct a parse forest is efficiency: the number of parse trees for a given sentence can be enormous. In addition to this, in most applications the objective will not be to obtain *all* parse trees, but rather the *best* parse tree. Thus, the final component of the parser consists of a procedure to select these best parse trees from the parse forest.

In order to select the best parse tree from a parse forest, we assume a parse evaluation function which assigns a score to each parse. In section 6 we describe some initial experiments with a variety of parse evaluation functions. A naive algorithm constructs all possible parse trees, assigns each one a score, and then selects the best one. Since it is too inefficient to construct all parse trees, we have implemented the algorithm which computes parse trees from the parse forest as a best-first search. This requires that the parse evaluation function is extended to partial parse trees. In order to be able to *guarantee* that this search procedure indeed finds the best parse tree, a certain monotonicity requirement should apply to this evaluation function: if a (partial) tree s is better than s', then a tree t which contains s should be better than t' which is just like t except it has s' instead of s. However, instead of relying on such a requirement, we implemented a variant of a best-first search algorithm in such a way that for each state in the search space, we maintain the b best candidates, where b is a small integer (the *beam*). If the beam is decreased, then we run a larger risc of missing the best parse (but the result will typically still be a relatively 'good' parse); if the beam is increased, then the amount of computation increases too. Currently, we find that a value of $b = 4$ is a good compromise between accuracy and efficiency. In table 2 the effect of various values for b is presented for two development treebanks. The grammar assigns on average about 33 parse trees per sentence for the `cdbl10` corpus. This number increases rapidly for longer sentences: for the `cdbl20` corpus it is at least 340.[5]

[5]This is the average number after creating all parse trees for each sentence with a maximum of 1000 parse trees per sentence.

6 Disambiguation

The best-first unpack strategy described in section 5 depends on a parse evaluation function which assigns scores to (partial) parse trees. We have experimented with a number of disambiguation techniques on the `cdbl10` and `cdbl20` development treebanks described earlier.

Penalty rules. The simplest disambiguation method consists of hand-written 'penalty' rules which implement a variety of preferences. Each such penalty rule describes a partial parse tree. For a given parse tree, the system computes how often a sub-tree matches with a penalty rule, giving rise to the total penalty of that parse. The following lists characterizes some of the penalty rules:

- complementation is preferred over modification
- subject topicalization is preferred over object topicalization
- long distance dependencies are dis-preferred
- certain rules are dis-preferred (e.g. rules which coordinate categories without an explicit coordinator)
- certain lexical entries are dis-preferred (e.g. the preposition readings for the words `aan, bij, in, naar, op, uit, voor, tussen` are preferred over the adjectival, noun and/or verb readings).
- certain guesses for unknown words are preferred over others

As can be concluded from the preliminary results presented in table 3, it appears to be the case that about 60% of the disambiguation problem can be solved using this very simple technique.

Dependency relations We also experimented with statistical models based on dependency relations encoded in the dependency structure. The model assigns a probality to a parse by considering each dependency relation. For this purpose, dependency relations d are 5-tuples $d = \langle w_h, p_h, r, w_a, p_a \rangle$ where w_h is the head word, p_h is the corresponding part-of-speech tag taken from a small set of part-of-speechs $\{v, n, a, adv, p, \ldots\}$, r is the name of the relation taken from a small set of relation names $\{su, obj1, obj2, vc, mod, det, \ldots\}$; w_a is the argument word, and p_a is its part of speech.

The probability of a parse y given a sentence x might then be defined as:

$$p(y|x) = \frac{1}{Z(x)} \prod_{d \in y} p(r, w_a, p_a | w_h, p_h)$$

For disambiguation, the normalizing factor $Z(x)$ is the same for every parse of a given sentence and can be ignored.

Due to the occurrence of reentrancies, dependency structures are generally not trees but graphs. Therefore, the product above gives poor results because it will have an unjustified bias against such reentrancies (a reentrancy gives rise to an additional dependency relation). For this reason, we have chosen to score parse trees by determining the *mean* value of $-\log p$ for each tuple; this improved results considerably. The probability of a dependency is calculated as follows:

$$p(r, w_a, p_a | w_h, p_h) = p(r|w_h, p_h) * p(p_a|w_h, p_h, r) * p(w_a|w_h, w_p, r, p_a)$$

The three components are each calculated using a linear back-off strategy, where the weights are determined by frequency and diversity (formula 2.66 of (Collins 1999)). The quantities we use for backing off are given in the following table:

back-off level	$p(r\|w_h, p_h)$	$p(p_a\|w_h, p_h, r)$	$p(w_a\|w_h, w_p, r, p_a)$
1	$p(r\|p_h)$	$p(p_a\|p_h, r)$	$p(w_a\|w_p, r, p_a)$
2	$p(r)$	$p(p_a\|r)$	$p(w_a\|r, p_a)$
3		$p(p_a)$	$p(w_a\|p_a)$
4			$p(w_a)$

Because the size of the treebanks we have currently available is much too small to estimate these quantities accurately, we have chosen to do our estimation using unsupervised learning. We have parsed a large corpus ('de Volkskrant' newspaper text: first four months of 1997) using the penalty rules described in the previous section as our disambiguator. This corpus contains about 350,000 sentences and 6,200,000 words. We only used those sentences that the system could analyse as a single constituent, and within a reasonable amount of time. This meant that we could use the results of about 225,000 sentences. We estimated the quantity p using the best parse (according to the penalty rules) for each of these sentences. Collecting the 225,000 dependency structures took about one month of CPU-time (using the high-performance computing cluster of the University of Groningen).

As can be concluded from table 3, such a model performs much better than the baseline. Moreover, a combined model in which we simply add the rule penalties to the quantity p performs better than either model in isolation.

Log-linear models. While the model described in the previous section offers good performance and conceptual simplicity, it is not without problems. In particular, the strategies for dealing with reentrancies in the dependency structures and for combining scores derived from penalty rules and from dependency relation statistics are ad hoc. Log-linear models, introduced to natural language processing by Berger, Della Pietra and Della Pietra (1996) and Della Pietra, Della Pietra and Lafferty (1997), and applied to stochastic constraint-based grammars by Abney (1997) and Johnson, Geman, Canon, Chi and Riezler (1999), offer the potential to solve both of these problems. Given a conditional log-linear model, the probability of a sentence x having the parse y is:

$$p(y|x) = \frac{1}{Z(x)} \exp\left(\sum_i \lambda_i f_i(x, y)\right)$$

technique	cdbl10 precision	cdbl10 recall	cdbl10 f-score	cdbl20 precision	cdbl20 recall	cdbl20 f-score
baseline	62.3	63.3	62.8	58.5	59.6	59.0
log linear	76.0	76.6	76.3	66.3	67.6	66.0
penalties	78.6	79.3	78.9	73.1	73.3	73.2
dependency rel's	78.9	79.7	79.3	69.7	71.1	70.4
heur. + dep-rel's	80.9	81.7	81.3	74.6	75.4	75.0
maximum	89.1	90.0	89.6	83.2	84.1	83.7

Table 3: Preliminary results on the `cdbl10` and `cdbl20` development treebanks for a number of disambiguation techniques. The *baseline* row lists the percentages obtained if we select for each sentence a random parse tree from the parse forest. The *maximum* row lists the percentages obtained if we take for each sentence the best parse tree. These two numbers thus indicate the lower and upper bounds for parse selection.

As before, the partition function $Z(x)$ will be the same for every parse of a given sentence and can be ignored, so the score for a parse is simply the weighted sum of the property functions $f_i(x,y)$. What makes log-linear models particularly well suited for this application is that the property functions may be sensitive to any information which might be useful for disambiguation. Possible property functions include syntactic heuristics, lexicalized and backed-off dependency relations, structural configurations, and lexical semantic classes. Using log-linear models, all of these disparate types of information may be combined into a single model for disambiguation. Furthermore, since standard techniques for estimating the weights λ_i from training data make no assumptions about the independence of properties, one need not take special precautions when information sources overlap.

The drawback to using log-linear models is that accurate estimation of the parameters λ_i requires a large amount of annotated training data. Since such training data is not yet available, we instead attempted unsupervized training from unannotated data. We used the Alpino parser to find all parses of the 82,000 sentences with ten or fewer words in the 'de Volkskrant' newspaper corpus. Using the resulting collection of 2,200,000 unranked parses, we then applied Riezler et al.'s (2000) 'Iterative Maximization' algorithm to estimate the parameters of a log-linear model with dependency tuples as described in the previous section as property functions. The results, given in table 3, show some promise, but the performance of the log-linear model does not yet match that of the other disambiguation strategies. Current work in this area is focused on expanding the set of properties and on using supervised training from what annotated data is available to bootstrap the unsupervised training from large quantities of newspaper text.

7 Conclusions

Alpino aims at providing a wide-coverage, accurate, computational grammar for Dutch. The linguistic component of the system consists of a lexicalist feature-based grammar for Dutch, a wide-coverage and detailed lexicon, and a method for constructing dependency treebanks. The parser contains a lexical analysis module and a method for reconstructing parses from a parse forest using beam search, which allows the linguistic knowledge to be applied efficiently and robustly to unrestricted text. Finally, we have presented preliminary experiments aimed at providing accurate disambiguation.

In the near future, we hope to address a number of additional issues. The valency information in the lexicon is in many ways incomplete. We hope to obtain a more complete lexicon by acquiring dependency frames from corpora. Lexical analysis currently uses hand-written filter rules to reduce the number of tags for lexical items. An obvious alternative is to use a corpus-based part-of-speech tagger to arrive at the relevant filters. Finally, the work on disambiguation can profit from the availability of more annotated material. This suggests that our efforts at creating a dependency treebank may lead to improved results in the future.

References

Abney, S. P.(1997), Stochastic attribute-value grammars, *Computational Linguistics* **23**, 597–618.

Baayen, R. H., Piepenbrock, R. and van Rijn, H.(1993), *The CELEX Lexical Database (CD-ROM)*, Linguistic Data Consortium, University of Pennsylvania, Philadelphia, PA.

Berger, A., Della Pietra, S. and Della Pietra, V.(1996), A maximum entropy approach to natural language processing, *Computational Linguistics* **22**(1), 39–72.

Bouma, G. and van Noord, G.(1998), Word order constraints on verb clusters in German and Dutch, *in* E. Hinrichs, T. Nakazawa and A. Kathol (eds), *Complex Predicates in Nonderivational Syntax*, Academic Press, New York, pp. 43–72.

Bouma, G., Malouf, R. and Sag, I.(2001), Satisfying constraints on adjunction and extraction, *Natural Language and Linguistic Theory* **19**, 1–65.

Calder, J.(2000), Thistle and interarbora, *Proceedings of the 18th International Conference on Computational Linguistics (COLING)*, Saarbrücken, pp. 992–996.

Carroll, J., Briscoe, T. and Sanfilippo, A.(1998), Parser evaluation: A survey and a new proposal, *Proceedings of the first International Conference on Language Resources and Evaluation (LREC)*, Granada, Spain, pp. 447–454.

Carter, D.(1997), The TreeBanker: A tool for supervised training of parsed corpora, *Proceedings of the ACL Workshop on Computational Environments For Grammar Development And Linguistic Engineering*, Madrid.

Collins, M.(1999), *Head-Driven Statistical Models for Natural Language Parsing*, PhD thesis, University Of Pennsylvania.

Della Pietra, S., Della Pietra, V. and Lafferty, J.(1997), Inducing features of random fields, *IEEE Transactions on Pattern Analysis and Machine Intelligence* **19**, 380–393.

Groot, M.(2000), Lexiconopbouw: microstructuur. Internal report Corpus Gesproken Nederlands.

Johnson, M., Geman, S., Canon, S., Chi, Z. and Riezler, S.(1999), Estimators for stochastic "unification-based" grammars, *Proceedings of the 37th Annual Meeting of the ACL*, College Park, Maryland, pp. 535–541.

Moortgat, M., Schuurman, I. and van der Wouden, T.(2000), CGN syntactische annotatie. Internal report Corpus Gesproken Nederlands.

Oostdijk, N.(2000), The Spoken Dutch Corpus: Overview and first evaluation, *Proceedings of Second International Conference on Language Resources and Evaluation (LREC)*, pp. 887–894.

Pollard, C. and Sag, I.(1994), *Head-driven Phrase Structure Grammar*, University of Chicago / CSLI.

Riezler, S., Prescher, D., Kuhn, J. and Johnson, M.(2000), Lexicalized stochastic modeling of constraint-based grammars using log-linear measures and em, *Proceedings of the 38th Annual Meeting of the ACL*, Hong Kong, pp. 480–487.

Sag, I.(1997), English relative clause constructions, *Journal of Linguistics* **33**(2), 431–484.

Skut, W., Krenn, B. and Uszkoreit, H.(1997), An annotation scheme for free word order languages, *Proceedings of the Fifth Conference on Applied Natural Language Processing*, Washington, DC.

Uit den Boogaart, P. C.(1975), *Woordfrequenties in geschreven en gesproken Nederlands*, Oosthoek, Scheltema & Holkema, Utrecht. Werkgroep Frequentie-onderzoek van het Nederlands.

van Noord, G.(1997), An efficient implementation of the head corner parser, *Computational Linguistics* **23**(3), 425–456. cmp-lg/9701004.

van Noord, G.(2001), Robust parsing of word graphs, *in* J.-C. Junqua and G. van Noord (eds), *Robustness in Language and Speech Technology*, Kluwer Academic Publishers, Dordrecht.

van Noord, G. and Bouma, G.(1994), Adjuncts and the processing of lexical rules, *Proceedings of the 15th International Conference on Computational Linguistics (COLING)*, Kyoto, pp. 250–256. cmp-lg/9404011.

van Noord, G., Bouma, G., Koeling, R. and Nederhof, M.-J.(1999), Robust grammatical analysis for spoken dialogue systems, *Journal of Natural Language Engineering* **5**(1), 45–93.

Veldhuijzen van Zanten, G., Bouma, G., Sima'an, K., van Noord, G. and Bonnema, R.(1999), Evaluation of the NLP components of the OVIS2 spoken dialogue system, *in* F. van Eynde, I. Schuurman and N. Schelkens (eds), *Computational Linguistics in the Netherlands 1998*, Rodopi Amsterdam, pp. 213–229.

Revolution in Computational Linguistics

Towards a Genuinely Applied Science

Pius ten Hacken

Abteilung für Geisteswissenschaftliche Informatik, Universität Basel

Abstract

Among people working in Computational Linguistics (CL) around 1990 and still active in the field now, there is a widely shared feeling that they have witnessed a revolution. This paper shows which developments are responsible for this perception and which elements are central in the actual revolution. In order to avoid terminological confusion, the concept of revolution as it is used here is clarified first. Then the development in the subfield of Machine Translation is studied in some detail. It is argued that the actual revolution consists in a shift of attention from the application of theoretical knowledge to the solution of practical problems. To the extent that this shift is representative of more general developments in the field, the conclusions can be generalized to CL as a whole.

Among people working in Computational Linguistics (CL) around 1990 and still active in the field now, there is a widely shared feeling that they have witnessed a revolution. The purpose of this paper is to show which developments are responsible for this perceived revolution and how the consequences of these developments for the field can be evaluated. Section 1 creates a basis by establishing which sense of revolution is meant in the title and how such a phenomenon can be recognized in general. The position of Machine Translation (MT) in CL and the general orientation of CL before the revolution are sketched in section 2. Some aspects of four MT systems representative of the development in the 1980s and 1990s are outlined in section 3 and analysed in section 4. From this analysis, a more general characterization of the revolution in CL is derived in section 5.

1 Revolutions

The concept of *revolution* is one loaded with a large connotative value, which tends to hamper its successful application in a specific context such as the question of whether and how exactly CL has undergone a revolution in the past decade.

A revolution can be described generally as a radical change in the orientation of a system. In a sufficiently broad interpretation of *system*, this definition even covers the sense of 'rotating movement', as in a motor. More to the point are the cases in which 'system' refers to a sociologically organized complex. In this context an interesting parallel can be observed between political revolutions and scientific revolutions. The interest resides in the possibility of identifying some key concepts of revolutions which can be used successfully in both contexts.

While political revolutions are always radical changes in the orientation of the political system of a country, not every radical change amounts to a revolution. When Mitterand won the French presidential elections in 1981 and his socialist party won a landslide victory in the subsequent parliamentary elections, this certainly caused a radical reorientation of the French political landscape. Nevertheless, it was not a revolution. By contrast, when in 1830 King Charles X was overthrown and replaced by King Louis Philippe, the change in political orientation was probably much less radical, but it was certainly a revolution (cf. Louessard, 1990). The main difference between these events is that the system in place in 1981 catered for a changeover of power of the type which took place, whereas in 1830 the changeover was not foreseen by the rules of the system.

In the context of science, the term was originally used in a definite sense, '*the* scientific revolution', referring to the emergence of science in the modern sense after the Middle Ages (cf. Rossi 1997). This is certainly not the sense in which CL was revolutionized in the 1990s. More relevant is the concept of revolution as discussed by Kuhn (1970). This sense of (scientific) revolution has more in common with the notion of (political) revolution sketched above. Kuhn showed that a science at a given point in its existence has a specific system of rules, which regulates what counts as normal, accepted behaviour, more or less like its political counterpart. This system determines how science is done, what counts as progress in the development of science, and what is good science. A scientific revolution is the change of this reference system for a science in a sense not foreseen by the rules of the system itself.

In politics and in science, the underlying system is not a purpose in itself, but rather a background for doing something else. It requires strong motivation to spend a lot of time and energy reworking this background rather than making progress along better known lines. Therefore a revolution is always caused by a crisis. It is not necessary that this crisis is felt by everyone involved in the system, nor can a definite threshold be set when a revolution will start (much less when it will be successful), but revolutions do not occur at random.

Only when a group of scientists perceive their way of science as not promising sufficient progress any more will they start investing time in a revision of the underlying system of assumptions. As a consequence, a revolution is often accompanied by a general spirit of optimism among this group, because they believe that their radical measures will bring a faster road to progress. By itself, observing such a spirit need not be a sign of a revolution, however. Here a parallel with politics can be drawn. A similar type of optimism could be observed in France after the 1981 elections (at least in one part of society), for which we established previously that it did not constitute a revolution.

As a scientific revolution involves a change in reference system which determines how scientific practice should be evaluated, it is not possible to make a fair comparison of theories developed before and after the revolution by applying the standards of one reference system to the theories formulated on the basis of the other. Kuhn (1970) calls this the incommensurability of theories inherent in the comparison of different paradigms or disciplinary matrices. It should be emphasized that this means not only that the 'old' theory is judged unfairly with the new evaluation criteria, but also that the 'new' theory will probably be bad in terms of the evaluation criteria of the old reference system.

Mutual misunderstanding is often a sign of incommensurability. Thus, the following statements from the discussion between Householder (1965) and Chomsky & Halle (1965) provide a strong argument for the analysis of the emergence of Chomskyan linguistics as a scientific revolution. After a review of different aspects of Chomsky & Halle's phonological theory, Householder's conclusion is (1). In a detailed reaction to Householder's argument we find such remarks as (2).

> (1) "on matters of phonology, their claims and assertions, if all wholly true, would tend to make all phonological work impossible *on any known lines*." [Householder (1965:13), my emphasis].
>
> (2) "We have no idea what this comment means, and therefore make no attempt to discuss it." [Chomsky & Halle (1965:118)]

A consequence of incommensurability is that in a scientific revolution the newly emerging framework cannot be expected to encompass everything the old framework was able to deal with. A revolution always involves both progress and losses (cf. Chen 1997). If the revolution is successful the scientific community apparently considers the progress promised by the new framework greater than the losses it induces. Such a judgement cannot be fully rational, however, because it involves the choice between two standards of evaluation. There does not exist a common set of criteria to choose between two scientific paradigms.

Returning to CL, in order to show that a revolution took place, we should look for a radical change in the system of assumptions underlying scientific work. Properties of such a change include the incommensurability of results of work before and after the revolution.

2 Computational Linguistics before the Revolution

CL is special as a science because it requires more than just a theory. Whatever is produced in CL should work. In this sense, the opposition between CL and theoretical linguistics can be compared to the one between electrical engineering and theoretical physics. Despite the opposition, linguistics is usually understood as including CL, and physics as including electrical engineering. In addition, fields such as CL and electrical engineering share some important goals and properties with science at large. Science is about the extension of knowledge. In the list of priorities for this extension, there is a tension between two types of argument. Scientists are primarily looking for interesting knowledge, e.g. knowledge which extends the scope or precision of a theory. Their financial supporters are first of all attracted by the possibility of useful knowledge, e.g. knowledge which is beneficial for society or commercially attractive. Therefore, scientists usually try to convince potential financial supporters of the usefulness of what they find interesting.

This fundamental dilemma governs the relationship between empirical science, which is concerned with explaining data, and applied science, which is concerned with the solution of practical problems. The track record of past successes in producing useful knowledge determines to a large extent how directly the immediate applicability of the envisaged results influences the research agenda of a particular science. Physics has in the course of the centuries established a solid reputation that its results are useful in the long run, even if no immediate application is in sight. Computational Linguistics (CL) is in a more difficult position, not only because of its shorter history, but also because it has repeatedly disappointed the expectations of its financial supporters.

The early history of Machine Translation (MT) offers a number of clear examples. The upsurge of MT in the USA in the 1950s enabled research teams to get a rather large amount of money, but when the ALPAC (1966) report concluded that the promised results were not forthcoming, financial resources were withdrawn. In the 1970s and 1980s, the availability of linguistic theories of a new kind constituted a new promise. However, the TAUM group in Montréal only managed to secure funding for its celebrated Météo project by making a compromise in which much of the linguistic knowledge was sacrificed to a useful application. When the subsequent Aviation project, in which more of the linguistic knowledge could be applied, did not produce results fast enough, funding stopped (cf. Isabelle 1987).

For the 1970s and 1980s it is not too much to claim that the overall goal of CL was perceived by people working in the field as the modelling of human language on a computer. This is the picture arising from conferences such as Coling (1984) and textbooks such as Grishman (1986) and Pereira & Shieber (1987). Thus, at Coling, Shieber (1984:362) remarked that "The goal of natural-language processing research can be stated quite simply: to endow computers with human language capacity.", and, in the introduction to his widely used textbook, Grishman (1986:4) states that "Computational linguistics is the study of computer systems for understanding and generating natural language." Characteristic of the general approach of this period is Kay's (1973) MIND system. This system consists of a number of modules for different aspects of language, which can be connected in different ways so as to perform different tasks. Pereira & Shieber (1987) take as their point of departure the task of "natural language analysis", which can indeed be considered the central task of CL in this approach.

Scientific work can be analysed in general as solving problems. The scope of the work is then determined by the type of problem chosen, the type of knowledge used for the solution, and the type of solution aimed at. In CL as it functioned in the 1970s and 1980s, these parameters were set as in (3):

(3) a. Problem: Understanding human language processing
b. Knowledge: Contemporary linguistic theories
c. Solution: A running program on a computer

MT had a relatively important position in CL in this period. There are at least two reasons for this. First, whereas it is difficult to check how much a computer has understood after processing a sentence, it is much easier to check whether a particular task can be carried out. Translation is a task which uses a large part of the input and results in a representation which is open to easy human inspection.

Second, translation is a task which can easily be explained to potential financial supporters and which has economic value.

This position of MT within CL explains why translation theory as it had developed in the 1960s and 1970s was largely ignored in MT. The main focus of interest was not translation as such. Rather translation was used as an excuse for syntactic and semantic research. Thus, Lehrberger and Bourbeau (1988:1) claim that "The obstacles to translating by means of the computer are mainly linguistic." Translation was modelled (in most cases implicitly) as a fairly simple meaning equivalence.

By the end of the 1980s, this type of MT research had entered a crisis. A sign of this crisis is the fact that financial support for a number of projects ran out. Around 1990 all three of the major MT projects represented in the Netherlands - Eurotra, Rosetta, and DLT - were phased out.

3 Four MT Systems

In order to illustrate how the general trend in MT is reflected in individual systems, let us consider some relevant aspects of four systems in more detail. Eurotra, Rosetta, the statistical system developed at IBM, and Verbmobil represent different attitudes to the crisis in MT as it arose at the end of the 1980s.

Eurotra had its roots in the late 1970s. By the time the signs of a crisis were apparent, the project had entered its final phase. Major design decisions had been taken and also much of the linguistic theory had been established and 'frozen' so as not to hamper development by undermining this basis. At the time of its inception, Eurotra had been innovative in being a large-scale, truly multilingual transfer system. The scale of the organization contributed to a certain inertia in view of the emerging crisis. In fact, the organization was designed to optimize the coordination of results of interesting linguistic research rather than foundational issues of translation. Even so, the project leadership felt obliged to mention the problem of the choice of a translation theory in an overview of the project, as in (4):

> (4) "Any machine translation system, be it a research prototype or an operational system, builds upon some notion of theory of translation, implicitly or explicitly. [...] Unfortunately, we have found no theory of human translation which could be taken over and formalized." [Maegaard & Perschke (1991:75)]

While at the start of the project the question of what constitutes a translation had been taken for granted, (4) shows that towards the end of the project the lack of an answer had come to be felt as a drawback.

As Kuhn (1970) states, within established circles in a science there is a large resistance to fundamental changes. As long as the need for changes is not strongly imposed by a crisis, scientists will go on with business as usual.

Rosetta existed at around the same time as Eurotra, but it was much smaller. In addition, the director of the project, Jan Landsbergen, put a particular emphasis on formal correctness from the beginning. Rosetta (1994) describes and motivates decisions in the design and theoretical development of the system systematically and in detail. As discussed more extensively in ten Hacken (to appear), the major design decisions such as the choice of an interlingua model and the tuning of grammars of different languages to each other were the subject of controversial discussion in the field of MT, but the explicit model of the translation problem was not. Rosetta assumes sentences as the input to the translation process, sets of possible translations as output, and compositional translation as the relation between an element of the input and an element of the output. In Rosetta a formal model of natural languages and their semantic correspondence is constructed. For the evaluation of such a model, internal and external criteria can be used. Internal evaluation criteria justified by the approach in Rosetta concern the formal consistency of the models of the individual languages and the formal correctness of the mapping between them. External evaluation criteria concentrate on the correspondence between the model and the actual language or the actual input to the system.

The translation theory of Rosetta is characteristic of the approach adopted more or less generally in the 1970s and 1980s. The most remarkable feature was its explicitness. Although other MT systems did not necessarily accept every detail of it, it was not attacked in its outline and no alternative statement was proposed. Proposals for comparative system evaluation such as Melby (1988) are based on the same presuppositions about the correct (external) evaluation criteria.

In terms of Kuhn (1970) the lack of discussion is less remarkable than the fact that such an explicit, detailed statement of the underlying assumptions of an MT system was made at all. It can well be interpreted as a sign of a crisis. As Kuhn describes it, a crisis brings about an atmosphere where we find on the one hand a group of people exploring new avenues, on the other hand a group which defends the traditional approach, for example by explicitly stating its foundational principles. Rosetta (1994) definitely belongs to the latter group.

An example of the former reaction to the crisis is found in the statistical MT system developed at IBM. Deliberately provocative in their presentation, Brown et al. (1988) at first outlined the possibility of doing MT without linguistic analysis. In later presentations, they suggest a type of collaboration with more traditional approaches (cf. below). Despite its resolutely innovative choice of a source of knowledge, the IBM system is rather traditional in other respects. In particular, translation is still considered as a matter of producing a target language sentence corresponding to the source language sentence in the input. This correspondence is still understood in terms of equivalence of meaning. The central evaluation criterion proposed is the percentage of correctly translated sentences, i.e. sentences which have the desired meaning. Only the calculation of the correspondence is meaning-independent, in accordance with Shannon's (1948) information theory. The external evaluation criteria for Rosetta can be used successfully for the IBM system as well, resulting in a measure of correctness of the output which can be compared by the same standards.

Verbmobil offers us an example of yet another type of reaction to the crisis.

In their study, which sketches the goals of the prototype to be pursued, Kay et al. (1994) devote a rather long section (one eighth of the entire text) to the argument that the fact that language is situated makes translation difficult. To professional translators this point is obvious. The reason why it has to be argued in so much detail is that it contradicts one of the central assumptions of what MT is as commonly understood among people working in this field at the time. In their overview of MT systems, the main criticism of Rosetta focuses on their use of possible translations, stating that "this whole line of argument carries to an extreme that fallacy of thinking of translation as a function from a source to a target text." (Kay et al. 1994:85). By contrast, they propose that the intention of a message rather than the meaning of a sentence should be rendered in translation.

Instead of the traditional transfer, interlingua, or even direct architectures for MT, which all assume a unidirectional mapping from source to target language, Kay et al. (1994:93) propose a negotiation model. Such a model, should offer the possibility to compare different analyses and different target language renderings before deciding on the best one in the given context. Moreover, they propose to exploit the situational context of a dialogue system. The fact that language is situated, so that the intention underlying a message cannot be fully retrieved without considering the situational context, complicates the analysis from a traditional point of view, but it can also be used as a strategy to support the solution of a real-life problem. Human communicative behaviour in a regular dialogue among people is marked by questions for clarification and confirmations of conclusions, communicative mechanisms which can also be used by an MT system to solve ambiguities and confirm analyses.

In his introduction to the volume presenting the results of the project, Wahlster (2000) represents the multi-engine architecture as the principal innovation reflecting this proposed new approach to translation. The negotiation model is reflected in packed representations of ambiguities at all stages, which can be unpacked when the negotiation process requires it. Perhaps the change in understanding of what constitutes successful translation is even more fundamental as an innovation. Once accepted, however, it is hardly spectacular enough to present it as such.

4 The Nature of the Revolution in Computational Linguistics

Let us now return to the question of what the revolution in CL in the 1990s amounts to. As a starting point, let us consider how the four MT systems whose general approach is described in section 3 relate to the description of pre-revolutionary CL in section 2, and in particular to the parameters in (3), repeated here for convenience.

(3)	a.	Problem:	Understanding human language processing
	b.	Knowledge:	Contemporary linguistic theories
	c.	Solution:	A running program on a computer

The problem of MT in the sense in which it is taken by Eurotra and Rosetta can be seen as an instantiation of the problem of understanding human language processing. These systems select the knowledge to be used from among linguistic theories, supplemented by contrastive studies for the translation part. Insofar as these theories say anything about processing, they are concerned with human processing. The goal of producing a running program on a computer has to be stated explicitly in order to distinguish research in Eurotra and Rosetta from purely theoretical linguistic research.

The emergence of probabilistic approaches in CL is often felt as a revolution. In MT this development is instantiated by the IBM system of Brown et al. (1988, 1990, 1993). In terms of the parameters in (3) the central difference from Eurotra and Rosetta is the type of knowledge used. Although the statistical modelling of natural language can be seen as a linguistic theory in the broadest sense, it does not reflect the theories which are the subject of debate in linguistics. In particular, it is not intended as a valid model for human language processing. Therefore, in at least one sense, the selection of knowledge in probabilistic approaches implies a change in the problem of CL as well.

In a narrower sense, however, the problem remains the same: the same external evaluation criteria can be applied to Eurotra, Rosetta, and the IBM system. In fact, the percentage of correctly translated sentences is used as a basis for the claims about the performance of statistical MT by Brown et al. (1990:83f.) in the same way as it had long been done for conventional systems based on linguistic theories. The acceptance of these figures by both sides indicates that there is a level of problem statement on which they agree. The main difference is that in the probabilistic approach the problem of matching corresponding sentences from two languages is taken in a literal sense, rather than as an instantiation of the problem of understanding and modelling human language processing.

Another indication showing whether a revolution separates two approaches is the way they behave towards each other. Clearly, ideologically oriented antagonism is not sufficient as a proof of a revolution. We also find it in French politics around 1981, although we established in section 1 that Mitterand's election as president was not a revolution. The same goes for the general spirit of optimism. A further sign might be taken from the type of collaboration between people working in the two frameworks. Here some care is needed to interpret the observations correctly.

Even in generally accepted cases of scientific revolutions the new approach will try to take over results from the old one. The large extent to which this took place in the Copernican Revolution is described in detail by Kuhn (1957). Thus Copernicus continued to use epicycles developed by Ptolemy, and Kepler based his hypothesis of elliptical orbits around the sun on Tycho Brahe's observations within a geocentric framework. In a linguistic context, Chomsky took over a significant part of the analyses and rule types used in the Post-Bloomfieldian framework, despite the separation by the Chomskyan revolution illustrated by (1) and (2). A more extensive justification of the analysis of the emergence of Chomskyan linguistics as a revolution is given in ten Hacken (1997, 2000). Laudan (1977) explains in more detail why new frameworks after a revolution can and even must take over certain insights from the preceding ones.

Against this background, the fact that Brown et al. (1993:294f.) explain the need to include morphological knowledge in a probabilistic system and Brown et al. (1990:84) even suggest including syntactic trees does not provide decisive evidence against the analysis of the emergence of probabilistic approaches as a revolution. More pertinent indications are the analysis of this emergence in Gazdar (1996), who observes a "merger" of the two frameworks, and the work exemplified by Klavans & Resnik (1996), which illustrates this merger. The central difference can be described as follows. When a new framework after a revolution takes over knowledge from the old one, the new framework is dominant and what is taken over is a mixture of data, formal mechanisms, and low-level analyses, which are generally reinterpreted quite drastically. In the case of linguistic and probabilistic approaches exemplified by Eurotra, Rosetta, and the IBM system, there is enough agreement on the basic question to be answered that a competition of approaches can take place in the components of a common framework. The typical kind of collaboration is that for components such as morphological analysis, syntactic analysis, semantic analysis, and translational disambiguation probabilistic and linguistic approaches compete in order to produce an overall system which is better than one which is entirely probabilistic or entirely linguistic in its choice of knowledge.

In conclusion, the emergence of probabilistic approaches in CL, exemplified by the IBM system for statistical MT, does not constitute a revolution, but only a radical change in the choice of knowledge.

Finally let us turn to Verbmobil. As noted in section 3 above, a strong attack at the foundations of traditional MT is at the root of this project. As opposed to the IBM project, the focus of the attack is not primarily the type of knowledge used but the very problem as it is modelled. Thus, Verbmobil's alternative to (3b) is not dramatically different, but (3a) is. Instead of language processing in isolation, it is a particular problem with its practical context which is the starting point. As a result, (3c) is also changed quite radically. It is no longer sufficient to have a running program as a proof that the proposed model of language processing is possible. Instead, only a fully usable, practical solution is an acceptable outcome.

The contrast in the position of the practical application stands out most clearly in comparison with the treatment by Rosetta (1994). Rosetta suggests that given the core solution of the translation problem in the project, consisting of a set of possible translations for each input sentence, the context-dependent choice of the best translation might be supported by an interactive interface or approximated by whatever technique turns out best. For Verbmobil there cannot be a separation between core solution and practical application, because the practical application motivates not only the enterprise as such but also the structure of the solution.

As a result of the radical break with the traditional choices in (3a) and (3c), it is no longer possible to use the same evaluation criteria for a fair comparison of Verbmobil and any of the other systems discussed. An evaluation of Verbmobil on the basis of the percentage of correctly translated sentences would be entirely beside the point. For the evaluation of systems such as Eurotra and Rosetta in a practical context, Krauwer (1993) uses the metaphor of a gearbox. It is not possible to evaluate gearboxes without building cars around them. In this metaphor,

Verbmobil is intended as a car.

We can therefore conclude that the revolution in CL is instantiated in MT by the emergence of systems such as Verbmobil. What remains to be explained is the fact that, in the perception of many people working in MT, the revolution is rather associated with the emergence of probabilistic methods. The reason for this is that the emergence of probabilistic methods changed the tasks of these people and the tools for performing them quite radically. However, the term *revolution* is used here for an epistemological change, not a practical change. While we can say informally that the invention of the telescope revolutionized astronomy, its role in the Copernican revolution as an epistemological process is minor. It only served to confirm certain predictions, when the actual change of mind had already taken place (cf. Kuhn 1957). Similarly, while the emergence of probabilistic techniques revolutionized work in MT only in an informal sense, the revolution as an epistemological process is associated with the reorientation from a principled solution to the abstract problem of translation to the practical solution of a practical problem involving translation.

5 Computational Linguistics after the Revolution

After this analysis of the repercussions of the revolution in CL in the subfield of MT, we are now in a position to broaden our scope and consider which general change in CL the revolution in MT reflects. On the basis of our observations in the field of MT, we can hypothesize the following set of assumptions for the new orientation of CL corresponding to (3).

(5)	a.	Problem:	A practical problem occurring in real life
	b.	Knowledge:	Whatever turns out to be helpful in a solution
	c.	Solution:	A system or program in practical use

The most striking difference between (3) and (5) is the relative importance of the choice of knowledge. In the older type of CL, based on (3), ideological oppositions were most often associated with the preference for one theory or another. In the new type of CL, based on (5), there is hardly any room for ideological oppositions on this basis, because what counts is the practical use of the solution.

At the same time, in connection with this reduced importance of the choice of knowledge, we find a change in the status of practical applications. In the older type of CL, a suggestion of how the program might be used in practice was considered enough in most cases. If the question was addressed in more depth, this was typically because financial support required it. In the new type of CL, the practical use of the product is part of the conception of the problem from the start.

As noted in section 1, a scientific revolution is always associated with progress in the field, but certain possibilities are also lost compared to the older framework. If progress is measured in terms of the amount of money invested and the number of people working in the field, the 1990s certainly featured substantial progress in CL. While ten Hacken (to appear) observes a relative decrease in the number of papers on MT at Coling conferences from 1988 to 1998, this is largely (and perhaps entirely) due to the diversification of the field, in which a greater variety of problems are taken on than ever before. The 1990s also saw the emergence of specialized conferences on a scale never seen before. Finally, the practical use of solutions produced by CL has increased. This is not surprising if the formulation of problems is guided not by the theoretical knowledge to be applied but directly by the observation of the problem in real life. What is lost in this development is the close connection between computational and theoretical approaches to language. The determinism which depends on the validity of formal correctness as a goal is lost.

In conclusion, the revolution in CL in the 1990s consisted in the reorientation of the field from knowledge to problems. Before the revolution, CL was performing theoretical linguistics by slightly different means. If practical applications played a role at all, as in Météo, it was a compromise imposed by financial constraints. Since the revolution, researchers in CL have discovered how interesting practical problems are. Taking into account what works in practice needs no longer to be imposed after the fact, but guides the research from the start. Many of the tasks concerning details have remained the same, but the overall design of CL projects has changed.

It is interesting to compare this development to what happened in electrical engineering. The Leyden jar, invented by Pieter van Musschenbroek in 1746, was a device which can be said to work in the sense that it is not merely theoretical. Its only use at the time, however, was in classroom demonstrations showing that there is such a thing as electricity. By contrast, when Thomas Edison invented the carbon-filament lamp in 1879, it was the conclusion of a search for a solution to the problem of producing electric light. This problem had occupied a host of researchers for fifty years or so. CL before the revolution can be compared to electrical engineering in the 18th century. It produced working systems which like the Leyden jar did not have an immediate practical function but could be used to demonstrate certain theoretical notions. In MT, the emphasis was on linguistic theory rather than on the practical problem of translation. Since the revolution, CL has become more like electrical engineering in the 19th century. It is no longer sufficient that a system works, it must also be usable in practice. Therefore, the starting point of CL research has shifted from applying linguistic theory to solving practical problems. Arguably, only since the revolution has CL really become an applied science.

References

ALPAC [Automatic Language Processing Advisory Committee] (1966), *Language and Machines: Computers in Translation and Linguistics*, Washington (DC): National Academy of Sciences.

Brown, Peter; Cocke, John; Della Pietra, Stephen; Della Pietra, Vincent J.; Jelinek, Fredrick; Mercer, Robert L. & Roossin, Paul S. (1988), 'A Statistical Approach to Language Translation', in Vargha (ed.), p. 71-76.

Brown, Peter; Cocke, John; Della Pietra, Stephen; Della Pietra, Vincent J.; Jelinek, Fredrick; Lafferty, John D.; Mercer, Robert L. & Roossin, Paul S. (1990), 'A Statistical Approach to Machine Translation', *Computational Linguistics* 16:79-85.

Brown, Peter F.; Della Pietra, Stephen A.; Della Pietra, Vincent J. & Mercer, Robert L. (1993), 'The Mathematics of Statistical Machine Translation: Parameter Estimation', *Computational Linguistics* 19:263-311.

Chen, Xiang (1997), 'Thomas Kuhn's Latest Notion of Incommensurability', *Journal for General Philosophy of Science* 28:257-273.

Chomsky, Noam & Halle, Morris (1965), 'Some controversial questions in phonological theory', *Journal of Linguistics* 1:97-138.

Coling (1984), *Proceedings of Coling84, 10th International Conference on Computational Linguistics, 22nd Annual Meeting of the Association of Computational Linguistics*, Stanford CA: Stanford University.

Gazdar, Gerald (1996), 'Paradigm Merger in Natural Language Processing', in Wand, Ian & Milner, Robin (eds.), *Computing Tomorrow: Future research directions in computer science*, Cambridge: Cambridge University Press, p. 88-109.

Grishman, Ralph (1986), *Computational Linguistics: An Introduction*, Cambridge: Cambridge University Press.

Hacken, Pius ten (1997), 'Progress and Incommensurability in Linguistics', *Beiträge zur Geschichte der Sprachwissenschaft*, 7:287-310.

Hacken, Pius ten (2000), *Reusability and Research Programmes in Computational Linguistics*, Habilitationsschrift, Universität Basel (Switzerland).

Hacken, Pius ten (to appear), 'Has There Been a Revolution in Machine Translation ?', to appear in *Machine Translation*.

Householder, Fred W. (1965), 'On some recent claims in phonological theory', *Journal of Linguistics* 1:13-34.

Isabelle, Pierre (1987), 'Machine Translation at the TAUM Group', in King, Margaret (ed.), *Machine Translation Today: The State of the Art*, Edinburgh: Edinburgh University Press, p. 247-277.

Kay, Martin (1973), 'The MIND System', in Rustin, Randall (ed.), *Natural Language Processing: Courant Computer Science Symposium 8, December 20-21, 1971*, New York: Algorithmics Press, p. 155-188.

Kay, Martin; Gawron, Jean Mark & Norvig, Peter (1994), *Verbmobil: A Translation System for Face-to-Face Dialog*, Stanford (Calif.): CSLI.

Klavans, Judith L. & Resnik, Philip (eds.) (1996), *The Balancing Act: Combining Symbolic and Statistical Approaches to Language*, Cambridge (Mass.): MIT Press.

Krauwer, Steven (1993), 'Evaluation of MT Systems: A Programmatic View', *Machine Translation* 8:59-66.

Kuhn, Thomas S. (1957), *The Copernican Revolution: Planetary Astronomy in the Development of Western Thought*, Harvard University Press, Cambridge (Mass.).

Kuhn, Thomas S. (1970), *The Structure of Scientific Revolutions*, Second Edition, Enlarged, Chicago: University of Chicago Press.

Laudan, Larry (1977), *Progress and Its Problems: Towards a Theory of Scientific Growth*, Berkeley: University of California Press.

Lehrberger, John & Bourbeau, Laurent (1988), *Machine Translation: Linguistic characteristics of MT systems and general methodology of evaluation*, Amsterdam: Benjamins.

Louessard, Laurent (1990), *La révolution de juillet 1830*, Spartacus.

Maegaard, Bente & Perschke, Sergei (1991), 'Eurotra: General System Design', *Machine Translation* 6:73-82.

Melby, Alan K. (1988), 'Lexical Transfer: Between a Source Rock and a Hard Target', in Vargha, (ed.), p. 411-413.

Pereira, Fernando C.N. & Shieber, Stuart M. (1987), *Prolog and Natural-Language Analysis*, Stanford: CSLI.

Rosetta, M.T. (1994), *Compositional Translation*, Dordrecht: Kluwer Academic.

Rossi, Paolo (1997), *La nascita della scienza moderna in Europa*, Roma / Bari: Laterza.

Shannon, Claude S. (1948) 'The mathematical theory of communication', *Bell Systems Technical Journal* 27:379-423 and 27:623-656.

Shieber, Stuart M. (1984) 'The Design of a Computer Language for Linguistic Information', in Coling (1984), p. 362-366.

Vargha, Dénes (ed.) (1988) *Coling Budapest: Proceedings of the 12th International Conference on Computational Linguistics*, (2 vol.), Budapest: John von Neumann Society for Computing Sciences.

Wahlster, Wolfgang (2000) 'Mobile Speech-to-Speech Translation of Spontaneous Dialogs: An Overview of the Final Verbmobil System', in Wahlster, Wolfgang (ed.), *Verbmobil: Foundations of Speech-to-Speech Translation*, Berlin: Springer.

Syntactic Annotation for the Spoken Dutch Corpus Project (CGN)

Heleen Hoekstra, Michael Moortgat, Ineke Schuurman, Ton van der Wouden

UiL-OTS, Utrecht University and CCL, KULeuven

Abstract

Of the ten million words of contemporary standard Dutch in the Spoken Dutch Corpus (Corpus Gesproken Nederlands, CGN), a selection of one million words of natural spoken language will be annotated syntactically. In the present paper we discuss the tag sets and the annotation procedures that are currently being developed and tested. The annotation tags provide information about syntactic constituents and about the semantic relations (dependencies) between these constituents. The annotation graphs allow crossing branches, which makes it possible to represent dependencies independently of surface word order. Moreover, constituents can carry multiple dependency roles, a feature that is exploited in the annotation of non-local dependencies and ellipsis. The annotation process is carried out semi-automatically, using an interactive annotation environment developed within the NEGRA project, a syntactically annotated corpus of German newspaper texts. We illustrate the approach with some real life examples from the CGN corpus, focusing on how some typical spoken language phenomena are dealt with.

1 Introduction: about the CGN

The aim of the Spoken Dutch Corpus project (abbreviated as CGN, from the Dutch name *Corpus Gesproken Nederlands*) is to build an annotated corpus of about one thousand hours of continuous speech, which amounts to 10 million words. The project started in June 1998, and runs for five years. It is a collaborative effort of several Dutch and Flemish universities (Goedertier, Goddijn and Martens 2000, Oostdijk 2000a, Oostdijk 2000b).

The corpus is intended as a major resource both for linguistic research and for language and speech technology. To serve this dual purpose, it contains materials recorded in a variety of communicative settings: spontaneous face-to-face and telephone dialogues, interviews, discussions, debates, lectures, news broadcasts and book passages read aloud. Two-thirds of the material is collected in the Netherlands, one third in the Dutch speaking part of Belgium. Upon completion, the corpus will be the largest and most diverse database of spoken Dutch collected so far.

The project envisages different levels of annotation. The complete corpus is orthographically transcribed; also, every word receives a (contextually disambiguated) part-of-speech (POS) tag (Van Eynde, Zavrel and Daelemans 2000). In addition, broad phonetic transcription and syntactic annotation is provided for a representative selection of 10 percent of the data — the so-called core corpus. One quarter of the core corpus receives a prosodic annotation as well. In this paper, we focus on the syntactic annotation.

2 CGN syntactic annotation

The syntactic annotation structures to be stored with the CGN sound files and the other types of annotations are derived semi-automatically. This annotation process is described in the following sections. Note that the most important aim of the enterprise is the annotation structures rather than the parser used in deriving them.

2.1 Input: POS-tagged orthographic transcription

Input for the syntactic annotation is a POS-tagged orthographic transcription of the primary sound files. The material is segmented in annotation units. POS-tagging is done in a way comparable to the syntactic annotation, viz., semi-automatically: the output of an ensemble of automatic taggers, using some 400 different morphosyntactic tags and with an accuracy around 95%, is checked and corrected by hand. (For details of POS-Tagging and lemmatization within the CGN project we refer to (Van Eynde 2000, Van Eynde et al. 2000).) We give a real life example below in (1). For expository purposes, we have picked a short 14-word unit.[1]

(1) *Ik zal u gaan uitleggen hoe we dat zo'n beetje hebben*
I will you go explain how we that such-a bit have
aangepakt dat probleem .
approached that problem.
'I will explain to you how we more or less approached it, that problem'

The POS-tagged material has a rather straightforward line-oriented format shown below. The leftmost column has the complete sentence in a one word per line manner, the middle column contains the POS-information (main category in caps, features within brackets), the last column has the lexical lemma's.

```
 <au id=1 t=0.000 sp=N00052>
ik          VNW(pers,pron,nomin,vol,1,ev)               ik
zal         WW(pv,tgw,ev)                               zullen
u           VNW(pers,pron,nomin,vol,2b,getal)           u
gaan        WW(inf,vrij,zonder)                         gaan
uitleggen   WW(inf,vrij,zonder)                         uitleggen
hoe         BW()                                        hoe
we          VNW(pers,pron,nomin,red,1,mv)               we
dat         VNW(aanw,pron,stan,vol,3o,ev)               dat
zo'n        VNW(aanw,det,stan,prenom,zonder,agr)        zo'n
beetje      N(soort,ev,basis,onz,stan)                  beetje
hebben      WW(pv,tgw,mv)                               hebben
aangepakt   WW(vd,vrij,zonder)                          aanpakken
dat         VNW(aanw,det,stan,prenom,zonder,evon)       dat
probleem    N(soort,ev,basis,onz,stan)                  probleem
.           LET()                                       .
```

[1]Real life annotation units are anywhere between one and more than 150 words; in the data parsed so far, the average length of an annotation unit is around 15 words.

2.2 The CGN annotation graphs

The CGN syntactic annotation enriches the material with category information and dependency information. We call the annotation graphs *dependency structures*. At the input side, the annotation schemes should be maximally simple in order to minimize the work load involved in annotation and correction. At the output side, the CGN users should be offered annotation information that is maximally rich. We therefore opted for a theory neutral primary annotation level in terms of dependency structures (cf. also (Skut, Krenn and Uzkoreit 1997)). This primary annotation can be enriched with information from the POS tagging and from the CGN lexicon. The combination of these sources of information yields a number of output formats tailored to the wishes of various user groups. The dependency structures used in the CGN syntactic annotation are developing into a *de facto* standard for the computational analysis of Dutch: cf. (Bouma, van Noord and Malouf 2001).[2]

Formally, a CGN dependency structure $D = \langle V, E \rangle$ is a labeled directed acyclic graph. Node labels V and edge labels E are taken from disjunct sets CAT and DEP, respectively.

- Nodes: CAT = POSCAT ∪ PHCAT: category labels (c-labels), the union of lexical (POS) and phrasal labels.

- Edges: DEP: dependency labels (d-labels).

We distinguish between atomic and composite dependency structures. Atomic dependency structures are simply nodes decorated with a c-label from POSCAT. They are the leaves of our annotation graphs. The label set POSCAT is a reduced version of the full set of CGN part-of-speech labels, which contains more than 300 tags. We condense this to a POSCAT set of some 50 labels, retaining distinctions that are relevant for the syntactic annotation procedure.[3] The set of POSCAT labels currently used is given in the Appendix.

The basic building blocks of composite dependency structures we call *local dependency domains*. The mother node of such a domain carries a phrasal label from PHCAT; the daughters have c-labels from CAT. The d-labels for the mother-daughter edges consist of a *head*, together with the *complements* and the *modifiers* of that head.

Head. The head of a dependency domain projects the c-label of the mother node.

Complements. The complementation pattern determines the interpretation of the head in terms of thematic structure. A complement label occurs at most once in a local dependency domain.

Modifiers. Modifying elements do not change the c-label of the mother node; they can be left out without affecting the thematic structure. There can be

[2] Syntactic details of the annotation are spelled out in (Moortgat, Schuurman and van der Wouden 2001).

[3] As the reader will see later, the original POS-labels are preserved in the 'morphology' field of the annotation.

multiple occurrences of a given modifier label within a local dependency domain.

The tags sets PHCAT and DEP currently used are given in full in the Appendix. As the reader will notice, the terminology follows traditional grammatical practice rather closely. To keep the DEP set small, we use some overloading. The tag OBJ1, for example, labels the 'direct object' of transitive verbs, but also the 'first complement' of prepositions and adjectival heads.

The tag sets make provision for phenomena that are typical for spoken language: the *c*-label DU ('discourse unit'), for example, makes it possible to categorize asyndetic constructions; dependency articulation within DU is given in terms of *d*-labels such as NUCL (nucleus) versus SAT (satellite), TAG, or DLINK (discourse link).

We now draw the reader's attention to some properties of the CGN annotation that follow from the two-dimensional analysis (form/categorial information versus function/dependency information).

Shallow annotation structures. Taking together complementation and modification within one and the same local dependency domain yields flat annotation structures. Specifically,

- a new local domain (hierarchical level) will only be opened if there is a new head;
- complementation and modification are *relations* between phrases and a head: if there are no complements or modifiers, there is no reason for (non-branching) projections.

The CGN treatment of verbal projections is a good illustration of this shallow approach. Following the custom in Dutch traditional grammar and elsewhere, we distinguish level between *finite* and *non-finite* verbal projections at the *c*-label. The inflected verb (= POS tag) is head of the finite clausal types; the infinitive or participle (= POS tag) is head of the non-finite ones. In finite clauses, there is no need then for an intermediate VP level.[4]

Lexical anchoring. A point related to the above is that, in the unmarked case, local dependency domains are lexically rooted: the *c*-label of the head is a leaf label from POSCAT. As the head projects the *c*-label of the mother node, we can use the *d*-label of the head to disambiguate in cases where the information we get from the POS-annotation is underdetermined. For example, in the POS annotation, no distinction is made between *te* as a preposition, i.e. head of a preposition phrase (PP), on the one hand, and as head of a non-finite verbal projection, the *te*-infinitive (TI):[5] both are labeled T701, which is an abbreviation for VZ(INIT),

[4]As a reviewer correctly observes, one would not expect a distinct VP level in a dependency structure either.

[5]The jury is still out on the exact status of *te*, but we have chosen to call it a complementizer.

i.e., preposition. The syntactic annotation disambiguates the word *te* by means of the *d*-label: the head of the TI is labeled CMP (for complementizer).[6]

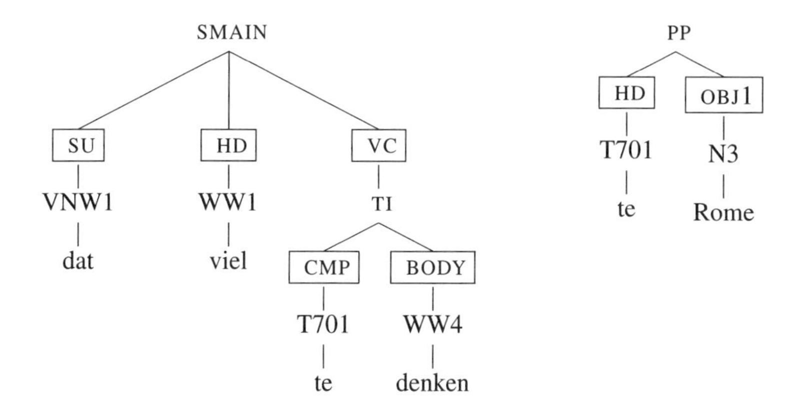

Crossing and multiple dependencies. We stress once again that the CGN annotation is a graph, not a tree. Graphs with crossing branches are used to annotate dependency relations that are at odds with surface word order and/or constituency. By assigning constituents multiple dependency roles, we can annotate non-local dependencies as they are found in e.g. relative clauses and constituent questions.[7]

- On the one hand, the elements introducing these kinds of configurations (constituents containing a WH-element or relative pronoun) determine the *c*-label of the mother node; therefore, they are dependency heads.
- On the other hand, we also want to be able to indicate the role these elements play in the rest of the clause; the relevant local dependency domain may be embedded arbitrarily deep.

Examples of crossed and multiple dependencies are given in the next section.

2.3 The annotation process

Our goal is to syntactically annotate a (balanced, representative) sub-corpus of one million words. In order to yield a maximally consistent result in the time allotted, the task is carried out (semi-)automatically. We use the interactive ANNOTATE tool, which was developed in Saarbrücken in the context of the NEGRA project (cf. (Plaehn 1998), and see www.coli.uni-sb.de/sfb378/negra-corpus/annotate.html). The functionality of this tool is very well adapted to the two-dimensional annotation philosophy we have adopted in the CGN project:

[6] *c*-labels are given in SMALL CAPS, *d*-labels are boxed. The *d*-labels decorate the *arcs* of the annotation graph: they are not *nodes*. POS information is taken directly from the POS annotation and will not always be spelled out.

[7] Specification of other types of non-local dependencies such as the resolution of pronouns and the interpretation of control structures is postponed to a later phase in the project.

> Annotate is a tool for the efficient semi-automatic annotation of corpus data. It facilitates the generation of context-free structures and additionally allows crossing edges. Functions for the manipulation of such structures are provided. Terminal nodes, non-terminal nodes, and edges are labeled. In the NEGRA project, these labels are used for parts-of-speech and morphology (terminal nodes), phrase categories (non-terminal nodes), and grammatical functions (edges). Type and number of labels are defined by the user. Annotated corpora are stored in an SQL database. Annotate has a specified interface for communication with external taggers and parsers. (Plaehn 1998)

For an illustration, we return to our real life example (1). With the tag sets given in the Appendix, ANNOTATE allows us to produce the graph of Figure 1 (on the next page).
The example illustrates some salient features of the annotation we have discussed in the previous section.

- The question word *hoe* ('how') has two parent nodes: it is the head of the subordinate interrogative WHSUB, and at the same time it plays the role of modifier within the PPART (past participle phrase) embedded in the body of that interrogative. The two edge labels WHD and MOD connecting the question word to the parent nodes WHSUB and PPART respectively, encode this double dependency role.[8]

- The dependency articulation is independent of surface order and constituency: the temporal auxiliary verb *hebben* ('have') selects the past participle phrase PPART as a complement, but it occurs within that phrase (between the direct object and the participle head) in surface order, leading to crossing dependecies in the annotation graph.

- Phenomena such as "right dislocation" are not seen as part of clausal syntax proper, but rather as belonging to discourse. The discourse coherence between the "main clause" and the "dislocated constituent" (in this case the noun phrase *dat probleem* 'that problem') is expressed by grouping these consituents under the label DU (for Discourse Unit) where they are assigned the dependency roles of NUCL and SAT respectively. If, in a later phase of the annotation process, anaphoric relations are going to be marked as well, a link may be made between the pronominal element *dat* in the nucleus component, and the satellite full noun phrase *dat probleem*.

[8]Nothing precludes, in principle, the possibility of an element having more than two dependency roles.

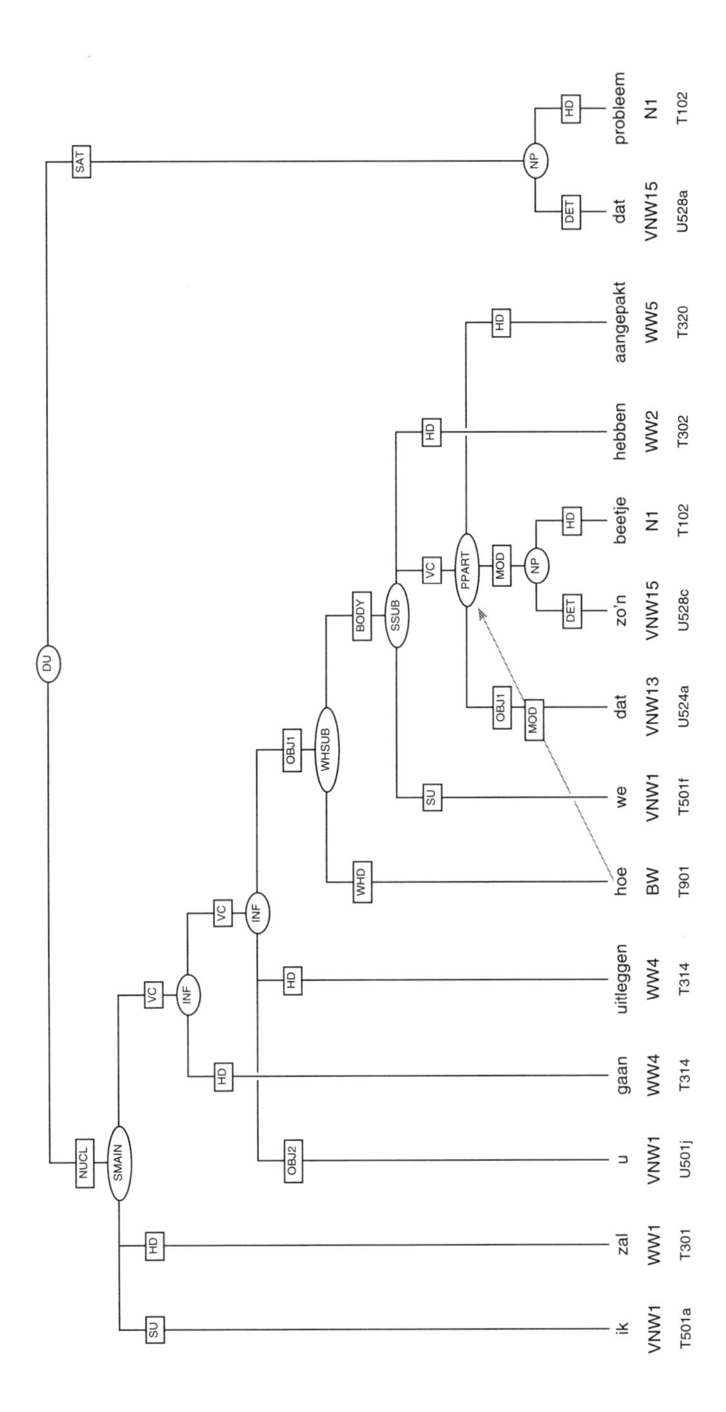

Figure 1: Example annotation

The ANNOTATE tools are designed to work together with parsers supporting the manual annotation and running in the background via a defined interface. In this phase of the project, we work with Thorsten Brant's (Brants 1999) Cascaded Markov Models (CMMs) approach which supports learning on the basis of an existing annotated corpus (a tree bank). The CMM approach implements a bootstrapping strategy: starting off with a small corpus, using the hypotheses of the parser to gain speed and quality in manually annotating the next part, add this part to the corpus and let the program refine its hypotheses, and so forth. In later phases of the project, the CMM approach will be used in combination with other parsers, so that we can integrate the rich information of the CGN lexicon with the statistical approach.

Currently, the parser is parsing the first subset of the CGN. The Spring 2001 CGN release already contained annotations for some 50.000 words, two thirds from the Netherlands, one third from Belgium, all checked by hand.

Given the fact, however, that even the most successful statistical POS-tagging algorithms reach only accuracy rates between 96 and 97% for new, unseen texts (Brants 1999), it may not be expected that the output of CMM parsing, which probably is a much more difficult task than mere POS-tagging, will be completely trustworthy. Therefore, all output will be checked and, whenever necessary, corrected by humans, who will often return to the sound signal for disambiguation clues. Tools have been developed to check for inconsistencies in the corrected output, which will again be fed into the parser's database in order to further increase the quality.

2.4 Customized export formats

The ANNOTATE environment has a line-oriented export format, which makes it possible to interface with other applications. Our running example is exported as follows:

```
%% word       tag      morph   edge   parent   secedge   secparent
#BOS 41 6 984562209 0
ik            VNW1     T501a   SU     507
zal           WW1      T301    HD     507
u             VNW1     U501j   OBJ2   505
gaan          WW4      T314    HD     506
uitleggen     WW4      T314    HD     505
hoe           BW       T901    WHD    504      MOD       502
we            VNW1     T501f   SU     503
dat           VNW13    U524a   OBJ1   502
zo'n          VNW15    U528c   DET    500
beetje        N1       T102    HD     500
hebben        WW2      T302    HD     503
aangepakt     WW5      T320    HD     502
dat           VNW15    U528a   DET    501
probleem      N1       T102    HD     501
.             LET      T007    --     0
#500          NP       --      MOD    502
#501          NP       --      SAT    508
#502          PPART    --      VC     503
#503          SSUB     --      BODY   504
#504          WHSUB    --      OBJ1   505
#505          INF      --      VC     506
#506          INF      --      VC     507
#507          SMAIN    --      NUCL   508
#508          DU       --      --     0
#EOS          41
```

We stress that this output is fully equivalent (modulo the interpunction, which is not a genuine part of the of the transcription *per se*, but rather an artifact of it) to the annotation graph in (1). Some clarification, however, may be appropriate. The structure of this table is as follows: each line describes one element in the data structure. The first line, for example, tells us that there is an end node valued *ik* with POS-label VNW1 (a personal pronoun) and morphological information T501 (which is a shorthand for the original POS-tag, cf. above) which fulfills the SU (subject) role with respect to some mother node 507. In one of the last lines we see that this node 507 itself is of category SMAIN (main clause), that it has no morphological information (what could it possibly be?) which functions as the NUCL (nucleus) of a DU (discourse unit).

Another element, *hoe* in line 8, has a POS-label BW (adverb) and functions as WHD (head of an interrogative clause) whose mother node carries the label 504; additionally (this information is in the final columns), it functions as a MOD (modifier) in the structure headed by node 502.

The primary annotation can be enriched with information from the POS tagging and from the CGN lexicon. The combination of these three information sources can lead towards a number of customized output formats for various user groups:

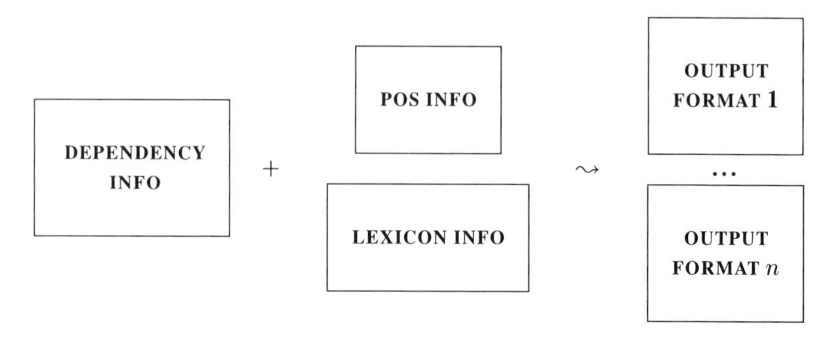

As regards the derived output formats mentioned, one may think of

- enriching category labels (c-labels) with morphosyntactic feature information;
- enriching dependency labels (d-labels) with 'deep' dependencies (e.g.: semantic control information);
- present surface constituent trees in a user friendly notation (with or without 'empty elements' etc.);
- presentation matters: choices as regards the 'language' of the label sets (Dutch, English, ...) and of the output (HTML, MSWORD, LaTeX, Postscript, XML, ...).
- (Moortgat and Moot 2001) discuss the feasability of deriving type-logical grammatical representations from the CGN output;
- etc.

Of course, the possibility of realizing such customized output formats depends heavily on other annotation levels, such as lemmatization (i.e. the linking up of all words with a rich lexicon), POS-tagging and prosodic annotation on the one hand, and the planned CGN exploitation software module on the other. In this paper, however, we have concentrated on the primary dependency annotation.

3 Concluding remarks

In this paper, we have given an overview of the CGN approach to syntactic annotation of a subset of the 10 million word spoken Dutch corpus. We stress once again that the goal of the annotation enterprise is not to build a maximally efficient, ninety odd percent trustworthy real time annotating tool, but rather to produce a ninety nine odd percent trustworthy output which is maximally useful for the maximal number of users. Given the current state of affairs in computational linguistics, this is only possible by means of human intervention. The output is a set of 'theory neutral' dependency trees, which are input to other modules producing data structures useful for users from various theoretical backgrounds and with various practical aims.[9]

References

Bouma, G., van Noord, G. and Malouf, R.(2001), Alpino: Wide-coverage computational analysis of Dutch. available via http://odur.let.rug.nl/alfa/papers/papers/.

Brants, T.(1999), Cascaded Markov Models. In *Proceedings of the 9th Conference of the European Chapter of the Association for Computational Linguistics EACL-99*, Bergen, Norway, 1999.

Goedertier, W., Goddijn, S. and Martens, J.-P.(2000), Orthographic transcription of the Spoken Dutch Corpus. Proceedings LREC 2000.

Moortgat, M. and Moot, R.(2001), CGN to Grail. extracting a type-logical lexicon from the CGN annotation, this volume.

Moortgat, M., Schuurman, I. and van der Wouden, T.(2001), Syntactische annotatie. Internal working document CGN, Utrecht, May 2001.

Oostdijk, N.(2000a), Building a corpus of spoken Dutch, *in* P. Monachesi (ed.), *Computational Linguistics in the Netherlands 1999. Selected Papers from the Tenth CLIN Meeting*, Utrecht University, Utrecht Institute of Linguistics OTS, Utrecht, pp. 147–157.

Oostdijk, N.(2000b), The Spoken Dutch Corpus. Overview and first evaluation. Proceedings LREC 2000.

Plaehn, O.(1998), Annotate: Bedienungsanleitung. Document Projekt C3 Nebenläufige Grammatische Verarbeitung. Universität des Saarlandes, FR 8.7 Computerlinguistik.

Skut, W., Krenn, B. and Uzkoreit, H.(1997), An annotation scheme for free word order languages, *Proceedings of the Fifth Conference on Applied Natural Language Processing*, Washington, D.C. available via http://arxiv.org/format/cmp-lg/9702004.

Van Eynde, F.(2000), Part of speech tagging en lemmatisering. Internal working document CGN, Centrum voor Computerlinguïstiek K.U. Leuven, May 2000.

Van Eynde, F., Zavrel, J. and Daelemans, W.(2000), Lemmatisation and morphosyntactic annotation for the spoken dutch corpus, *in* P. Monachesi (ed.), *Computational Linguistics in the Netherlands 1999. Selected Papers from the Tenth CLIN Meeting*, Utrecht University, Utrecht Institute of Linguistics OTS, Utrecht, pp. 53–62.

[9]See the CGN web site at http://lands.let.kun.nl/cgn/ehome.htm for general information on the CGN corpus and how to receive the current corpus materials. A free viewer for ANNOTATE analyses can be downloaded from the Utrecht CGN site http://cgn.let.uu.nl/.

Appendix: The tag sets

POS-labels

The next table contains all part of speech labels: presently, four types of nouns are distinguished (common nouns and proper nouns, singular and plural), twelve types of adjectives (differentiating between attributive and predicative usage, and various morphological variants, including comparative and superlative forms), six (morphologically defined) verb forms, ordinals and cardinals, and many types of pronouns (morphologically defined). The first column shows the abbreviation we use, the second column gives a more verbose variant, the third column offers some information in English.

POS-labels

N1	N(soort,ev)	common noun, singular
N2	N(soort,mv)	common noun, plural
N3	N(eigen,ev)	proper noun, singular
N4	N(eigen,mv)	common noun, singular
ADJ1	ADJ(prenom,basis)	prenominal adjective, base form
ADJ2	ADJ(prenom,comp)	prenominal adjective, comparative form
ADJ3	ADJ(prenom,sup)	prenominal adjective, superlative form
ADJ4	ADJ(nom,basis)	nominalized adjective, base form
ADJ5	ADJ(nom,comp)	nominalized adjective, comparative
ADJ6	ADJ(nom,sup)	nominalized adjective, superlative
ADJ7	ADJ(postnom,basis)	postnominal adjective, base form
ADJ8	ADJ(postnom,comp)	postnominal adjective, comparative form
ADJ9	ADJ(vrij,basis)	adjective used predicatively, base form
ADJ10	ADJ(vrij,comp)	
ADJ11	ADJ(vrij,sup)	
ADJ12	ADJ(vrij,dim)	adjective, diminutive form
WW1	WW(pv,ev)	inflected verb form, singular
WW2	WW(pv,mv)	inflected verb form, plural
WW3	WW(pv,met-t)	inflected verb form with *-t*
WW4	WW(inf)	infinitive
WW5	WW(vd)	past participle
WW6	WW(od)	present participle
TW1	TW(hoofd)	ordinal number
TW2	TW(rang)	cardinal number
VNW1	VNW(pers,pron)	personal pronoun
VNW2	VNW(pr,pron)	
VNW3	VNW(refl,pron)	reflexive pronoun
VNW4	VNW(recip,pron)	reciprocal pronoun
VNW5	VNW(bez,det)	possessive pronoun
VNW6	VNW(vrag,pron)	question word
VNW7	VNW(betr,pron)	relative pronoun
VNW8	VNW(vb,pron)	
VNW9	VNW(vb,adv-pron)	
VNW10	VNW(excl,pron)	exclamative pronoun
VNW11	VNW(vb,det)	
VNW12	VNW(excl,det)	
VNW13	VNW(aanw,pron)	demonstrative pronoun

VNW14	VNW(aanw,adv-pron)	
VNW15	VNW(aanw,det)	
VNW16	VNW(onbep,pron)	indefinite pronoun
VNW17	VNW(onbep,adv-pron)	
VNW18	VNW(onbep,det)	
VNW19	VNW(onbep,grad)	
LID	LID	determiner
VZ	VZ	preposition
VG1	VG(neven)	coordinating element
VG2	VG(onder)	subordinating element
BW	BW	adverb
TSW	TSW	interjection
SPEC	SPEC	rest category
LET	LET	interpunction

Category labels

The next table contains all category labels currently in use. The first column shows the label, the second one an explanation in Dutch, with one in English below it.

Node labels (category information)

SMAIN	declaratieve zin (V2) main clause (V2)
SSUB	bijzin (V-finaal) subordinate clause (verb-final)
SV1	zin met V op de eerste plaats any sentence with a sentence-initial inflected verb
INF	kale-infinitiefgroep short infinitive group
PPART	voltooid/passief-deelwoordgroep past/passive participle group
PPRES	tegenwoordig-deelwoordgroep present participle group
CP	zinsdeel ingeleid door onderschikkend vw. of vw./vz. v. verg. clause headed by any kind of complementizer
MWU	merged-word-unit ('drie en twintig', 'Jan van den Berg') merged-word-unit (used for complex numbers and names)
TI	te-infinitiefgroep long infinitive group
OTI	om-te-infinitiefgroep long infinitive group headed by *om* (∼ *for to*)
AHI	aan-het-infinitiefgroep long infinitive group headed by *aan het* ('a Dutch progressive form')
ADVP	bijwoordgroep (alleen voor echte bijwoorden) adverbial phrases
DETP	determinatorgroep ('bijna alle' in 'bijna alle boeken') determiner group
AP	adjectiefgroep (ook voor adverbiaal gebruikte adjectieven) adjectival group

PP	prepositiegroep prepositional group
NP	nominale groep nominal group
SVAN	van-zin (complement in directe rede) subordinate clause headed by *van*
REL	relatiefzin relative clause
WHREL	hoofdloze relatiefzin headless relative
WHQ	constituentvraag: hoofdzin WH-question, V2
WHSUB	constituentvraag: bijzin embedded WH-question
CONJ	conjunctie conjunction
DU	discourse-unit (asyndetische constructie) discourse-unit
LIST	asyndetische conjunctie asyndetic conjunction
COMPP	zinsdeel met ‘meer’ of ‘even’ als hoofd en CP als complement various comparative constructions

Edge labels

The next table contains all edge labels currently in use. The first column shows the label, the second one an explanation in Dutch, with one in English below it.

Edge labels (dependency information)

HD	hoofd head
HDF	staart (scheidbaar deel) van circumpositie second part of a circumposition (*tot hier **toe***)
DET	determinator determiner
PART	partitief partitive
SU	subject, onderwerp subject
SUP	voorlopig subject provisional subject
OBJ1	direct object van V, (eerste) complement van P, A, N direct or first object
POBJ1	voorlopig OBJ1 provisional direct or first object
OBJ2	secundair object (IO, EO, BO) secondary object
SE	verplicht reflexief object obligatory reflexive object

SVP	scheidbaar deel van werkwoord verbal particle
PREDC	predicatief complement predicative complement
PC	voorzetselvoorwerp prepositional complement
VC	verbaal complement, beknopte bijzin verbal complement
LD	locatief of directioneel complement locational or directional complement
ME	maat(/duur/gewicht)-complement measure complement
CMP	complementeerder/hoofd van CP, SVAN, TI, OTI of AHI grammatical complementizer
RHD	complementeerder/hoofd van (hoofdloze) relatiefzin complementizer heading (headless) relative
WHD	complementeerder/hoofd van WHQ of WHSUB complementizer heading WH question
BODY	romp van CP, SVAN, TI, OTI, AHI, REL, WHQ of WHSUB body of subordinate clause
PREDM	bepaling v. gesteldheid 'tijdens de handeling' secondary predicate
MOD	algemeen label voor bepaling/modificeerder modifier
CRD	nevenschikker coordinator
CNJ	lid van nevenschikking member of conjunction
NUCL	kernzin (in DU) nuclear clause
SAT	satelliet: aan- of uitloop (in DU) met binding in NUCL satelite
TAG	aanhangsel, voor- of tussenvoegsel tag
DP	elk der delen van een DU any part of a DU
PRT	elk der delen van een partikelgroep any part of a particle group
OBCOMP	vergelijkingscomplement (compl. van 'meer'/'even') comparative complement
APPOS	bijstelling apposition
LP	elk der delen van een LIST any part of a LIST
DLINK	"en", "maar", "want" o.i.d. aan het begin van een uiting discourse particles joining discourse fragments
MWP	elk der delen van een MWU any part of a MWU

930300

Part-of-Speech Tagging with Two Sequential Transducers

André Kempe

Xerox Research Centre Europe

Abstract

The article presents a method of constructing and applying a cascade consisting of a left- and a right-sequential finite-state transducer, T_1 and T_2, for part-of-speech disambiguation. In the process of POS tagging, every word is first assigned a unique ambiguity class that represents the set of alternative tags that this word can occur with. The sequence of the ambiguity classes of all words of one sentence is then mapped by T_1 to a sequence of reduced ambiguity classes where some of the less likely tags are removed. That sequence is finally mapped by T_2 to a sequence of single tags. Compared to a Hidden Markov model tagger, this transducer cascade has the advantage of significantly higher processing speed, but at the cost of slightly lower accuracy. Applications such as Information Retrieval, where speed can be more important than accuracy, could benefit from this approach.

1 Introduction

We present a method of constructing and applying a cascade consisting of a left- and a right-sequential finite-state transducer (FST), T_1 and T_2, for part-of-speech (POS) disambiguation.

In the process of POS tagging, we first assign every word of a sentence a unique ambiguity class c_i that can be looked up in a lexicon encoded by a sequential FST. Every c_i is denoted by a single symbol, e.g. "`[ADJ NOUN]`", although it represents a set of alternative tags that a given word can occur with. The sequence of the c_i of all words of one sentence is the input to our FST cascade (Fig. 1). It is mapped by T_1, from left to right, to a sequence of reduced ambiguity classes r_i. Every r_i is denoted by a single symbol, although it represents a set of alternative tags. Intuitively, T_1 eliminates the less likely tags from c_i, thus creating r_i. Finally, T_2 maps the sequence of r_i, from right to left, to an output sequence of single POS tags t_i. Intuitively, T_2 selects the most likely t_i from every r_i (Fig. 1).

Compared to a Hidden Markov model (HMM) (Rabiner 1990), this FST cascade has the advantage of significantly higher processing speed, but at the cost of slightly lower accuracy. Applications such as Information Retrieval, where speed can be more important than accuracy, could benefit from this approach.

Although our approach is related to the concept of bimachines (Schützenberger 1961) and factorization (Elgot and Mezei 1965), we proceed differently in that we build two sequential FSTs directly and not by factorization.

This article is structured as follows. Section 2 describes how the ambiguity classes and reduced ambiguity classes are defined based on a lexicon and a training corpus. Then, Section 3 explains how the probabilities of these classes in the context of other classes are calculated. The construction of T_1 and T_2 is shown in Section 4. It makes use of the previously defined classes and their probabilities.

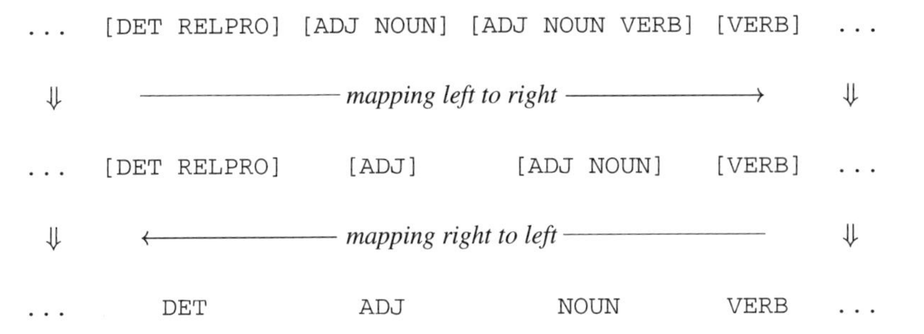

Figure 1: Part of an input, an intermediate, and an output sequence in the FST cascade (example)

Section 5 describes the application of the FSTs to an input text, and Section 6 finally compares the FSTs to an HMM tagger, based on experimental data.

2 Definition of Classes

Instead of dealing with lexical probabilities of individual words (Church 1988), many POS taggers group words into *ambiguity classes* and deal with lexical probabilities of these classes (Cutting, Kupiec, Pedersen and Sibun 1992, Kupiec 1992). Every word belongs to one ambiguity class that is described by the set of all POS tags that the word can occur with. For example, the class described by {NOUN, VERB} includes all words that could be analyzed either as noun or verb depending on the context. We follow this approach.

Some approaches make a more fine-grained word classification (Daelemans, Zavrel, Berck and Gillis 1996, Tzoukermann and Radev 1996). Words that occur with the same alternative tags, e.g., NOUN and VERB, can here be assigned different ambiguity classes depending on whether they occur more frequently with one or with the other tag. Although this has proven to increase the accuracy of HMM-based POS disambiguation, it did not significantly improve our method. After some investigations in this direction, we decided to follow the simpler classification above.

Before we can build the FST cascade, we have to define ambiguity classes, that will constitute the input alphabet of T_1, and *reduced ambiguity classes*, that will form the intermediate alphabet of the cascade, i.e., the output of T_1 and the input of T_2.

Ambiguity classes c_i are defined from the training corpus and lexicon, and are each described by a pair consisting of a tag list $\hat{t}(c_i)$ and a probability vector $\vec{p}(c_i)$:

$$\hat{t}(c_i) = \langle t_{i1}, t_{i2}, ..., t_{i,n} \rangle \qquad \vec{p}(c_i) = \begin{bmatrix} p(t_{i1}|c_i) \\ p(t_{i2}|c_i) \\ \vdots \\ p(t_{i,n}|c_i) \end{bmatrix} \tag{1}$$

For example:

$$\hat{t}(c_1) = \langle \texttt{ADJ}, \texttt{NOUN}, \texttt{VERB} \rangle \qquad \vec{p}(c_1) = \begin{bmatrix} 0.29 \\ 0.60 \\ 0.11 \end{bmatrix} \tag{2}$$

which means that the words that belong to c_1 are tagged as ADJ in 29 %, as NOUN in 60 %, and as VERB in 11 % of all cases in the training corpus.

When all c_i are defined, a class-based lexicon, that maps every word to a single class symbol, is constructed from the original tag-based lexicon, that maps every word to a set of alternative tag symbols. In the class-based lexicon, the above c_1 (Eq. 2) could be represented, e.g., by the symbol "[ADJ NOUN VERB]".

We describe a reduced ambiguity classes r_i also by a pair consisting of a tag list $\hat{t}(r_i)$ and a probability vector $\vec{p}(r_i)$. Intuitively, an r_i can be seen as a c_i where some of the less likely tags have been removed. Since at this point we cannot decide which tags are less likely, all possible subclasses of all c_i are considered. To generate a complete set of r_i, all c_i are split into all possible subclasses s_{ij} that are assigned a tag list $\hat{t}(s_{ij})$ containing a subset of the tags of $\hat{t}(c_i)$, and an (un-normalized) probability vector $\vec{p}(s_{ij})$ containing only the relevant elements of $\vec{p}(c_i)$. For example, the above c_1 (Eq. 2) is split into seven subclasses s_{1j} :

$$\begin{aligned} \hat{t}(s_{1,0}) &= \langle \texttt{ADJ}, \texttt{NOUN}, \texttt{VERB} \rangle & \vec{p}(s_{1,0}) &= \begin{bmatrix} 0.29 \\ 0.60 \\ 0.11 \end{bmatrix} \\ \hat{t}(s_{1,1}) &= \langle \texttt{NOUN}, \texttt{VERB} \rangle & \vec{p}(s_{1,1}) &= \begin{bmatrix} 0.60 \\ 0.11 \end{bmatrix} \\ \hat{t}(s_{1,2}) &= \langle \texttt{ADJ}, \texttt{VERB} \rangle & \vec{p}(s_{1,2}) &= \begin{bmatrix} 0.29 \\ 0.11 \end{bmatrix} \\ &etc. \end{aligned} \tag{3}$$

Different c_i can produce a s_{ij} with the same tag list $\hat{t}(s_{ij})$ but with different probability vectors $\vec{p}(s_{ij})$; e.g., the classes with the tag lists $\langle \texttt{ADJ}, \texttt{NOUN}, \texttt{VERB} \rangle$, $\langle \texttt{NOUN}, \texttt{VERB} \rangle$, and $\langle \texttt{ADJ}, \texttt{ADV}, \texttt{NOUN}, \texttt{VERB} \rangle$ can all produce a subclass with the tag list $\langle \texttt{NOUN}, \texttt{VERB} \rangle$. To reduce the total number of subclasses, all s_{ij} with the same tag list $\hat{t}(s_{ij})$ are clustered, based on the *centroid method* (Romesburg 1989, p. 136), using the *vector cosine* as the similarity measure between clusters (Salton and McGill 1983, p. 201). Each final cluster constitutes a reduced ambiguity class

r_y. If we obtain, e.g., three r_y with the same tag list $\hat{t}(r_y) = \langle \texttt{NOUN}, \texttt{VERB} \rangle$ but with different (re-normalized) probability vectors:

$$\vec{p}(r_1) = \begin{bmatrix} 0.89 \\ 0.11 \end{bmatrix} \qquad \vec{p}(r_2) = \begin{bmatrix} 0.57 \\ 0.43 \end{bmatrix} \qquad \vec{p}(r_3) = \begin{bmatrix} 0.09 \\ 0.91 \end{bmatrix} \tag{4}$$

we represent them in an FST by three different symbols, e.g., "`[NOUN VERB]_R_1`", "`[NOUN VERB]_R_2`", and "`[NOUN VERB]_R_3`".

3 Contextual Probabilities

T_1 will map a sequence of c_i, from left to right, to a sequence of r_i. Therefore, the construction of T_1 requires estimating the most likely r_i in the context of both the current c_i and the previous r_{i-1} (wrt. the current position i in a sequence). To determine this r_i, a probability $P_{T_1}(t_{ij})$ is estimated for every POS tag t_{ij} in c_i. In the initial position, $P_{T_1}(t_{ij})$ depends on the preceding sentence boundary $\#_{i-1}$ and the current c_i which are assumed to be mutually independent:

$$\begin{aligned} P_{T_1}(t_{ij}) &= p(t_{ij} | \#_{i-1}\ c_i) \\ &= \frac{p(t_{ij}\ \#_{i-1}\ c_i)}{p(\#_{i-1}\ c_i)} \\ &= \frac{p(\#_{i-1}\ c_i | t_{ij}) \cdot p(t_{ij})}{p(\#_{i-1}\ c_i)} \\ &\approx \frac{p(\#_{i-1} | t_{ij}) \cdot p(c_i | t_{ij}) \cdot p(t_{ij})}{p(\#_{i-1}) \cdot p(c_i)} \\ &= \frac{\frac{p(\#_{i-1}\ t_{ij})}{p(t_{ij})} \cdot \frac{p(c_i\ t_{ij})}{p(t_{ij})} \cdot p(t_{ij})}{p(\#_{i-1}) \cdot p(c_i)} \\ &= \frac{p(t_{ij}\ \#_{i-1}) \cdot p(t_{ij}\ c_i)}{p(t_{ij}) \cdot p(\#_{i-1}) \cdot p(c_i)} \\ &= \frac{p(t_{ij} | \#_{i-1}) \cdot p(t_{ij} | c_i)}{p(t_{ij})} \end{aligned} \tag{5}$$

The latter $p(t_{ij}|c_i)$ can be extracted from the probability vector $\vec{p}(c_i)$, and $p(t_{ij}|\#_{i-1})$ and $p(t_{ij})$ can be estimated from the training corpus.

In another than the initial position, $P_{T_1}(t_{ij})$ depends on the preceding r_{i-1} and the current c_i which are assumed to be mutually independent:

$$P_{T_1}(t_{ij}) = p(t_{ij} | r_{i-1}\ c_i) \approx \frac{p(t_{ij} | r_{i-1}) \cdot p(t_{ij} | c_i)}{p(t_{ij})} \tag{6}$$

The latter $p(t_{ij}|r_{i-1})$ is estimated by:

$$p(t_{ij}|r_{i-1}) \quad = \quad \sum_k p(t_{ij}|t_{i-1,k}) \cdot p(t_{i-1,k}|r_{i-1}) \qquad (7)$$

$$\text{with} \quad t_{ij} \in \hat{t}(c_i) \; ; \; \; t_{i-1,k} \in \hat{t}(r_{i-1})$$

where $p(t_{ij}|t_{i-1,k})$ can be estimated from the training corpus, and $p(t_{i-1,k}|r_{i-1})$ can be extracted from the probability vector $\vec{p}(r_{i-1})$ of the preceding r_{i-1}.

To evaluate all tags of the current c_i, a list $\hat{\mathcal{P}}(c_i)$ containing pairs $\langle\, t_{ij} \,,\; P_{T_1}(t_{ij}) \,\rangle$ of all tags t_{ij} of c_i with their probabilities $P_{T_1}(t_{ij})$ (Eq.s 5, 6), is created:

$$\hat{\mathcal{P}}(c_i) \quad = \quad \begin{pmatrix} \langle\, t_{i,1} \,,\; P_{T_1}(t_{i,1}) \,\rangle \\ \langle\, t_{i,2} \,,\; P_{T_1}(t_{i,2}) \,\rangle \\ \vdots \\ \langle\, t_{i,j} \,,\; P_{T_1}(t_{i,j}) \,\rangle \\ \vdots \end{pmatrix} \qquad (8)$$

Every tag t_{ij} in $\hat{\mathcal{P}}$ is compared to the most likely tag $t_{i,m}$ in $\hat{\mathcal{P}}$. If the ratio of their probabilities is below a threshold τ , t_{ij} is removed from $\hat{\mathcal{P}}$:

$$\frac{P_{T_1}(t_{ij})}{P_{T_1}(t_{i,m})} \quad < \quad \tau \qquad (9)$$

Removing less likely tags leads to a reduced list $\hat{\mathcal{P}}_r(c_i)$ that is then split into a reduced tag list $\hat{t}_r(c_i)$ and a reduced probability vector $\vec{p}_r(c_i)$ that jointly describe a reduced ambiguity class r_y . From among all predefined r_i (cf. e.g. Eq. 4), we select the one that has the same tag list $\hat{t}(r_i)$ as the "ideal" reduced class r_y and the most similar probability vector $\vec{p}(r_i)$ according to the cosine measure. This r_i is considered to be the most likely among all predefined r_i in the context of both the current c_i and the previous r_{i-1}.

T_2 will map a sequence of r_i, from right to left, to a sequence of tags t_i. Therefore, the construction of T_2 requires estimating the most likely t_i in the context of both the current r_i and the following t_{i+1}. To determine this t_i, a probability $P_{T_2}(t_{ij})$ is estimated for every tag t_{ij} of the current r_i . In the final position, $P_{T_2}(t_{ij})$ depends on the current r_i and on the following sentence boundary $\#_{i+1}$:

$$P_{T_2}(t_{ij}) = p(t_{ij}|r_i \; \#_{i+1}) \approx \frac{p(t_{ij}|\#_{i+1}) \cdot p(t_{ij}|r_i)}{p(t_{ij})} \qquad (10)$$

In another than the final position, $P_{T_2}(t_{ij})$ depends on the current r_i and the following tag t_{i+1} :

$$P_{T_2}(t_{ij}) = p(t_{ij}|r_i \; t_{i+1}) \approx \frac{p(t_{ij}|t_{i+1}) \cdot p(t_{ij}|r_i)}{p(t_{ij})} \qquad (11)$$

The latter $p(t_{ij})$, $p(t_{ij}|t_{i+1})$, and $p(t_{ij}|\#_{i+1})$ are estimated from the training corpus, and $p(t_{ij}|r_i)$ is extracted from the probability vector $\vec{p}(r_i)$.

The t_i with the highest probability $P_{T_2}(t_i)$ is the most likely tag in the context of both the current r_i and the following t_{i+1} (Eq.s 10, 11).

4 Construction of the FSTs

The construction of T_1 is preceded by defining all c_i and r_i, and estimating their contextual probabilities. In this process, all words in the training corpus, that are initially annotated with POS tags, are in addition annotated with ambiguity classes c_i.

In T_1, one state is created for every r_i (output symbol), and is labeled with this r_i (Fig. 2a). An initial state, not corresponding to any r_i, is created in addition. From every state, one outgoing arc is created for every c_i (input symbol), and is labeled with this c_i. The destination of every arc is the state of the most likely r_i in the context of both the current c_i (arc label) and the preceding r_{i-1} (source state label) which is estimated as described above. All arc labels are then changed from simple symbols c_i to symbol pairs $c_i : r_i$ (mapping c_i to r_i) that consist of the original arc label and the destination state label. All state labels are removed (Fig. 2b). Those r_i that are unlikely in any context disappear from T_1 because the corresponding states have no incomming arcs. T_1 accepts any sequence of c_i and maps it, from left to right, to the sequence of the most likely r_i in the given left context.

Figure 2: Two stages in the construction of T_1

The construction of T_2 is preceded by annotating the training corpus in addition with reduced ambiguity classes r_i, by means of T_1. The probability vectors $\vec{p}(r_i)$ of all r_i are then re-estimated. The contextual probabilities of tags, are estimated only at this point (Eq.s 10, 11).

In T_2, one state is created for every t_i (output symbol), and is labeled with this t_i (Fig. 3a). An initial state is added. From every state, one outgoing arc is created for every r_i (input symbol) that occurs in the output language of T_1, and is labeled with this r_i. The destination of every arc is the state of the most likely t_i in the context of both the current r_i (arc label) and the following t_{i+1} (source state label) which is estimated as described above. Note, this is the following tag, rather than the preceding, because T_2 will be applied from right to left. All arc labels are then changed into symbol pairs $r_i : t_i$ and all state labels are removed (Fig. 3b), as was done in T_1. T_2 accepts any sequence of r_i, generated by T_1, and maps it, from right to left, to the sequence of the most likely t_i in the given right context.

Figure 3: Two stages in the construction of T_2

Both T_1 and T_2 are sequential. They can be minimized with standard algorithms. Once T_1 and T_2 are built, the probabilities of all t_i, r_i, and c_i are of no further use. Probabilities do not explicitly occur in the FSTs, and are not directly used at run time. They are, however, "reflected" by the structure of the FSTs.

5 Application of the FSTs

Our FST tagger uses the above described T_1 and T_2, a class-based lexicon, and possibly a guesser to predict the ambiguity classes of unknown words (possibly based on their suffixes). The lexicon and guesser are also sequential FSTs, and map any word that they accept to a single symbol c_i representing an ambiguity class (Fig. 1). If a word cannot be found in the lexicon, it is analyzed by the guesser. If this does not provide an analysis either, the word is assigned a special c_i for unknown words that is estimated from the m most frequent tags of all words that occur only once in the training corpus.

The sequence of the c_i of all words of one sentence is the input to our FST cascade (Fig. 1). It is mapped by T_1, from left to right, to a sequence of reduced ambiguity classes r_i. Intuitively, T_1 eliminates the less likely tags from c_i, thus creating r_i. Finally, T_2 maps the sequence of r_i, from right to left, to an output sequence of single POS tags t_i. Intuitively, T_2 selects the most likely t_i from every r_i.

6 Results

We compared our FST tagger on English, German, and Spanish with a commercially available (foreign) HMM tagger (Table 1). The comparison was made on the same non-overlapping training and test corpora for both taggers (Table 3). The FST tagger was on average 10 times as fast but slightly less accurate than the HMM tagger (45 600 words/sec and 96.97% versus 4 360 words/sec and 97.43%). In some applications such as Information Retrieval a significant speed increase could be worth the small loss in accuracy.

		English	German	Spanish	Average
Speed (words/sec)	T_1+T_2	47 600	42 200	46 900	45 600
	HMM	4 110	3 620	5 360	4 360
Accuracy (%)	T_1+T_2	96.54	96.79	97.05	96.97
	HMM	96.80	97.55	97.95	97.43

Computer: SUN Workstation, Ultra2, with 1 CPU

Table 1: Processing speed and accuracy of the FST and the HMM taggers

	English	German	Spanish	Average
# States	615	496	353	488
# Arcs	209 000	197 000	96 000	167 000
# Tags	76	67	56	66
# Ambiguity classes	349	448	265	354
# Reduced ambiguity classes	724	732	465	640

Table 2: Sizes of the FST cascades and their alphabets

	English	German	Spanish	Average
Training corpus size (words)	20 000	91 000	16 000	42 000
Test corpus size (words)	20 000	40 000	15 000	25 000

Table 3: Sizes of the training and test corpora

References

Church, K. W.(1988), A stochastic parts program and noun phrase parser for unrestricted text, *Proceedings of the 2nd Conference on Applied Natural Language Processing (ANLP)*, Association for Computational Linguistics, Austin, TX, USA, pp. 136–143.

Cutting, D., Kupiec, J., Pedersen, J. and Sibun, P.(1992), A practical part-of-speech tagger, *Proceedings of the 3rd Conference on Applied Natural Language Processing (ANLP)*, Association for Computational Linguistics, Trento, Italy, pp. 133–140.

Daelemans, W., Zavrel, J., Berck, P. and Gillis, S.(1996), MBT: A memory-based part-of-speech tagger-generator, *Proceedings of the 4th Workshop on Very Large Corpora*, Special Interest Group for Linguistic Data and Corpus-based Approaches (SIGDAT) of the ACL, Copenhagen, Denmark, pp. 14–27.

Elgot, C. C. and Mezei, J. E.(1965), On relations defined by generalized finite automata, *IBM Journal of Research and Development* pp. 47–68.

Kupiec, J. M.(1992), Robust part-of-speech tagging using a hidden markov model, *Computer, Speech, and Language* **6**(3), 225–242.

Rabiner, L. R.(1990), A tutorial on hidden markov models and selected applications in speech recognition, *in* A. Waibel and K.-F. Lee (eds), *Readings in Speech Recognition*, Morgan Kaufmann, pp. 267–296.

Romesburg, H. C.(1989), *Cluster Analysis for Researchers*, Krieger Publishing Company, Malabar, FL, USA.

Salton, G. and McGill, M. J.(1983), *Introduction to Modern Information Retrieval*, McGraw-Hill Advanced Computer Science Series, McGraw-Hill Publishing Company, New York, USA.

Schützenberger, M. P.(1961), A remark on finite transducers, *Information and Control* **4**, 185–187.

Tzoukermann, E. and Radev, D. R.(1996), Using word class for part-of-speech disambiguation, *Proceedings of the 4th Workshop on Very Large Corpora*, Special Interest Group for Linguistic Data and Corpus-based Approaches (SIGDAT) of the ACL, Copenhagen, Denmark, pp. 1–13.

Different approaches to Cross-Language Information Retrieval

Wessel Kraaij and Renée Pohlmann

TNO TPD

Abstract

This paper describes two experiments in the domain of Cross-Language Information Retrieval. Our basic approach is to translate queries word by word using machine readable dictionaries. The first experiment compared different strategies to deal with word sense ambiguity: i) keeping all translations and integrate translation probabilities in the model, ii) a single translation is selected on the basis of the number of occurrences in the dictionary iii) word by word translation after word sense disambiguation in the source language. In a second experiment we constructed parallel corpora from web documents in order to construct bilingual dictionaries or improve translation probability estimates. We conclude that our best dictionary-based CLIR approach is based on keeping all possible translations, not by simple substitution of a query term by its translations but by creating a structured query and including reverse translation probabilities in the retrieval model.

1 Introduction

Within the framework of the TREC and recently also the CLEF information retrieval evaluation initiatives, TNO TPD has tested several approaches to cross-language information retrieval (CLIR). Our basic approach is to translate queries word by word using machine readable dictionaries. The first experiment compared different strategies to deal with word sense ambiguity: i) keeping all translations and integrate translation probabilities in the model, ii) a single translation is selected on the basis of the number of occurrences in the dictionary iii) word by word translation after word sense disambiguation in the source language. In a second experiment we constructed parallel corpora from the web in order to construct bilingual dictionaries or improve translation probability estimates.

1.1 CLIR

Cross-Language Information Retrieval is receiving an increasing amount of attention in IR research. The goal of a CLIR system is to retrieve relevant documents from a multilingual document base in response to a query, irrespective of the language the documents are written in. Most CLIR systems either use query translation or document translation, cf. (Oard 1997). A third option would be to translate both queries and documents into a language independent representation (interlingua). Although this seems an attractive option, since queries and/or documents only need to be translated once and only one index needs to be maintained, in practice this last option is hardly ever used in other than very small scale, semi-automatic systems for well-defined domains, e.g. (Ruiz, Diekema and Sheridan 2000), because devising and maintaining such an interlingua for applications with very diverse documents, e.g. WWW search engines, would be infeasible. Both query translation and document translation have (dis)advantages. Theoretically, it seems that document translation would be superior to query translation. Documents provide more context for resolving ambiguities and the translation of source documents into all the languages supported by the IR system effectively reduces cross-language retrieval to a monolingual task. Furthermore, document translation has the added advantage that document content is accessible to users in different languages (one of which may even be their mother tongue). Document translation, however, is inherently slower than query translation but, unlike query translation, it can be done off-line and translation speed may therefore not be crucial. Document translations need to be stored for indexing though, and storage space may be a limiting factor, especially if many languages are involved. Query translation on the other hand can be improved by consulting the user during translation, an option that is clearly not available for document translation. For realistically sized CLIR document collections like, for instance, the TREC CLIR collection which consists of 2 Gb of text, document translation is usually not considered a viable option, the majority of CLIR systems therefore apply a form of query translation, cf. (Braschler, Peters and Schäuble 2000), although two research groups have demonstrated the great potential of document translation: IBM (Franz, McCarley and Roukos 1999) with a fast statistical MT system optimised for CLIR and Eurospider (Braschler and Schäuble 2001) who translated the full CLEF collection with a commercial MT system.

1.2 CLIR evaluation conferences

Evaluation is a key activity for IR research. It gives researchers the opportunity to test new ideas on new data, while minimising the risk of tuning systems to a specific data set. The development of test corpora is a time consuming task, because human assessors are employed to set a 'gold standard'. In IR experiments, assessors decide whether retrieved documents are relevant for a certain query or not. The size of current test collections makes it impossible to do complete relevance judgements, so usually it is assumed that most relevant documents have been retrieved by a set of diverse systems. The quality of this *pool* is to a large extent dependent on the number and variety of retrieval systems that contribute to it (Hiemstra and Kraaij 1999). Since 1992 the Text REtrieval Conference (TREC) organised by NIST[1] has built a tradition of carefully controlled IR experiments. The first years were aimed at developing test procedures for two main tasks: Ad-Hoc queries and Routing queries. In later years, new tasks were introduced. The bilingual Spanish-English task at TREC-5 in 1995 can be considered the first small scale comparative CLIR evaluation experiment. In 1996, SIGIR hosted a successful CLIR workshop which stimulated groups to participate in the new CLIR task (the CLIR track in TREC terminology) at TREC-6. This first CLIR track was based on a new data set with French and German documents, originating from the Swiss News Agency SDA, a Swiss German newspaper and the AP document

[1] `http://trec.nist.gov`

set from TIPSTER. The topic set consisted of 24 queries, which were available in 5 languages. Groups were allowed to do any combination of topic and document language except EN-EN. The evaluation was quite successful, because a lot of new groups participated. The organisation of the track proved to be more difficult than monolingual evaluations. Firstly, the topic development had to be synchronised over several languages, secondly, relevance judgements were spread over different languages and carried out at different institutes, because NIST lacked enough native speakers of German and French. In terms of cross-group comparability, the CLIR task structure had some problems. Because the availability of corpora in 3 languages and topics in 5 languages, groups from different nationalities generally chose to work in their own languages. Apart from lack of comparability, this also had an adverse effect on the reliability of the evaluation, because the number of runs per document language pool was quite low. But TREC-6 proved to be the starting point of a new stream of IR research for non English languages, also drawing attention from statistical MT researchers. The organisation decided to have a more controlled evaluation at TREC-7. The TREC-7 task showed three major changes:

1. The extension with Italian as a new document language. The Italian document collection also originated from the Swiss news agency SDA.

2. Instead of a free choice of tasks, groups were stimulated to do a multilingual run, i.e. retrieving relevant documents in multiple languages based on a query in a single language.

3. The start of the "GIRT" subtask, which focused on CLIR in a domain specific document collection. GIRT is a document collection consisting of documents from the social sciences, which are indexed by a domain specific multilingual thesaurus.

A similar set-up was maintained at the CLIR task of TREC-8. The new set-up was successful, although there were still some problems. First of all, only a few groups were able to do the multilingual task, because it required a lot of resources. Comparability of the runs improved considerably, but it is still a question whether one can really compare the performance of an English query on the document collection in 4 languages with the performance of a German query on the same collection. This was caused by the fact that the English document collection was much larger than the other subcollections, and yielded most of the relevant documents. There were also problems with quality control of the topics in the different languages, because sometimes translations were done by non-native speakers, or some query translations were not done from the source language. But, the quality of the evaluation matured steadily every year.

In 2000, the organisation of the CLIR evaluation moved to Europe, in order to acquire independent European funding and to attract more European participants. The new name of the evaluation is "Cross-Language Evaluation Forum (CLEF)". Not surprisingly, CLEF focuses on European languages. The organisation stimulated participation of new groups by including bilingual and mono-

	TREC-8		CLEF2000	
Nr. topics	28		40	
doc language	source	total docs	source	total docs
English	AP	242,866	LA Times	110,250
German	SDA	185,099	Frankfurter Rundschau, Der Spiegel	153,694
French	SDA	141,637	Le Monde	44,013
Italian	SDA	62,359	La Stampa	58,051

Table 1: Description of test collections

lingual tasks for languages other than English. The number of participants has grown indeed while improving the quality of the evaluation: CLEF had more topics and larger pools for the relevance assessments. CLEF 2001 seems to continue the growth curve with 30 registered participants. Apart from CLEF, several other Cross-Language Evaluation forums exist: NTCIR which focuses on Asian languages, Chinese–English is also the focus of cross-language tasks at TREC and TDT sponsored by the American TIDES program, and Amaryllis, a French CLIR research program. Links to these activities can be found on the CLEF webpage: `http://www4.eurospider.ch/CLEF/resources.html`

In this paper we will present results from experiments run in the context of the CLIR track at TREC-8 and at CLEF 2000. Table 1 gives an overview of the two document collections.

1.3 TNO engine & Retrieval Model

IR research at TNO started with the development of the Twenty-One retrieval system, a cross-language retrieval system initially developed for dissemination and retrieval of documents in the field of sustainable development (Agenda 21). The development of the Twenty-One system was started in the context of an EU project in the Telematics Application Programme. Besides TNO TPD, project partners included the Universities of Twente and Tübingen, DFKI, Xerox, Getronics and several environmental organisations. Both document translation and query translation approaches to CLIR were explored in the development of the Twenty-One retrieval system. The first prototype was largely based on document translation. Using existing Machine Translation resources (Logos), source documents were translated and stored in the database. This early prototype of the Twenty-One system was not tested as such in the TREC CLIR evaluation task. Instead, all experiments were carried out with an information retrieval system based on a simple unigram language model (Hiemstra and Kraaij 1999). The basic idea is that documents can be represented by simple statistical language models. Now, if a query is more probable given a language model based on document d_1, than given a language model based on document d_2, then we hypothesise that document d_1 is more relevant to the query than document d_2. Thus the probability of generating a certain query given a document-based language model can serve as a score to rank documents with respect to relevance.

$$(1) \quad P(T_1, T_2, \cdots, T_n|D_k)P(D_k) = P(D_k)\prod_{i=1}^{n}(1-\lambda_i)P(T_i) + \lambda_i P(T_i|D_k)$$

Formula 1 shows the basic idea of this approach to information retrieval, where the document-based language model is interpolated with a background language model to compensate for sparseness. In the formula, each query term is modeled by a random variable T_i ($1 \leq i \leq n$, where n is the query length), whose sample space is the set $\{t^{(0)}, t^{(1)}, \cdots, t^{(m)}\}$ of all terms in the collection. The probability measure $P(T_i)$ defines the probability of drawing a term at random from the collection, $P(T_i|D_k)$ defines the probability of drawing a term at random from the document; and λ_i defines the importance of each query term. For our experiments we worked with a simplified model where we used the same constant λ_i for each query term. The optimal λ (0.15) was found by tuning on several test collections. The a-priori probability of relevance $P(D_k)$ is usually taken to be a linear function of the document length, modelling the empirical fact that longer documents have a higher probability of relevance.

The retrieval model has been extended for the CLIR task, by integrating a statistical translation step into the model (Hiemstra 2001). The CLIR extension is presented in the following formula:

$$(2) \quad P(D_k, S_1, S_2, \cdots, S_n) =$$

$$P(D_k)\prod_{i=1}^{n}\sum_{j=1}^{m}P(S_i|T_i=t^{(j)})((1-\lambda_i)P(T_i=t^{(j)}) + \lambda_i P(T_i=t^{(j)}|D_k))$$

Here S_i refers to terms in the source (query) language and T_i refers to terms in the target (document) language, $P(S_i|T_i = t^{(j)})$ represents the probability of translating a term from the target language $t^{(j)}$ to a source language term S_i.[2]

An informal paraphrase of the extension is: the relevance of a document in a target language with respect to a query in a different source language can be modelled by the probability that the document generates the query. We know that several words T_j in the target language can be translated into the query term S_i, we also assume for the moment that we know their respective translation probabilities. The calculation of the probability involves an extra step: the probability of generating a certain query term is the sum of the probabilities that a document in the target language generates a word which in turn is translated to the query term. These probabilities are a product of the probability $P(T_j)$ as in Formula

[2]Note that the notions of source and target language are a bit confusing here, because the CLIR retrieval model contains a translation component, which translates *target* language terms to *source* language terms.

1 with the translation probability $P(S_i|T_j)$. We refer to (Kraaij, Pohlmann and Hiemstra 2000) and (Hiemstra 2001) for a technical description of the model. Section 2.1.1 explains how these translation probabilities are estimated. The retrieval model is implemented in the TNO retrieval engine, allowing for a fast and efficient retrieval procedure.

2 CLIR Experiments

Within the framework of the TREC and recently also the CLEF information retrieval evaluation initiatives, TNO TPD has tested several approaches to cross-language information retrieval. Our main approach to CLIR for TREC and CLEF has been query translation. We experimented with two basic variants:

- Dictionary-based query translation using the VLIS lexical database developed by Van Dale Lexicography
- Corpus-based translation using parallel corpora

We will describe our experiments with these query translation techniques in the next sections.

2.1 Dictionary-based query translation

Our dictionary-based query translation strategies are based on the Van Dale VLIS database. The VLIS database is a relational database which contains the lexical material that is used for publishing several bilingual translation dictionaries, i.e. Dutch $\rightarrow$ German, French, English, Spanish. The database contains 270k simple and composite lemmas for Dutch corresponding to about 513k concepts. These concepts, Lexical Entities (LEs) in Van Dale terminology, are linked by several typed semantical relations, e.g. hyperonymy, synonymy, antonymy, effectively forming a concept hierarchy. All concepts have corresponding translations in French, Spanish, German and English. In Table 2 below, some statistics for the VLIS database are given.

language	simple lemmas	composite lemmas	total
English	260k	40k	300k
German	224k	24k	248k
French	241k	23k	264k
Spanish	139k	28k	167k

Table 2: number of translation relations in the VLIS database

Before translation, queries are pre-processed in a series of steps:

1. Tokenizing: The query string is separated into individual words and punctuation characters.

2. Part of speech tagging: Words are annotated with their part of speech. We use the the Xelda toolkit developed by Xerox Research Centre in Grenoble for tagging and lemmatisation.

3. Lemmatisation: Inflected word forms are lemmatised (replaced with their base form).

4. Stopword removal: So-called stopwords, i.e. frequent non-content bearing words like articles, auxilliaries etc, are removed.

The remaining query terms are subsequently translated into the different target languages. We used three different strategies to create queries in the target languages using the VLIS database: 1) all translations, where we did not select a particular translation for each query term but created a structured query with all the options and assigned a probability to each of them[3], 2) "most probable" translation, where we selected the translation with the highest probability without using context information and 3) word sense disambiguation, where we used context information in the source language to try to select the correct sense and the corresponding translation(s) of each query term. These three strategies will be discussed in the next sections.

2.1.1 All translations

For almost every lemma the VLIS lexical database lists a number of senses, each again possibly with several translations. In one experiment we decided to use all possible translations to search for relevant documents as this might at least lead to higher recall. We used disjunction to combine all possible translations of each query term, whereas conjunction was used to link the translations in a way that reflects the original query. For example:

bosbranden Sydney $\rightarrow$ (forest OR wood) AND fire AND Sydney

These "Boolean" queries are generated automatically in the translation process, no hand-coding of operators is required. We do not actually use the Boolean operators "OR" and "AND" but they are implicitly encoded in the structure of the translated query. We developed an algorithm that inputs queries in conjunctive normal form and assigns a probability of relevance to documents given these queries. The algorithm takes into account the relative probabilities of translations. These probabilities are estimated in the following way. Some lemmas have identical translations for different senses. The Dutch lemma *bank*, for example, translates to *bank* in English in five different senses: "institution", "building", "sand bank", "hard layer of earth" and "dark cloud formation". Other translations include *bench, couch, pew*, etc. Since our retrieval model is based on the probability that a document (in the target language) generates a query (in the source language), cf. Section 1.3 above, translation probabilities are computed in the following way.

[3]No real translation probabilities are used but an approximation strategy.

First, we select all lemmas in the target language that translate to the query term in the source language. We subsequently translate the target language lemmas to the source language and count the number of times that the target lemma translates to the literal query term, e.g.

query: bank (Dutch)

bank (English) →	bank (2x), oever, reserve, rij etc.
pew (English) →	(kerk)bank, stoel
couch (English) →	bank, sponde, (hazen)leger, etc.

In the example above, the probability that *bank* (E) translates to *bank* (NL) is twice as high as the probability that *bank* (E) translates to *oever* (NL). Furthermore, some combinations of translations of query terms are more likely to occur together in documents than others. Documents containing such combinations of query terms will be ranked higher than others by the retrieval model. In this way the document collection itself is used for implicit disambiguation of possible translations (Hull 1997).

2.1.2 Most probable translation

In our "most probable" translation strategy we select a single translation for each query term based on the number of occurrences of translations in the dictionary. When a lemma has several identical translations for different senses, e.g. in the "bank" example in Section 2.1.1 above, this "most probable" translation is selected. If no translation occurs more than once, the first translation is chosen by default. The implicit assumption in this strategy is that the number of occurrences of a translation in the dictionary may serve as a rough estimate of an actual translation probability. Ideally, these probabilities should of course be estimated from actual corpus data.

2.1.3 Word sense disambiguation

We also experimented with a rather crude word sense disambiguation technique. In this approach, dictionary-based word senses are disambiguated in the source language using corpus information. First, the original query is used for retrieval on a monolingual corpus in the source language. All unique non-stopwords in the top N documents produced by this run are saved. We experimented with different values of N for this initial monolingual retrieval run, 20 turned out to be the best choice. Subsequently, all query terms are looked up in the VLIS database. The semantic relations defined in VLIS are used to look up synonyms, hyponyms and hyperonyms of each different sense of a query term. In this way we gather a group of words associated with each particular sense of a query term. These groups are expanded further using words from example sentences which illustrate the use of a particular word sense, which are also provided in the VLIS database. See Table 3 for examples of these word sense groups.

LEs	word sense groups
bank_1	concern business enterprise deposit mortgage loan
bank_2	rise elevation mound sandbank shoal aground stuck
pipe_1	duct funnel nozzle tube supply drain eustachian
pipe_2	tobacco peace clay water hookah opium

Table 3: example word sense groups

The groups of words associated with each possible sense of a query term are subsequently compared with the words from the monolingual retrieval run and "evidence" for each sense is computed based on the overlap between the two sets of words. The sense for which the most evidence is found is selected. If no evidence is found at all or all senses score equally, the first sense is selected by default. Query translation is now fairly straightforward. The translations for the selected word senses are looked up in the VLIS database, if more than one translation is given for a particular sense they are all included in a structured query (c.f. section 2.1.1 above).

2.1.4 Results

strategy	avp E-E	avp E-F	avp E-G	avp E-I	average	merged
alltrans	0.313	0.367	0.251	0.312	0.308	0.279
mprobtrans	0.313	0.332	0.205	0.312	0.288	0.252
disamtrans	0.313	0.310	0.181	0.312	0.276	0.241
monoling	0.313	0.551	0.410	0.362	0.409	0.323

Table 4: Results of the cross-lingual runs

In Table 4 the results of our submission for the TREC-8 CLIR track are presented. We chose to submit CLIR runs with English as the source language. English queries were run on the four target language document collections: English, German, French and Italian. Note that the E-E runs are monolingual runs without any form of translation. Because Italian is not included in the VLIS database, we did not use any of the translation strategies described above for the E-I runs, we used the Systran MT system instead. For comparison, we also include the results for the monolingual counterparts of all the cross-language runs. They provide an indication of the upper bound in performance that can be reached using our retrieval model. We present two different scores for the final results of the CLIR runs: average and merged. Average is simply the average score of the individual runs for the different target languages. The CLIR task, however, requires that the result list of a CLIR run consists of the top 100 documents in the four target languages *ordered by relevance, irrespective of language*. The result lists for the four different target languages therefore need to be merged in some way in order to obtain the final result list. A whole range of possible merging strategies have been proposed so far and research is still very much going on in this area. For TREC-8 we used a merging strategy based on document rank. We will not go into the details here but refer to (Kraaij et al. 2000).

If we look at the results for the different translation strategies we can conclude that the strategy where all translations are kept performs best for both French and German (the results for English and Italian are not relevant for this comparison). The second best strategy is the "most probable" strategy and the disambiguation strategy performs worst. We tentatively conclude that it is best not to select a particular translation unless one is very sure it is the correct one. Apparently, the CLIR retrieval process is not damaged nearly as much by adding extra incorrect translations as it is by leaving out correct ones. We were somewhat surprised by the results for disambiguation compared to the most probable translation strategy. It seems counterintuitive that simply picking the most probable translation, irrespective of context, should outperform the context-sensitive disambiguation strategy. More experimentation and error analysis are needed to explain this result.

If we compare the cross-language runs with their monolingual counterparts on a per-query basis, there are a number of queries with very poor results for all three translation strategies. We have identified some factors which contributed to this effect.

- Phrases. The failure to recognise and translate phrases as a unit was especially detrimental for the English to German runs where English phrases have to be translated to German single word compounds, e.g. *World War* → *Weltkrieg*, *armed forces* → *Bundeswehr*.
- Tagging errors, e.g. *arms* (weapons) was tagged as the plural of *arm* (body part) by the Xerox tagger.
- Capitalisation. Since most words in query titles[4] were capitalised, we decided to convert titles to lower case to prevent the tagger from tagging all title words as proper nouns. This had the effect that those title words that were actually proper nouns were not tagged correctly, e.g. the proper name *Turkey* was translated as *Truthuhn* and *dindon* (bird) in German and French respectively.

2.2 Parallel corpora

We developed three parallel corpora based on web pages in close cooperation with RALI, Université de Montréal. RALI already had developed an English-French parallel corpus of web pages, so it seemed interesting to investigate the feasibility of a full multilingual system based on web derived lexical resources only. We used the PTMiner tool (Nie, Simard, Isabelle and Durand 1999) to find web pages

[4]TREC queries, or "topics" as they are called, are fairly extensive representations of an "information need". They consist of a title, description and narrative.

which have a high probability to be translations of each other. The mining process consists of the following steps:

1. Query a web search engine for web pages with a hyperlink anchor text "English version" and respective variants.

2. (For each web site) Query a web search engine for all web pages on a particular site.

3. (For each web site) Try to find pairs of path names that match certain patterns, e.g.:
`/department/tt/english/home.html` and `/department/tt/italian.html`.

4. (For each pair) download web pages, perform a language check using a probabilistic language classifier, remove pages which are not positively identified as being written in a particular language.

The mining process was run for three language pairs and resulted in three modestly sized parallel corpora. Table 5 lists sizes of the corpora during intermediate steps. Due to the dynamic nature of the web, a lot of pages that have been indexed, do not exist anymore. Sometimes a site is down for maintenance. Finally a lot of pages are simply place holders for images and are discarded by the language identification step.

language	# web sites	# candidate pages	# candidate pairs	# cleaned pairs
EN-IT	3651	1053649	23447	4768
EN-DE	3817	1828906	33577	5743
EN-NL	3004	1170082	24738	2907

Table 5: Intermediate sizes during corpus construction

These parallel corpora have been used in different ways: i) to refine the estimates of translation probabilities of a dictionary-based translation system (corpus based probability estimation) ii) to construct simple statistical translation models (IBM model 1) (Nie et al. 1999).

2.2.1 Results

Table 6 lists the results of the bilingual experiments. The base run for Dutch to English scored an average precision of 0.307. The experiment with corpus based frequencies yielded disappointing results. We first generated topic translations in a standard fashion based on VLIS. Subsequently we replaced the translation probabilities $P(w_{NL}|w_{EN})$ by rough corpus based estimates. We simply looked up all English sentences which contained the translation and determined the proportion of the corresponding (aligned) Dutch sentences that contained the original

run name	avp	description
ne1	0.307	standard NL→EN
ne2	0.276	corpus frequencies NL→EN
ei1	0.320	Systran MT EN→IT
ei2	0.275	corpus translations EN→IT

Table 6: Results of the bilingual runs

Dutch query word. If the pair was not found, the original probability was left unchanged. Unfortunately a lot of the query terms and translations were not found in the aligned corpus, because they were lemmatised whereas the corpus was not lemmatised. This mismatch probably hurt the estimates. The procedure resulted in high translation probabilities for words that did not occur in the corpus and low probabilities for words that did occur. Other bilingual experiments for Dutch to English are reported in (Hiemstra, Kraaij, Pohlmann and Westerveld 2001)

For English to Italian we compared a Systran MT run with a statistical MT run based on the small parallel web corpus. We were quite surprised by the performance of the statistical MT run, which was not much below the performance of the Systran run. Key conclusion from this run is that usable translation dictionaries can be built from parallel web corpora.

3 Conclusions

Our initial conclusions from these experiments are that, so far, our best dictionary-based CLIR approach is keeping all possible translations. Our approach is not based on simple substitution of a query term by its translations but on including (reverse) translation probabilities in the retrieval model. Other researchers have published good results with similar strategies (Pirkola 1998),(Sperer and Oard 2000). Another common ingredient with these approaches is that our CLIR queries are *structured* queries, unlike standard - bag of word - expanded queries, which seem to work well for monolingual retrieval tasks but do not yield similar results in a CLIR setting (Hiemstra 2001). The results of our experiments also seem to indicate that the effectiveness of the CLIR process is not reduced nearly as much by including incorrect translations of query terms as it is by excluding correct ones. Our system could probably be improved by a model for phrase translations, which are especially important for translations from English to e.g. German (compounds). Finally, our pilot experiment seems to indicate that parallel web corpora can be used to produce reasonable translation resources.

References

Braschler, M. and Schäuble, P.(2001), Experiments with the eurospider retrieval system for CLEF 2000, *in* C. Peters (ed.), *Proceedings of CLEF 2000*,

Springer. (to be published).

Braschler, M., Peters, C. and Schäuble, P.(2000), Cross-language information retrieval (CLIR) track overview, *in* E. Voorhees and D. Harman (eds), *The Eighth Text REtrieval Conference (TREC-8)*, National Institute for Standards and Technology. Special Publication 500-246.

Franz, M., McCarley, J. and Roukos, S.(1999), Ad hoc and multilingual information retrieval at IBM, *in* E. Voorhees and D. Harman (eds), *The Seventh Text REtrieval Conference (TREC-7)*, National Institute for Standards and Technology. Special Publication 500-242.

Hiemstra, D.(2001), *Using Language Models for Information Retrieval*, PhD thesis, University of Twente.

Hiemstra, D. and Kraaij, W.(1999), Twenty-one at TREC-7: Ad hoc and cross-language track, *in* E. Voorhees and D. Harman (eds), *The Seventh Text REtrieval Conference (TREC-7)*, National Institute for Standards and Technology. Special Publication 500-242.

Hiemstra, D., Kraaij, W., Pohlmann, R. and Westerveld, T.(2001), Translation resources, merging strategies and relevance feedback, *in* C. Peters (ed.), *Proceedings of CLEF 2000*, Springer. (to be published).

Hull, D.(1997), Using structured queries for disambiguation in cross-language information retrieval, *in* D. Hull and D. Oard (eds), *AAAI Symposium on Cross-Language Text and Speech Retrieval*, American Association for Artificial Intelligence. http://www.clis.umd.edu/dlrg/filter/sss/papers/.

Kraaij, W., Pohlmann, R. and Hiemstra, D.(2000), Twenty-one at TREC-8: using language technology for information retrieval, *in* E. Voorhees and D. Harman (eds), *The Eighth Text Retrieval Conference (TREC-8)*, National Institute for Standards and Technology. Special Publication 500-246.

Nie, J., Simard, M., Isabelle, P. and Durand, R.(1999), Cross-language information retrieval based on parallel texts and automatic mining of parallel texts on the web, *Proceedings of the 22nd Annual International ACM SIGIR Conference on Research and Development in Information Retrieval*, pp. 74–81.

Oard, D. W.(1997), Alternative approaches for cross-language text retrieval, *in* D. Hull and D. Oard (eds), *AAAI Symposium on Cross-Language Text and Speech Retrieval*, American Association for Artificial Intelligence. http://www.clis.umd.edu/dlrg/filter/sss/papers/.

Pirkola, A.(1998), The effects of query structure and dictionary setups in dictionary-based cross-language information retrieval, *Proceedings of the 21st Annual International ACM SIGIR Conference on Research and Development in Information Retrieval*, pp. 55–63.

Ruiz, M., Diekema, A. and Sheridan, P.(2000), CINDOR conceptual interlingua document retrieval, *in* E. Voorhees and D. Harman (eds), *The Eighth Text Retrieval Conference (TREC-8)*, National Institute for Standards and Technology. NIST Special Publication 500-246.

Sperer, R. and Oard, D. W.(2000), Structured translation for cross-language information retrieval, *Proceedings of the 23rd Annual International ACM SIGIR Conference on Research and Development in Information Retrieval*, pp. 120–127.

A New–Old Class of Linguistically Motivated Regulated Grammars

S. Marcus, C. Martín-Vide, V. Mitrana, Gh. Păun

Romanian Academy, Romania
Research Group in Mathematical Linguistics, Rovira i Virgili University, Spain
Faculty of Mathematics, University of Bucharest, Romania
Institute of Mathematics of the Romanian Academy, Romania

Abstract

The oldest restriction in the derivation of context-free grammars is believed to be the matrix control mechanism, introduced by S. Abraham in 1965. However, in a paper (with solid linguistic motivations) of I. Bellert, published in the same year, there are *in nuce* the ideas of several control mechanisms considered later, as well as an idea which we do not know to have been explored. In short, conditions about some of the paths from the root to leaf nodes in the derivation trees of a context-free grammar are considered. Here we investigate this type of control, with emphasis on a class which generates a mildly context-sensitive family of languages (in particular, a useful pumping lemma is provided).

1 Introduction

Regulated rewriting is one of the most developed branches of formal language theory, with roots in the mid-sixties and with several dozens of control mechanisms well investigated – see (Dassow and Păun 1989). The motivation started from the observation that many languages of interest, natural and programming languages included, are not context-free. Generating such languages by context-sensitive grammars is not a practical solution, because at the context-sensitive level we have many difficulties (e.g., many problems are undecidable), and, more important from a linguistic point of view, the derivation in a context-sensitive grammar cannot be described by a sufficiently easy to manipulate graph structure. The first restriction in the derivation of context-free grammars is believed to be that introduced by S. Abraham, in 1965, the *matrix grammars*. In short, sequences of rewriting rules are given, which are applied together in a derivation step (this considerably increases the power of context-free grammars).

It was a surprise for us to recently discover the paper by I. Bellert, also published in 1965 (submitted on November 19, 1964) in a quite visible journal, *Information and Control*, with a provocative title, where a class of regulated context-free grammars was introduced which were never – to our knowledge – studied after that. In particular, this paper is not mentioned in (Salomaa 1973), the first monograph having a chapter about regulated rewriting.

Two things are rather interesting in the paper (Bellert 1965). First, it is very well motivated, starting from the assertion that natural language is not context-free (this was a lenghtily debated issue in linguistics: it was "clear" in the sixties, based on arguments of Chomsky, Bar-Hillel, and others; later these arguments were contested, but it is agreed now that natural language contains at least typical constructions which are not context-free; the reader can consult the papers we have included in the bibliography, most of them with self-explanatory titles). However, the paper not only provides a theoretical study of this assertion, but, after introducing "relational grammars", a consistent case study is examined, using the new formalism for modelling several constructions from Polish. Bellert applies her relational grammar to the generation of Polish kernel sentences. In this application, 13 relations are considered, mainly concerning the agreement in gender, number or case between the noun and the predicate.

Second, the definition of relational grammars contained several different ideas which remind us of restrictions on derivation which were widely investigated later, under different names. Informally, the framework is the following one. One considers a context-free grammar $G = (N, T, S, P)$ and a way to select from all possible derivation trees in G only those trees with certain properties, specified by a set of *tuple-grammars* and a *relation* on the rules of these tuple-grammars. More specifically, one gives several k-tuples of context-free grammars, $(G_1, \ldots, G_k)$, of the form $G_i = (N_i, N \cup T, S_i, P_i)$. Note that these grammars have as the terminal alphabet the total alphabet of G. The grammars from such a tuple work in parallel, over separate sentential forms, also observing the restriction imposed by a relation $\rho \subseteq P_1 \times \ldots \times P_k$. In a derivation of the k-tuple of grammars $(G_1, \ldots, G_k)$ we have to use rules related by ρ. The k-tuples $(w_1, \ldots, w_k)$ of strings generated in this way by $(G_1, \ldots, G_k)$ are then used for selecting from the derivation trees of G only those trees which have paths starting from a given node which are marked by $w_1, \ldots, w_k$.

Rather complex, but the reader can see here the idea of tuple grammars, investigated later in a series of papers by several authors, the idea of a matrix grammar (in the tuples of rules specified by the relation ρ), the idea of tree controlled grammars (we refer to Dassow and Păun (1989) for references), and to some extent, the idea of multi-component TAGs (Joshi 1987), where a set of auxiliary trees may be adjoined to an elementary tree. Of course, there are also essential differences between all these grammars.

We do not persist here in this direction, but we observe that the restriction from Bellert (1965) also contains an idea which we do not know to have been investigated in the regular rewriting area: to impose some restriction on the paths present in a derivation tree of a context-free grammar. This is the new–old restriction which we discuss here.

In short, we take two context-free grammars, G_1, G_2, where G_2 generates a language over the total alphabet of G_1. A string w generated by G_1 is accepted only if there is a derivation tree τ of w with respect to G_1 such that there exists a path in τ, from the root to a leaf node, which is marked by a string which is in $L(G_2)$. We say that such a pair $\gamma = (G_1, G_2)$ is a *path-controlled grammar.*

For an intuitive representation of this idea, one should have in mind the fact that a string w is generated by $\gamma = (G_1, G_2)$ by considering two derivation trees, τ_1, τ_2, the first one with respect to G_1 and the second one with respect to G_2; the first tree has w as the frontier, while the second tree is "orthogonal" to the first tree and its frontier string describes a path in the first tree. Figures 1, 2 contain illustrations of this idea.

Here we mainly investigate the generative power and the linguistically oriented properties of path-controlled grammars. When one of the grammars G_1, G_2 is regular, we do not obtain new families of languages, but more interesting are the cases when the two grammars are both linear or context-free. We prove that in the first case we get a family of mildly context-sensitive languages (a pumping lemma is used for obtaining the bounded growth property, while the polynomial parsability is obtained for the case when G_1 has a bounded degree of ambiguity), strictly included into the family of languages generated by matrix grammars (actually, this is true also for the case of using context-free grammars), not able to "count to five", but able to cope with the three basic non-context-free contructions: replication, crossed dependencies, and multiple agreements.

We close this introduction by also pointing out the remote similarity of path-controlled grammars (G_1, G_2), where the grammar G_1 is linear, with a variant of contextual grammars (Marcus 1969), the so-called external contextual grammars with a control language (Păun 1997), where contexts are added in the ends of a string, like in a linear grammar, in a sequence prescribed by a language on a set of labels for these contexts.

2 Path-Controlled Grammars

We use the standard formal language theory notions and notations, as available in many monographs. In particular, V^* is the free monoid generated by the alphabet V under the operation of concatenation, λ is the empty string, $|x|$ is the length of the string $x \in V^*$, and REG, LIN, CF are the families of regular, linear, and context-free languages, respectively. A grammar is given in the form $G = (N, T, S, P)$, where N is the nonterminal alphabet, T is the terminal alphabet, S is the axiom, and P is the set of rewriting rules. As usual, when comparing two languages, the empty string is ignored, that is, we consider L_1 equal to L_2 if $L_1 - \{\lambda\} = L_2 - \{\lambda\}$.

Given a context-free grammar $G = (N, T, S, P)$, with derivations in G we associate derivation trees in the well-known manner. Remember that each node in such a tree is marked by an element of N, with the exception of leaves, which are marked with elements of T; the root is marked with S. Let $S \Longrightarrow^* w$ be a terminal derivation in G and τ its associated tree. Each path from the root of τ to a leaf is described by a string of the form $SA_1, A_2, \ldots A_r a$, with $A_i \in N, 1 \leq i \leq r, r \geq 0$, and $a \in T$. We denote by $path(\tau)$ the language of all these strings, describing paths in τ, by $path(x)$ the union of all the languages $path(\tau)$, where τ is a derivation tree for x in G, and by $path(G)$ the union of all these languages.

Proposition 1 *If G is a context-free grammar, then* $path(G) \in REG$.

Proof. Starting from $G = (N, T, S, P)$, we construct the regular grammar

$G' = (\{S'\} \cup \{[A] \mid A \in N\}, N \cup T, S', P')$, with

$$\begin{aligned} P' &= \{S' \to S[S]\} \cup \{[A] \to B[B] \mid A \to uBv \in P,\ u,v \in (N \cup T)^*\} \\ &\cup\ \{[A] \to a \mid A \to uav \in P,\ u,v \in (N \cup T)^*\}. \end{aligned}$$

The equality $path(G) = L(G')$ is obvious, hence $path(G) \in REG$. ■

Let us now introduce the control mechanism we have announced: a *path-controlled* grammar is a pair $\gamma = (G, G')$, where $G = (N, T, S, P)$ and $G' = (N', N \cup T, S', P')$ are context-free grammars. The language generated by γ is

$$L(\gamma) = \{w \in L(G) \mid path(w) \cap L(G') \neq \emptyset\}.$$

That is, we accept a string w generated by G only if there is a derivation tree for w such that at least one path in this tree is described by a string which can be generated by G'. In other words, the language generated by γ is the yield of the tree language obtained from the derivation trees of G_1 which are "accepted" by G_2.

We denote by $PC(F_1, F_2)$ the family of languages $L(\gamma)$ generated by path-controlled grammars $\gamma = (G, G')$ with G of type F_1 and G' of type F_2, where F_1, F_2 can be one of *REG, LIN, CF*.

In Proposition 5 we will consider three (standard) examples, so we pass directly to investigating the power of path-controlled grammars.

When the control on paths is imposed only by regular grammars, we do not increase the power of regular, linear, or context-free grammars:

Proposition 2 *$F = PC(F, REG)$, for all $F \in \{REG, LIN, CF\}$.*

Proof. By taking G' a grammar which generates the language $(N \cup T)^*$, for any $\gamma = (G, G')$ one obtains $L(\gamma) = L(G)$, that is, $F \subseteq PC(F, REG)$ for all families F.

Also the converse inclusion is true: Let $\gamma = (G, G')$ be a path-controlled grammar with $G = (N, T, S, P)$ of type F and G' regular. Let $FA = (K, N \cup T, s_0, fin, \delta)$ be a deterministic finite automaton for the language $L(G')$ with the mapping δ totally defined. We construct the grammar $G'' = (N \times K, T \cup \{c\}, (S, s_0), P'')$, where c is a new symbol,

$$P'' = \{(A, s) \to X'_1, \ldots X'_n, \mid A \to X_1 \ldots X_n \in P, n \geq 1, X_i \in N \cup T, \text{ and}$$

$$X'_i = \begin{cases} (X_i, \delta(A, s)), & \text{if } X_i \in N, \\ X_i c, & \text{if } X_i \in T,\ \delta((A, s), X_i) \in fin,\ 1 \leq i \leq n\}. \\ X_i, & \text{otherwise,} \end{cases}$$

From this definition, one sees that the nonterminals of G'' together with the rules from P'' check the existence of strings describing paths in the derivation tree under construction which are in $L(G')$. Clearly, a path exists in a derivation tree of frontier w, with respect to G, if and only if a string having at least one occurrence of the new letter c, which can be reduced to w by removing all the occurrences of c, appears in the language generated by G''. We now define a gsm which removes all the occurrences of c in the input string and terminates successfully if at least one occurrence of c is removed. Consequently, the image of $L(G'')$ by this gsm is exactly $L(\gamma)$. Since all the families mentioned in the theorem statement are closed under gsm mappings, the proof is complete. ■

When the generating grammar of a path-controlled grammar is regular, the obtained language can be produced by a grammar of the same type as the control grammar.

Proposition 3 $PC(REG, F) \subseteq F$, *for all* $F \in \{LIN, CF\}$.

Proof. We present a proof for $F = LIN$ only, the case when $F = CF$ can be handled in a similar way. Let $\gamma = (G, G')$ be a path-controlled grammar with $G = (N, T, S, P)$ regular and G' a linear grammar such that $L(G') \subseteq \{S\}N^*T$. We consider the linear grammar $G_1 = (N_1, \{(A, B), (A, a) \mid A, B \in N, a \in T\}, S_1, P_1)$, $N_1 \cap N = \emptyset$, which generates the language

$$L(G_1) = \{(S, A_1)(A_1, A_2) \dots (A_{n-1}, A_n)(A_n, a) \mid SA_1A_2 \dots A_n a \in L(G')\}.$$

We now construct the linear grammar $G_2 = (N_2, T, S_2, P_2)$, where $N_2 = N \cup N_1 \cup \{S_2\}$ and P_2 contains the following rules:

1. $S_2 \to S_1,$ and $A \to S_1,$ for all $A \in N,$
2. $S_2 \to Aa,$ for all $A \to a \in P,$ and $B \to Aa,$ for all $A \to aB \in P,$
3. $A \to s(x),$ where $A \to x \in P_1$ and s is a finite substitution defined by $s((A, B)) = \{a \in T \mid A \to aB \in P\},$ $s((A, a)) = \{a \in T \mid A \to a \in P\},$ and $s(X) = \{X\},$ for all $X \in N_2.$

We obtain $L(G_2) = L(\gamma)$. If $w \in L(\gamma)$, then there exists a derivation

$$\begin{aligned} &S \Longrightarrow a_1A_1 \Longrightarrow a_1a_2A_2 \Longrightarrow \dots \Longrightarrow a_1a_2 \dots a_{n-1}A_{n-1} \Longrightarrow \\ &a_1a_2 \dots a_nB_1 \Longrightarrow a_1a_2 \dots a_na_{n+1}B_2 \Longrightarrow \dots \Longrightarrow a_1a_2 \dots a_{n+m} = w \end{aligned}$$

and $SA_1A_2A_{n-1}a_n \in L(G')$. It follows that $(S, A_1)(A_1, A_2) \dots (A_{n-1}, a_n) \in L(G_1)$. Moreover, the following derivation exists in G_2:

$$\begin{aligned} &S_2 \Longrightarrow B_ma_{n+m} \Longrightarrow \dots \Longrightarrow B_1a_{n+1}a_{n+2} \dots a_{n+m} \Longrightarrow \\ &S_1a_{n+1}a_{n+2} \dots a_{n+m} \Longrightarrow^* a_1 \dots a_na_{n+1} \dots a_{n+m} = w. \end{aligned}$$

The converse inclusion is obtained in the same way. ■

There are linear languages which cannot be generated by any path-controlled grammar $\gamma = (G, G')$, with G a regular grammar. Indeed, let us consider the linear language $L = \{a^nb^n \mid n \geq 1\} \cup \{a\}$, and assume that $\gamma = (G, G')$ generates L.

Clearly, Sa must be in $L(G')$, hence any derivation tree in G has a path described by a string, Sa, in $L(G')$, that is $L(\gamma) = L(G)$, a contradiction. However, the following result holds.

Proposition 4 *If L is a language in $F \in \{LIN, CF\}$ without words of length one, then $L \in PC(REG, F)$.*

Proof. Let us consider the grammar $G = (N, T, S, P)$, and the morphism $h : T^* \to \{[a] \mid a \in T\}^*$ defined by $h(a) = [a]$ for $a \in T$. For each $a, b \in T$, let $\partial^r_{ab}(L) = \{w \mid wab \in L\}$. We consider the language

$$L' = \{S\}(\bigcup_{a,b \in T} h(\partial^r_{ab}(L))\{(a)b\}).$$

Clearly, $L' \in F$; let $G' = (N', \{[a], (a) \mid a \in T\} \cup T \cup \{S\}, S, P')$ be a grammar of type F for this language. We also consider the regular grammar $G = (\{[a], (a) \mid a \in T\} \cup \{S\}, T, S, P)$, with the following rules:

$$P = \{S \to a[a],\ S \to a(a),\ [a] \to b[b],\ [a] \to b(b),\ (a) \to b \mid a, b \in T\}.$$

The grammar G generates the language T^* (remember that we ignore the empty string), and from all the derivation trees only paths which are described by strings of the form $S[a_1][a_2] \dots [a_n](a_{n+1})b$, for $a_i \in T, 1 \leq i \leq n+1, b \in T$, where $n \geq 1$, are in the language L'. By the definition of L', the string $a_1 a_2 \dots a_n a_{n+1} b$ belongs to L. However, this is exactly the string generated in the grammar G by the tree which has a path marked with $S[a_1][a_2] \dots [a_n](a_{n+1})b$. Consequently, for $\gamma = (G, G')$ we have $L(\gamma) = L$. ∎

Thus, from the generative point of view, the path-controlled grammars γ of types (F_1, F_2) with at least one of F_1, F_2 equal to REG are not very interesting. This is definitely not the case when F_1, F_2 are equal to LIN or to CF. It is known that the set of all derivation trees of a context-free grammar is a regular tree language and the yield of any regular tree language is context-free, see (Thatcher 1967). Next proposition states that the set of derivation trees of a linear grammar accepted by another linear grammar is not a regular tree language anymore.

At the same time we point out that the three usually discussed non-context-free constructions from natural language, duplication, crossed dependencies, and multiple agreements (up to four related positions) can be handled by path-controlled grammars of type (LIN, LIN).

Proposition 5 *The languages $L_1 = \{a^n b^n c^n d^n \mid n \geq 1\}$, $L_2 = \{a^n b^m a^n b^m \mid n, m \geq 1\}$, $L_3 = \{xcx \mid x \in \{a, b\}^+\}$ are in $PC(LIN, LIN)$.*

Proof. Let us consider the linear grammars:

$$\begin{aligned} G_1 &= (\{S, B, D\}, \{a, b, c, d\}, S, P_1), \text{ with} \\ P_1 &= \{S \to aSd, S \to aBd, B \to bBc, B \to D, D \to bc\}, \end{aligned}$$

$$\begin{aligned}
G_2 &= (\{S, A, B, C, D\}, \{a, b\}, S, P_2), \text{ with} \\
P_2 &= \{S \to aS, S \to aB, B \to Bb, B \to A, A \to bA, A \to C, \\
&\quad C \to Ca, C \to D, D \to a\}, \text{ and} \\
G_3 &= (\{S, A, B, C\}, \{a, b, c\}, S, P_3), \\
P_3 &= \{S \to Aa,\ A \to Sb,\ S \to B,\ B \to aC,\ C \to bB,\ B \to c\},
\end{aligned}$$

as well as the linear grammars G'_1, G'_2, G'_3 generating the languages

$$\begin{aligned}
&C_1 = \{S^n B^n Db \mid n \geq 1\}, \quad C_2 = \{S^n B^m A^m C^n Da \mid n, m \geq 1\}, \\
&C_3 = \{w\, h(mi(w))c \mid w \in \{S, A\}^*\},
\end{aligned}$$

respectively, where h is the morphism defined by $h(S) = B, h(A) = C$, and $mi(x)$ is the mirror image (the reversal) of x.

One can see that we have the equalities $L((G_i, G'_i)) = L_i, i = 1, 2, 3$.

The first two cases are left to the reader and we discuss here only the last one. Consider a terminal derivation in the grammar G_3. If the path from S to c in the associated derivation tree is in the language C_3, then it is described by a string of the form $S\alpha_1\alpha_2 \ldots \alpha_k B\beta_k \ldots \beta_2\beta_1 c$, where $\alpha_i \in \{S, A\}, \beta_i \in \{B, C\}$, such that $\beta_i = h(\alpha_i), 1 \leq i \leq k$. This means that the string $\beta'_k \ldots \beta'_2\beta'_1 c\alpha'_k \ldots \alpha'_2\alpha'_1$ is in the language $L(\gamma)$, where $\beta'_i = \alpha'_i = a$ if $\beta_i = S$ (hence $\alpha_i = B$), and $\beta'_i = \alpha'_i = b$ if $\beta_i = A$ (hence $\alpha_i = C$). This proves that all strings in $L(\gamma)$ are of the form $wcw, w \in \{a, b\}^*$. ■

However, the families $PC(F, F), F \in \{LIN, CF\}$, are not "too large". First, let us point out an "upper approximation" for them, the classic family MAT of languages generated by matrix grammars.

Proposition 6 $PC(CF, CF) \subseteq MAT$.

Proof. Let $\gamma = (G, G')$ be a path-controlled grammar with $G = (N, T, S, P)$, $G' = (N', N \cup T, S', P')$ being context-free grammars; without loss of the generality we may assume that $L(G') \subseteq \{S\}N^*T$. We define the matrix grammar $G'' = (N'', T'', S'', M)$, with

$$\begin{aligned}
N'' &= N \cup N' \cup \{\bar{X}, \hat{X} \mid X \in N \cup T\} \cup \{S''\}, \\
T'' &= T \cup \{[A, B] \mid A \in N, B \in N \cup T\}, \\
M &= \{(S'' \to \bar{S}S')\} \cup \{(r) \mid r \in P\} \cup \{(X \to h(x)) \mid X \to x \in P'\} \\
&\cup\ \{(\bar{A} \to u\bar{X}v, \hat{A} \to [A, X]) \mid A \in uXv \in P, X \in N \cup T\} \\
&\cup\ \{(\bar{a} \to a, \hat{a} \to a) \mid a \in T\}
\end{aligned}$$

where h is a morphism from $(N' \cup N \cup T)^*$ into $(N' \cup \{\hat{X} \mid X \in N \cup T\})^*$ defined by $h(X) = X$, if $X \in N'$, and $h(X) = \hat{X}$, if $X \in N \cup T$.

The idea behing this construction is the following: we start by constructing a string of the form $\bar{S}\hat{A}_1\hat{A}_2 \ldots \hat{A}_k\hat{a}$, where $A_1A_2 \ldots A_k a \in L(G_2)$; then we start a derivation in the grammar G_1 taking care that always when rewriting a barred symbol $\bar{A}_i$ which introduces a barred symbol $\bar{B}_i$ (always there is exactly one barred symbol), the corresponding symbol $\hat{A}_i$ is replaced by $[A_i, B]$. The derivation is finished only after removing all symbols with a hat. If in the obtained string the couple symbols $[A_i, B_i]$ are such that $B_i = A_{i+1}$, this means that the rules used in the derivation with respect to G_1 which contain barred symbols have followed a path which is described correctly by the string $A_1 A_2 \ldots A_k a \in L(G_2)$ constructed initially.

A more formal counterpart of this explanation can be given.

Claim. *A derivation $S \Longrightarrow^* xay, a \in T, x, y \in T^*$, with respect to G, with the derivation tree containing a path described by $A_1 A_2 \ldots A_m a \in L(G')$, exists if and only if $x\bar{A}_i y[A_1, A_2][A_2, A_3] \ldots [A_{i-1}, A_i]\hat{A}_i \hat{A}_{i+1} \ldots \hat{A}_m \hat{a} \in L(G'')$.*

We leave to the reader the technical task of proving (by induction on i) this claim, and we now define a gsm M which reads and leaves unchanged the prefix of its input string till the first symbol $[A, B]$ is met, then removes the rest of the input string, checking at the same time the following conditions (if one of them is not satisfied the machine is blocked and no output is produced): (i) For each consecutive symbols $[A, B][C, D]$ on the input tape, $B = C$ must hold. (ii) The last two symbols of the input string are $[A, a]a$ for some $A \in N$ and $a \in T$.

By the previous claim and since each terminal string produced by the matrix grammar is of the form $x[A_1, A_2][A_3, A_4] \ldots [A_{2n-1}, a]b$, $x \in T^*$, $a, b \in T$, $A_i \in N, 1 \leq i \leq 2n-1$, $A_1 = S$, it follows that the image of $L(G'')$ through the gsm M is equal to $L(\gamma)$. Because the family of matrix languages is closed under gsm mappings, the proof is complete. ■

Unfortunately, the fact that each path-controlled language is a matrix language does not say too much, because not so many (linguistically appealing) properties of matrix languages are know; in particular, no pumping property is known for matrix languages. Fortunately, such a property can be directly obtained for languages in the family $PC(CF, CF)$, with a stronger form for $PC(LIN, LIN)$.

Proposition 7 *If $L \subseteq V^*, L \in PC(CF, CF)$, then there are two constants p and q such that each string $z \in L$ with $|z| > p$ can be written in the form $z = u_1 v_1 u_2 v_2 u_3 v_3 u_4 v_4 u_5$, such that $0 < |v_1 v_2 v_3 v_4| \leq q$ and $u_1 v_1^i u_2 v_2^i u_3 v_3^i u_4 v_4^i u_5 \in L$ for all $i \geq 1$.*

Proof. Consider a path-controlled grammar $\gamma = (G, G')$, with context-free components $G = (N, T, S, P), G' = (N', N \cup T, S', P')$.

It is clear that without any loss of the generality, we may suppose that the grammar G' contains no λ-rule and no chain rule (rule of the form $A \to B$, for A, B nonterminals) – we deal with the language $L(G')$, not directly with the grammar G', hence we can apply classic erasing and chain rule reduction algorithms in order to obtain a grammar equivalent with G' and having these properties.

Now, if $L(\gamma)$ is finite, then the proposition holds by default. Assume that $L(\gamma)$ is infinite, and consider an arbitarily long string in $L(\gamma)$. (Because of space restriction, we give here only a partially formal argument – based on the so-called pigeon hole principle –, which can be followed on the graphical representation from Figure 1.) Consider a derivation tree τ for z with respect to the grammar G which has a path described by a string from the language $L(G')$. Denote by δ this path, and let $\alpha = SA_1A_2 \dots A_k a$ be the string from $L(G')$ which describes it, with $A_i \in N, 1 \leq i \leq k, a \in T$.

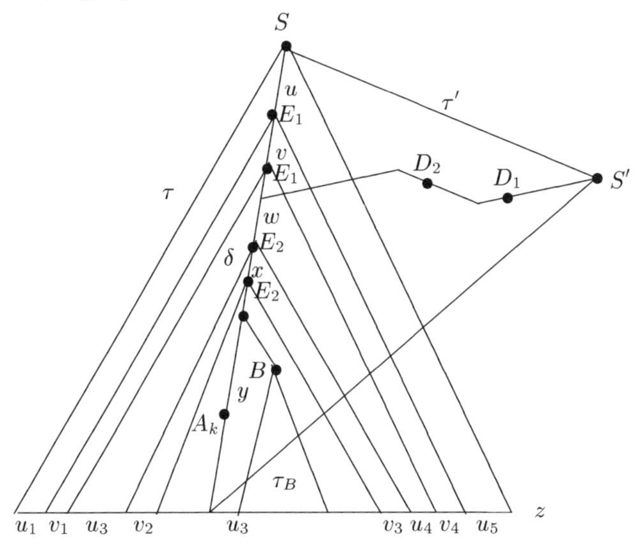

Figure 1

Consider the rules $A_i \to x_i A_{i+1} y_i$ used when passing from A_i to A_{i+1} on this path, as well as the rule $A_k \to x_k a y_k$ used in the last step of the derivation in G corresponding to the path δ. If any $x_i y_i$ contains a nonterminal B such that the substring of z derived from this nonterminal is long enough, then in the subtree τ_B we can find a recurrent nonterminal: there is a path from B to a leaf where a nonterminal $C \in N$ appears twice, hence the derivation in-between the two occurrences of C can be iterated – note that this path, as all paths in the subtree τ_B, is not under the control of G', because this subtree is independent of the path δ and the path δ ensures the correctness of all trees obtained from τ where the path δ is present). In this way, we have obtained a pair of pumped substrings of z in the usual way for context-free languages. The fact that the pumped substrings are bounded in length is ensured by the similar property from the pumping lemma for context-free languages.

Assume now that there is no such a nonterminal B. On the one hand, this means that all derivations starting from the nonterminals which are not appearing on the path δ are of a bounded length – denote this bound by r. On the other hand, the previous assumption implies that the path δ, and hence the string α describing it, are arbitrarily long.

This means that we can find a symbol $D \in N'$ which is repeated arbitrarily many times on a path in the tree τ'. Thus, we can find at least two such occurences of D, let us denote them by D_1, D_2, such that the corresponding subderivations $D_i \Longrightarrow^* \beta_{i,1} D_i \beta_{i,2}$ from τ' have $\beta_{i,1} = E_1, \beta_{i,2} = E_2, i = 1, 2$.

Consequently, the subderivation $D_1 \Longrightarrow^* E_1 \beta_{1,1} D_1 E_2 \beta_{2,1}$ can be iterated in the grammar G' and, also, the derivations corresponding to the substrings $E_1 \beta_{1,1}$ and $E_2 \beta_{2,1}$ of α can be iterated in G.

Therefore, we have found two substrings v and x of α such that $\alpha = uvwxy$ and the following two assertions hold: (1) $uv^i wx^i y \in L(G'), i \geq 1$, (2) for each i we can iterate a subderivation of the derivation in G described by τ such that the subderivations described by v and x are repeated.

Now, if we iterate the subderivations of τ which correspond to the iteration of v and x in the string α, this will lead to the pumping of four substrings of z, two in the left hand of the path δ and two in the right hand of this path (see again Figure 1). However, we have assumed that the derivations starting from nonterminals which are placed outside the path δ produce only substrings of a length bounded by the constant r. Also the strings v, x pumped in α can be bounded. Therefore, also the substrings of z which are obtained by starting from the nonterminals of v and x are bounded in length by a given constant, that is, the total length of the four pumped substrings of z is bounded by a constant, q. This concludes the proof. (The reader with a mathematical background can easily fill in the combinatorial arguments described in a rather informal manner here, following the classic proof of pumping lemma for context-free grammars). ■

The classic pumping lemma for context-free languages has a special form for linear languages: if $L \in LIN$, then there are $p, q \in \mathbf{N}$ such that each string $z \in L$ with $|z| > p$ can be written in the form $z = uvwxy$, with $0 < |vx| \leq |uvxy| \leq q$, such that $uv^i wx^i y \in L$ for all $i \geq 1$ (that is, the pumped positions can be chosen at a bounded distance from the ends of the string). As it is easy to see from the proof of Proposition 7, the same property can be obtained also for languages in the family $PC(LIN, LIN)$, just by choosing the iterated nonterminals D which are the closest to the root of the tree τ' with respect to G' (then, the iterated substrings of α will be close to the ends of the string, hence two of the iterated substrings of z will be close to the ends of z, too). Thus, we obtain:

Proposition 8 *If* $L \subseteq V^*, L \in PC(LIN, LIN)$, *then there are two constants* p *and* q *such that each string* $z \in L$ *with* $|z| > p$ *can be written in the form* $z = u_1 v_1 u_2 v_2 u_3 v_3 u_4 v_4 u_5$, *such that* $0 < |v_1 v_2 v_3 v_4| \leq q$, $|u_1 v_1 v_4 u_5| \leq q$, *and* $z_i = u_1 v_1^i u_2 v_2^i u_3 v_3^i u_4 v_4^i u_5 \in L$ *for all* $i \geq 1$.

There are several **consequences** of the previous pumping lemmas:

• The inclusion $PC(CF, CF) \subset MAT$ is proper. An example of a matrix language which does not have the pumping property from Proposition 7 is $\{a_1^n a_2^n a_3^n a_4^n a_5^n \mid n \geq 1\}$. This language also illustrates the next assertion.

• The path-controlled grammars, even with context-free components, "cannot count to five" (but, as we have seen in Proposition 5, path-controlled grammars with linear components "can count to four").

• The languages in the family $PC(CF, CF)$ (and hence also those from the family $PC(LIN, LIN)$ have the bounded growth property, for each infinite language $L \in PC(CF, CF)$ there is a constant r such that for each string $z \in L$ there is $z' \in L$ such that $|z'| - |z| \leq r$. This is important from a linguistical point of view, as languages with "jumps in length" do not look "natural", see (Joshi 1985).

• The family $PC(LIN, LIN)$ is not closed under concatenation: the language $L = \{a_1^n a_2^n a_3^n a_4^n \mid n \geq 1\}$ is in $PC(LIN, LIN)$ (Proposition 5), but LL is not, because it does not fulfill the condition in the pumping lemma for this family, see Proposition 8.

This last language is not context-free, but there also are context-free languages which are not in $PC(LIN, LIN)$. This can be proved by using another classic necessary condition for a language to be linear: if $L \subseteq V^*, L \in LIN$, then there are two regular languages L_1, L_2 such that $L \subseteq L_1 L_2$ and for each string $x \in L_1$ (each string $y \in L_2$) there is a string $y \in L_2$ (a string $x \in L_1$, respectively) such that $xy \in L$.

Proposition 9 *For each language $L \subseteq V^*, L \in PC(LIN, LIN)$, there are three linear languages $L_1 \subseteq V^*\{c\}V^*, L_2 \subseteq V^*\{c\}V^*, L_3 \subseteq V^*$, where $c \notin V$, such that:*

(i) $L \subseteq \{u_1 u_2 u_3 u_4 u_5 \mid u_1 c u_5 \in L_1, u_2 c u_4 \in L_2, u_3 \in L_3\}$,

(ii) *For each string $u_1 c u_5 \in L_1$ (for each string $u_2 c u_4 \in L_2$, for each string $u_3 \in L_3$) there are a string $u_2 c u_4 \in L_2$ and a string $u_3 \in L_3$ (a string $u_1 c u_5 \in L_1$ and a string $u_3 \in L_3$, respectively, a string $u_1 c u_5 \in L_1$ and a string $u_2 c u_4 \in L_2$) such that $u_1 u_2 u_3 u_4 u_5 \in L$.*

Proof. Instead of a completely formalized proof, we choose again to use a picture to explain the reasoning. Consider the situation illustrated in Figure 2, for a given path-controlled grammar $\gamma = (G, G')$ with linear grammars G, G', $G = (N, T, S, P)$.

We have a derivation tree τ with respect to the grammar G, where a path δ exists which is described by a string α from $L(G')$. Assume that this path ends when using a rule $B \to uay$. The language L_3 we look for is the union of all languages generated by the linear grammars $G_B = (N, T, B, P)$, B as above.

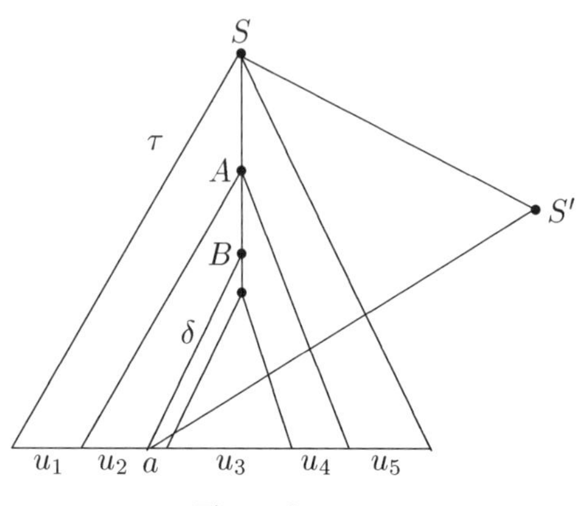

Figure 2

Now, consider the previously mentioned property for the linear language $L(G')$. Two regular languages R_1, R_2 exist such that $L(G') \subseteq R_1R_2$, and all strings from R_1, R_2 are useful, in the sense specified above. We construct two path-controlled grammars $\gamma_1 = (G_1, G'_1), \gamma_2 = (G_2, G'_2)$, where

$$G_1 = (N, T \cup \{c\}, S, P \cup \{A \rightarrow c \mid A \in N\}),$$
$$G_2 = (N, T \cup \{c\}, S_0, P \cup \{S_0 \rightarrow A, A \rightarrow c \mid A \in N\}),$$

and G'_1, G'_2 are regular grammars generating the languages $R_1\{c\}$ and $\{S_0\}(\bigcup_{a\in T} \partial^r_a(R_2))\{c\}$, respectively. Then, $L_1 = L(\gamma_1)$ and $L_2 = L(\gamma_2)$ have the desired properties. First, in view of Proposition 2, the languages L_1, L_2 are linear. Then, each string from $L(\gamma)$ can be obtained by interleaving strings from the three languages L_1, L_2, L_3: from the property of languages R_1, R_2, the path δ is cut into two parts, each one from one of the regular languages R_1, R_2. The definition of the path-controlled grammars γ_1, γ_2 follows this separation according to R_1, R_2. The derivations in G_1 start as any derivation with respect to G from S and end by introducing the symbol c. The derivations in G_2 start from the new axiom S_0, which directly introduces any nonterminal of G, and also ends by introducing the symbol c. These two derivations can be "concatenated", ignoring the symbols c, and can be completed with a derivation corresponding to the linear language L_3, so that the obtained derivation is correct with respect to γ. Because no string from R_1, R_2 is useless, no string from L_1, L_2 is useless; the same is true for the strings of L_3. ■

From this proposition we get two important consequences:

Proposition 10 (i) $CF - PC(LIN, LIN) \neq \emptyset$. (ii) *The inclusion* $PC(LIN, LIN) \subset PC(CF, CF)$ *is proper.*

Proof. The context-free language $\{a^{n_1}b^{n_1}a^{n_2}b^{n_2}\dots a^{n_6}b^{n_6} \mid n_1, \dots, n_6 \geq 1\}$ does not have the property from Proposition 9, as one can easily check. ■

Consequently, the family $PC(LIN, LIN)$ is incomparable with the family of context-free languages (and includes the family of linear languages). This corresponds to the speculation that this is probably the case with the classes of grammars which are adequate for modeling the syntax of natural language, see, e.g., (Manaster-Ramer 1999; Marcus, Martin-Vide and Păun 1998).

One of the most important properties of any class of grammars which aims to be considered a model of syntax is the polynomial parsability.

This can be achieved for path-controlled grammars $\gamma = (G, G')$ with linear components and such that G_1 *has a bounded ambiguity* (for each string in the language $L(G)$ there are at most k different derivation trees, for a given constant k) in the following manner. Let $G = (N, T, S, P), G' = (N', N \cup T, S, P')$. Assume that there is no derivations of the form $A \Longrightarrow^* B$ with respect to G (if such derivations exist, then we remove all chain rules from G by the well known algorithm, and this requires a polynomial time). We now construct a gsm M which scans strings from $\{S\}N^*T$ and, nondeterministically, for each symbol $A \in N$ either leaves it unchanged, or removes it provided that tere is a rule $B \rightarrow A$ in P and B was just scanned before A (this can be "remembered by the state of M). Therefore, substrings which correspond to recurrent derivations in G which produce nothing are either erased or not (the second case prevents the possibility to also have productive derivations with the same nonterminals). Consider the language $M(L(G'))$. Because LIN is closed under gsm mappings, this language is linear; let G'' be a grammar for it and consider the path-controlled grammar $\gamma' = (G, G'')$. The equality $L(\gamma) = L(\gamma')$ is obvious (note that we have $L(G') \subseteq M(L(G')))$.

Consider a string $w \in T^*$. We construct as above the path-controlled grammar γ' (this takes a polynomial time). The string w is generated by γ' if and only if there is a tree with respect to G of height at most $card(N)|w|$. Thus, we first decide whether or not $w \in L(G)$ (this can be done in polynomial time). If $w \notin L(G)$, then $w \notin L(\gamma)$. If $w \in L(G)$, then we consider all the derivation trees τ for w with respect to G. Because we have assumed that G has the degree of ambiguity at most k, the number of such trees τ at most k.

For each tree, we have $|w|$ paths from the axiom S to a leaf node. For each such a path we check whether or not it is described by a string in $L(G'')$. Because the height of the derivation trees we consider are bounded, the length of the paths in these trees are bounded, hence the membership of the associated strings to the language $L(G'')$ can be decided in polynomial time (with respect to the length of the strings, which in turn is polynomially bounded with respect to the length of w). If at least such a path, for at least a tree τ', exists, then $w \in L(\gamma)$, otherwise $w \notin L(\gamma)$.

In total, the decision takes a polynomial time. We formulate this important conclusion as a proposition.

Proposition 11 *If $\gamma = (G, G')$ is a path-controlled grammar with linear components G, G' and such that G has a bounded ambiguity, then the parsing of strings in $L(\gamma)$ can be done in polynomial time.*

It is a natural (and interesting) *open problem* whether or not the previous proposition can be extended to all path-controlled grammars, that is, without imposing the bounded ambiguity condition.

3 Final Remarks

Starting from an "old" paper by I. Bellert, which has introduced a (complicated) class of regulated context-free grammars in the aim of formalizing constructions from natural languages (with a detailed application to Polish), we have considered a new type of restriction in derivation: a derivation tree in a context-free grammar is accepted only if it contains a path which is described by a string which can be generated by another context-free grammar. We have found many properties of such devices (generative power, pumping properties, properties related to the mildly context-sensitive concept), but still many problems remain to be solved, both of a language theoretic type – for instance, closure and decidability properties – and of a linguistical type – concerning the adequacy/relevance of these grammars. Irrespective of the answer to such questions, we believe that at least from a historical point of view, this new-old type of regulated mechanism deserves to be investigated and further examined.

As the control by considering only one path from a derivation tree does not look very restrictive (also for capturing linguistics constraints), stronger controls could be of interest. Here are two posibilities: to have *all* path from a derivation tree described by strings in a given language, or, an intermediate case, to select *some* paths (by a "pre-condition", for instance, a regular language) and to impose a condition as above only to the selected paths. The formal study of such variants remains to be carried out; we hope to return to this topic in a forthcoming paper.

References

Abraham, S. (1965). Some questions of phrase-structure grammars, *Computational Linguistics*, 4, pp. 61–70.

Bellert, I. (1965). Relational phrase structure grammar and its tentative applications, *Information and Control*, 8, pp. 503–530.

Chomsky, N. (1956). Three models for the description of language, *IRE Trans. in Information Theory*, IT-2, 3, pp. 113–124.

Chomsky, N. (1957). *Syntactic Structures*, Mouton, The Hague.

Dassow, J. and Păun, Gh. (1989). *Regulated Rewriting in Formal Language Theory*, Springer-Verlag (Berlin).

Higginbotham, J. (1984). English is not a context-free language, *Linguistic Inquiry*, 15, pp. 119–126.

Joshi, A.K. (1985). How much context-sensitivity is required to provide reasonable structural descriptions? Tree adjoining grammars, *in* Dowty, D.R. et al. (eds), *Natural Language Processing: Psycholinguistic, Computational, and Theoretic Perspectives*, Cambridge Univ. Press (New York), pp. 206–250.

Joshi, A.K. (1987). An introduction to tree adjoining grammars, *in* Manaster Ramer, A. (ed), *Mathematics of Language*, John Benjamins (Amsterdam).

Manaster Ramer, A. (1999). Uses and misuses of mathematics in linguistics, *in* Martín-Vide, C. (ed), *Issues in Mathematical Linguistics*, John Benjamin, Amsterdam, pp. 73–130.

Marcus, S. (1969). Contextual grammars, *Rev. Roum. Math. Pures Appl.*, 14, pp. 1525–1534.

Marcus, S., Martin-Vide, C., and Păun, Gh. (1998). Contextual grammars as generative models of natural languages, *Computational Linguistics*, 24, 2, pp. 245–274.

Păun, Gh. (1997). *Marcus Contextual Grammars*, Kluwer (Dordrecht).

Pullum, G.K. (1985). On two recent attempts to show that English is not a CFL, *Computational Linguistics*, 10, pp. 182–186.

Pullum, G.K. and Gazdar, G. (1982). Natural languages and context-free languages, *Linguistics and Philosophy*, 4, pp. 471–504.

Rounds, W.C., Manaster Ramer, A. and Friedman, J. (1987). Finding natural languages a home in formal language theory, *in* Manaster Ramer (ed), *Mathematics of language*, John Benjamins (Amsterdam, Philadelphia), pp. 349–360.

Salomaa, A. (1973). *Formal Languages*, Academic Press (New York).

Shieber, S.M. (1985). Evidence against the context-freeness of natural languages, *Linguistics and Philosophy*, 8, pp. 333–343.

Thatcher, J.W. (1967). Characterizing derivation trees of context-free grammars through a generalization of finite automata theory, *J. Comput. Systems Sci.*, 1, pp. 317–322.

CGN to Grail

Extracting a Type-logical Lexicon From the CGN Annotation

Michael Moortgat and Richard Moot
Utrecht institute of Linguistics OTS

Abstract

The tag set for the CGN syntactic annotation is designed in such a way as to enable a transparent mapping to the derivational structures of current 'lexicalized' grammar formalisms. Through such translations, the CGN tree bank can be used to train and evaluate computational grammars within these frameworks.

In this paper we will discuss some preliminary work on the mapping between the CGN annotation graphs and the proof net format of the Grail parser/theorem prover (Moot 2001, Moot 1999). Grail is a general grammar development environment for type-logical categorial grammars (TLG, (Moortgat 1997, Morrill 1994, Carpenter 1998)). To a large extent, there is a straightforward transfer between the type-logical format and the analyses provided by other lexicalized grammar formalisms such as LTAG (lexicalized Tree Adjoining Grammars, (Sarkar 2001)) and MG (computational versions of Minimalist Grammars, (Stabler 1997)). An attractive feature of TLG, which is not shared by these other frameworks, is its full support for hypothetical reasoning.

In this paper, we exploit the hypothetical reasoning facilities to extract a type-logical grammar from the CGN annotation graphs. This task can be naturally divided in two subtasks. The first of these consists in solving type equations: in the TLG setting this means breaking up the CGN annotation graph into the subgraphs that correspond to lexical type assignments. In the presence of discontinuous dependencies, the lexical type assignments will not always be compatible with surface word order. The second subtask then consists in calibrating the lexicon in such a way that it has controlled access to the structural reasoning component of the grammar.

1 Introduction

The aim of the Spoken Dutch Corpus CGN (Corpus Gesproken Nederlands) is to build a database of contemporary spoken Dutch. The final version will contain around 10 million words. In addition to providing 1000 hours of audio, the corpus will be annotated in various ways: the entire corpus will be tagged for part-of-speech information, parts of the corpus will receive a phonetic transcription and be tagged for prosodic information, and so on.

In this paper we will focus on the syntactic annotation component. A total of one million words of the corpus will be syntactically annotated, part manually, part automatically. The annotation software used to this purpose is the *annotate* tool (Plähn 2000), which was developed at the university of Saarbrücken and which has been successfully used for the annotation of the NEGRA corpus.

For data exchange, *annotate* provides a line-oriented, ASCII based export format that can be efficiently processed by applications that want to make use of the annotation information. The philosophy behind the CGN syntactic annotation schema is to provide an informationally rich, but theory-neutral annotation level. The export format then allows users to convert the annotation information in the way which is most convenient for them; that is, we want to *derive* theory specific notions from the theory neutral export format.

As an illustration of this approach, we present a translation of the CGN annotation graphs into the type-assignments and proof nets of Type Logical Grammar (TLG, (Moortgat 1997, Morrill 1994, Carpenter 1998)). To a large extent, type-logical analyses are compatible with analyses within other lexicalized computational grammar formalisms—see for example (Moot 2000) on the encoding of TAGs into TLG proof nets, and (Vermaat 1999) on the embedding of Stabler-style Minimalist Grammars into TLG. But as a logic-based framework, TLG has extra inferential possibilities. In this paper, we will exploit the full support for *hypothetical reasoning* to induce a type-logical grammar from the CGN syntactic annotation. The first step is to extract a type-logical lexicon from the CGN annotation graphs: the approach described in §4 provides an algorithm based on hypothetical reasoning for solving the type-assignment equations. To make the solutions for these type equations compatible with surface word order, some form of structural reasoning is necessary. The CGN annotation graphs provide a tree bank to determine from data what the appropriate structural package would be. In §5, we discuss the fine-tuning of the interface between the lexicon and the structural reasoning component of the grammar.

2 CGN Annotation Graphs

The CGN annotation uses directed acyclic graphs (DAGs), where the vertices are labeled by syntactic categories and the edges labeled by dependency relations. We will only give a brief exposition of the basic ideas behind the annotation format, full details can be found in (Hoekstra, Moortgat, Schuurman and van der Wouden 2001) in this volume.

The annotation graphs allow us to specify structures which are unlike 'typical' tree-based grammatical descriptions. DAGs are allowed to be disconnected, DAGs can have discontinuous constituents or 'crossing branches' and DAGs can have multiple dependencies, where a single constituent plays a grammatical role in more than one domain. An example of a CGN annotation graph, which we will use as a running example throughout this article, is given in Figure 1. The direction of the edges is implicit in the graph; if we would draw the direction of the edges explicitly, they would all point downwards. Note that the *wh* word 'wat' (what) gives an example of multiple dependencies: it has the grammatical role of [whd], the head of the *wh* question WHQ, but at the same time it functions as the direct object [obj1] in the INF domain. The advantage of this form of annotation is that phrasal category and dependency information can be expressed without traces or other syntactic elements without phonological realization.

Another point worth noting is that we produce very flat annotation structures; a syntactic domain is only introduced when it is necessitated by a new head.

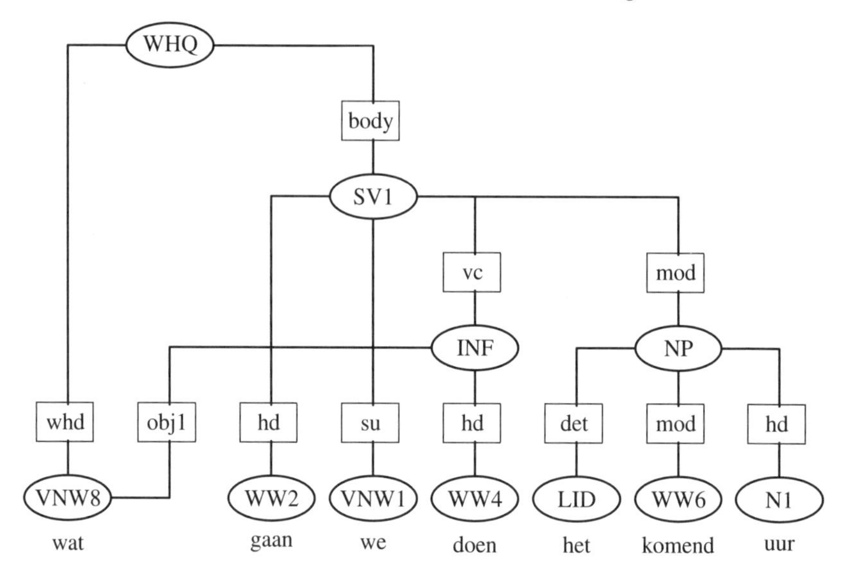

Figure 1: A CGN annotation graph

3 Categorial Proof Nets

The categorial proof nets presented in this section are essentially the same as those used by (Moot and Puite 2001). We refer the reader to that paper for formal results, showing soundness and completeness of these proof nets with respect to the sequent calculus for multimodal categorial grammar of (Moortgat 1997), and give only an informal introduction here.

Definition 1 *A* categorial proof net system *consists of the following:*

[Terminals] *Terminals are the lexical words of our grammar. We denote a word as a terminal by enclosing it in a square box, as follows.*

alcohol   Apeldoorn   reclame   ...

[Nonterminals] *Nonterminals denote the syntactic types of expressions.*

$$s, n, np, \ldots$$

[Constructors] *Finally, we have constructors which allow us to make complex expressions out of terminals and nonterminals. There are four basic binary constructors.*

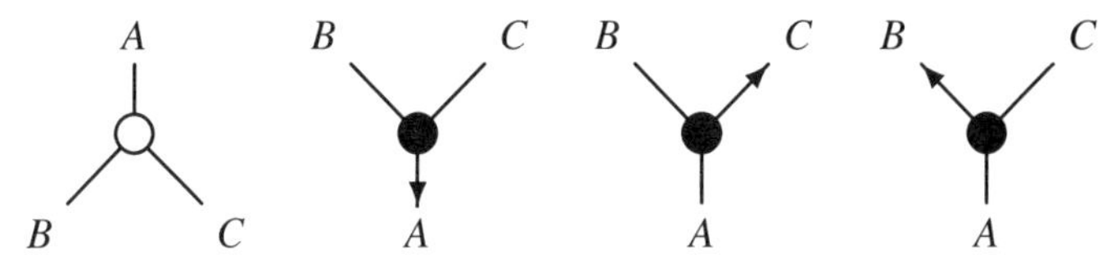

The downward branching constructor, the main *constructor, has no constraints associated with its use.*

The upward branching constructors, which we will call auxiliary *and which we draw with a black center, denote* constraints *on the use of their lexical entry, in a sense to be made precise later. The only difference between the three auxiliary constructors is which of the three points it connects is the output, as indicated by the arrow.*

More formally, a constructor C is a tuple $\langle Type, P, Q, p, q \rangle$, where $Type$ is either 0 (black) or 1 (white), P is a sequence of vertices which are 'above' C, Q is a sequence of vertices which are 'below' C, p is a subsequence of P, the outputs which are 'above' C, and q is a subsequence of Q, the outputs which are 'below' C, such that length(p) + length(q) ≤ 1, that is, a constructor has at most one output.

In this notation, we write the four constructors as $\langle 1, [A], [B, C], [], [] \rangle$, $\langle 0, [B, C], [A], [], [A] \rangle$, $\langle 0, [B, C], [A], [C], [] \rangle$ *and* $\langle 0, [B, C], [A], [B], [] \rangle$.

Definition 2 *A* lexical entry *for a categorial proof net system is a free tree made from constructor nodes such that*

1. *every root node (there can be multiple root nodes because of the auxiliary constructors) is labeled with a nonterminal symbol.*

2. *every leaf is labeled with either a nonterminal or a terminal symbol.*

3. *at least one leaf of every lexical entry is labeled with a terminal symbol.*

Because the auxiliary constructors have more than one parent node, they prevent the graph we are constructing from being a *rooted* tree. To remove these auxiliary constructors, we define the following graph contractions on the graphs in our system.

Definition 3 *We define the following* graph contractions *on categorial proof net systems, one for each of the auxiliary constructors. Whenever we find one of the following three configurations of constructors, we can contract this configuration to a single point.*

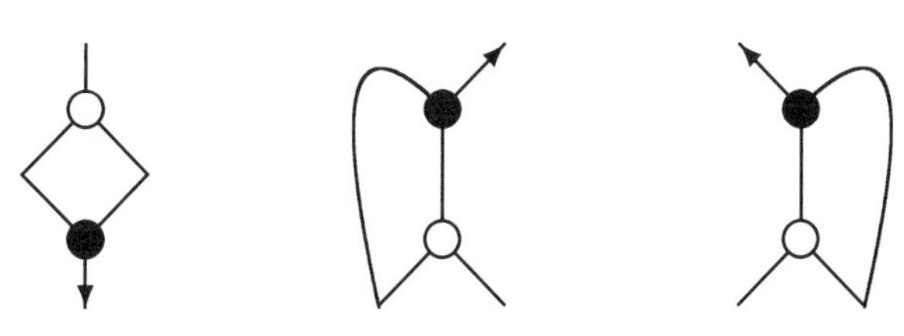

Note that all contractions are of the same general form: they combine an auxiliary constructor with a main constructor on both ends not marked by the arrow and in a way which respects the up-down and left-right ordering of the nodes.

Also note that drawing these graphs on a plane sometimes requires us to bend one of the connections, because we want to keep all up-down and left-right distinctions explicit in the graph. These bends disappear if we draw the graphs on a cylinder.

Definition 4 *A* grammatical expression *of type t in a proof net system is a graph which contracts to a rooted tree T, with t as its root, and where all leaves are labeled with terminals.*

Example 1 *An example lexicon for a categorial proof net system is given in Figure 2. We have simple lexical entries, like 'Albanië' (Albania) and 'politie' (police), which simply assign a syntactic category to a word, but also more complex lexical entries, like 'de' (the) which combines with a syntactic expression of category n to its right to form a syntactic expression of category np. Similarly, the transitive verb 'steunt' (supports) combines with an np to its right and with an np to its left to form an expression of type s.*

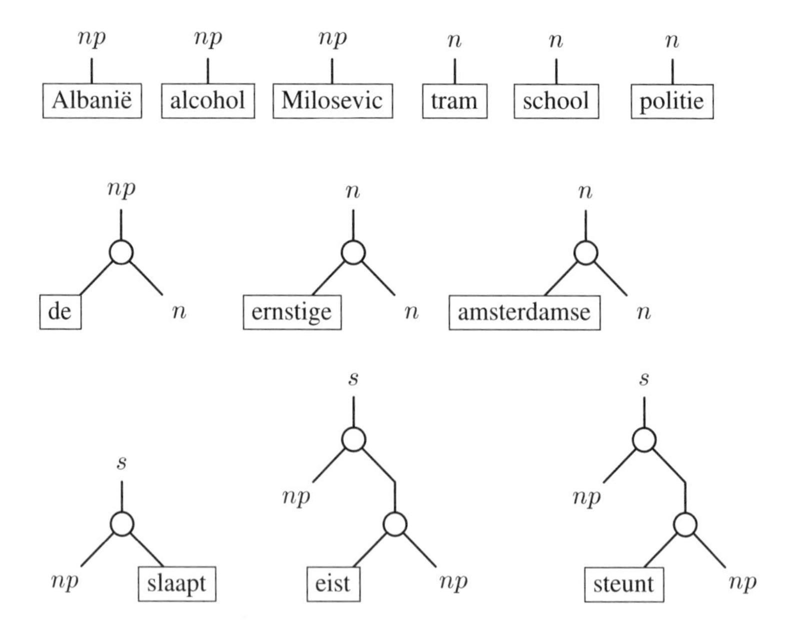

Figure 2: Some simple lexical graphs

We can use the auxiliary constructors to assign quantifiers like 'iemand' (someone) the lexical graph given in Figure 3.

This lexical entry indicates that 'iemand' selects an s to produce an s, where we can use an np inside this s, subject to the condition that the special constructor can

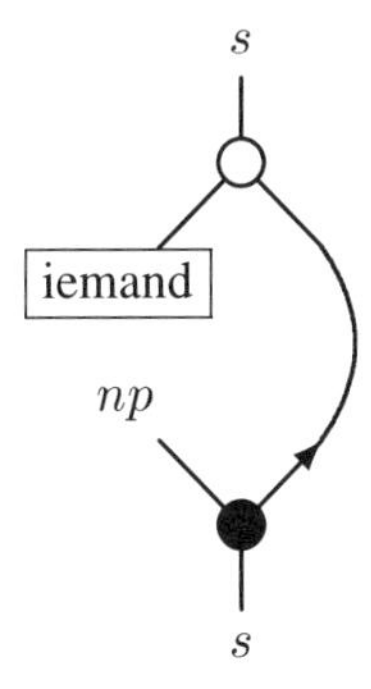

Figure 3: Lexical graph for a generalized quantifier

be contracted according to Definition 3. The difference between the assignment of 'iemand' to that of simple np's like 'Albanië' is that the assignment above allows 'iemand' to take scope at sentence level as a generalized quantifier.

Example 2 *We can derive 'iemand slaapt' (someone sleeps) to be a well-formed expression of type s by the derivation shown in Figure 4. First, we connect the bottom s of 'iemand' to the s of slaapt, which results in the structure on the left. After identifying the two np nonterminals, the structure will look as shown in the middle of Figure 4. Note that this structure is of the proper form to apply the contraction for the auxiliary constructor, as indicated by the dotted box around the redex. The resulting tree after the contraction is pictured on the right.*

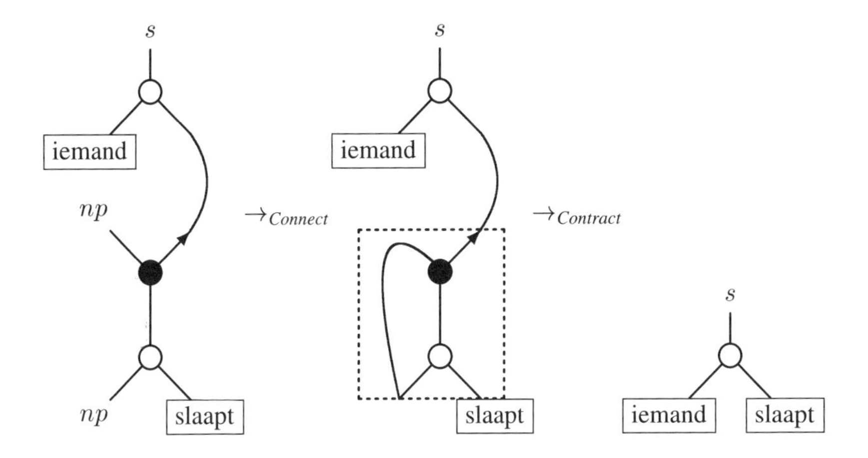

Figure 4: Derivation of 'iemand slaapt'

To give a direct correspondence to the multimodal sequent calculus, the full system described in (Moot and Puite 2001) is more extensive than the one described above in a number of ways. We will see later that we need some of these extensions for our proposed translation.

First of all, we allow our lexical graphs to have unary branches, which look as follows.

As with the binary constructors, the only difference between the unary auxiliary constructors is in the arrow which indicates the output connection. We can contract a main and an auxiliary unary connector if they are connected at the point which is not the output of the auxiliary constructor, just like with the binary constructors.

Secondly, we allow our constructors to have different modes of composition by writing an index i, out of a finite set of possible indices I, inside the constructor, as follows.

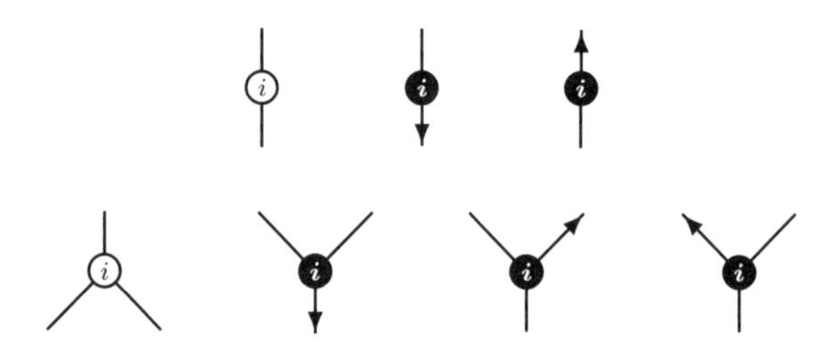

Finally, in addition to the contractions we allow a grammar to specify *structural conversions* which convert one tree of main constructors into another tree of main constructors with the same leaves. An example of a structural conversion, where 0 and 1 are elements of I, would be the following.

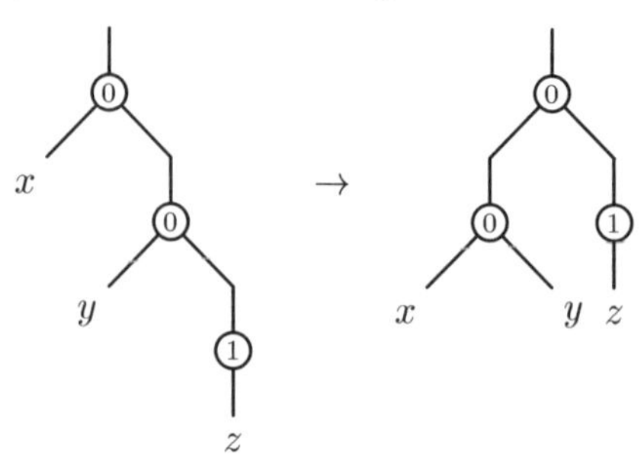

There is a straightforward correspondence between the nets described in this section in terms of unary and binary constructors and the type language of TLG

(Moortgat 1997), where we build complex types out of atoms by means of unary and binary connectives (indexed for composition modes, in the case of a multimodal system):

$$\mathsf{Type} ::= \mathsf{Atom} \mid \Diamond\mathsf{Type} \mid \Box\mathsf{Type} \mid \mathsf{Type}/\mathsf{Type} \mid \mathsf{Type} \bullet \mathsf{Type} \mid \mathsf{Type}\backslash\mathsf{Type}$$

As an example, type assignments corresponding to the lexical nets from (1) would take the following form:

$$\text{de} \vdash np/n \quad \text{amsterdamse} \vdash n/n \quad \text{steunt} \vdash (np\backslash s)/np \quad \ldots$$

This correspondence extends to the contractions and structural operations defined on nets. The deductive counterpart of the graph contractions of Definition 3 are the residuation laws below.

$$\Diamond A \vdash B \quad \text{iff} \quad A \vdash \Box B$$

$$A \vdash C/B \quad \text{iff} \quad A \bullet B \vdash C \quad \text{iff} \quad B \vdash A\backslash C$$

Structural conversions on the nets correspond to structural postulates (nonlogical axioms) in the deductive presentation. Below, as an example, the postulate corresponding to the structural rewriting we gave before. Note that the structural conversions perform, from the logical point of view, a type of backward chaining proof search and therefore the direction of the structure postulate needs to be reversed.

$$(A \bullet_0 B) \bullet_0 \Diamond_1 C \vdash A \bullet_0 (B \bullet_0 \Diamond_1 C)$$

Since it is proved in (Moot and Puite 2001) that the proof nets and the type language of TLG are two ways of expressing the same information, we will feel free in the rest of the paper to shift between the nets and the formula presentation where this is appropriate.

4 Extracting the lexicon

The remainder of this paper will be devoted to translating the DAGs of the CGN corpus into the proof nets of the previous section. This translation is parametric in a number of ways.

Firstly, we need to be able to identify the *functor* of every local domain. Usually, this will be the head, indicated by the edge label *hd*, but in some cases we might want to diverge from this.

Secondly, we need to be able to identify the *modifiers* of every domain. Usually modifiers will be indicated by the edge label *mod* but we might want to assign some other syntactic roles a modifier function.

A final parameter is whether we want to translate the annotated CGN graphs into a set of lexical graphs or into a single graph where all connections of nonterminals are already explicit. The first choice will be useful to test the predictions of the annotated corpus on new sentences, whereas the second choice will be useful to see which structural conversions we need to add to the system to produce the right word order. We return to this issue in §5.

4.1 Basic Entries

When translating the basic entries, the issue of granularity surfaces. The tags for some words differ only in the morphological information. For example, at the level of the leaves of the CGN annotation graphs, the syntactic category VNW for 'voornaamwoord' (pronoun) has 19 different instantiations depending on whether it is a personal pronoun, a reflexive pronoun, a demonstrative pronoun, and so on. Do we want to distinguish all of these in the translation, or do we want to conflate some of these distinctions?

Determining the appropriate level of granularity is a matter of grammatical fine-tuning. For expository purposes, we stay at a rather coarse level in this paper. We will translate the syntactic categories of our example sentence into nonterminal categories as follows.

VNW1 $\rightarrow np$
VNW8 $\rightarrow np$
N1 $\rightarrow n$
INF $\rightarrow inf$
SV1 $\rightarrow sv1$
WHQ $\rightarrow whq$

With this translation in hand, we can immediately assign two of the words of the example a lexical entry, as shown below.

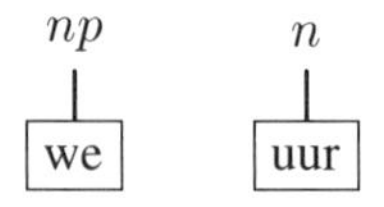

4.2 Modifiers

The example sentence of Figure 1 has two modifiers: 'komend' (next) is a modifier at the np level, whereas the phrase 'het komend uur' (the next hour) is a sentence level modifier. We repeat the relevant part of Figure 1 in Figure 5.

The n modifier is lexically anchored and is in fact the same lexical graph used for noun modifiers in the example lexicon in Figure 2. The translation for the $sv1$ modifier is still partial, since it depends on the translation of the functor of the NP domain.

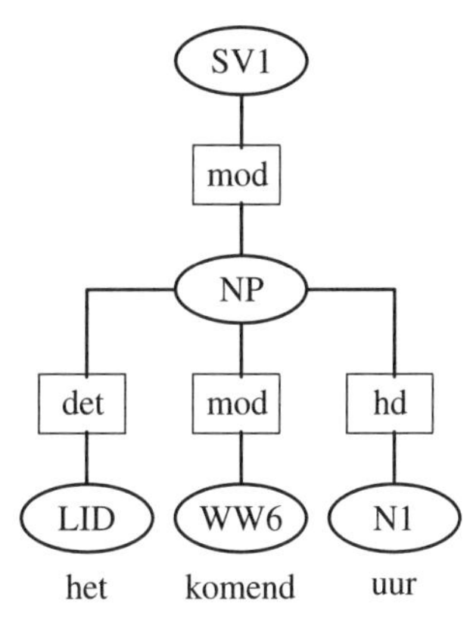

Figure 5: Modifiers from Figure 1

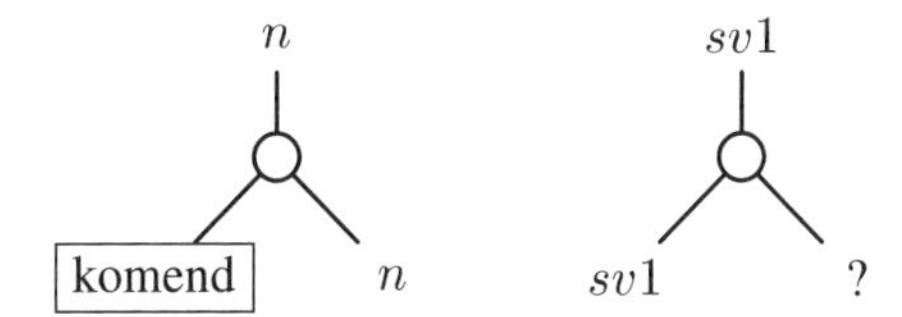

4.3 Functors

For functors, we again have to make a choice: do we want to follow the surface structure as much as possible and basically generate the words of the sentence in the right order, or do we want to assign functors a structure which is as canonical as possible, which would reduce the number of different lexical assignments and require us to *derive* the other possibilities from this canonical structure via some appropriate form of structural rewriting. For the moment we choose the first option and we defer the discussion of structural reasoning to §5.

The functor 'doen' (to do) selects a direct object np to its left to produce an *inf* category. This is coded by the following lexical graph.

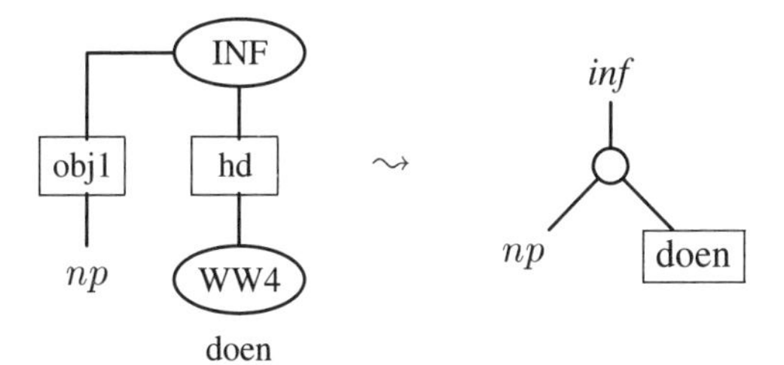

The functor 'het' (the) selects a noun to its right to produce the translation of the np category.

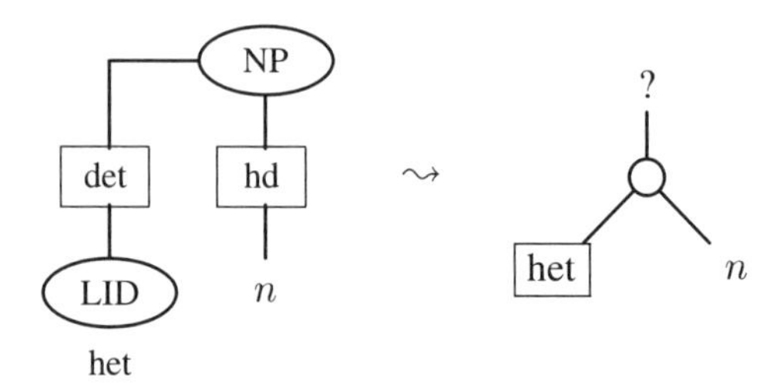

As we have seen in the previous section this translation is an $sv1$ modifier, so the final result will select an n to its right to produce an $sv1$ modifier as follows.

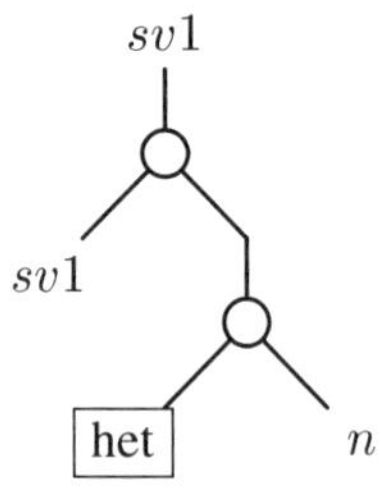

The auxiliary verb 'gaan' (go) selects for a subject np and an infinitival complement *inf*, which is translated as follows.

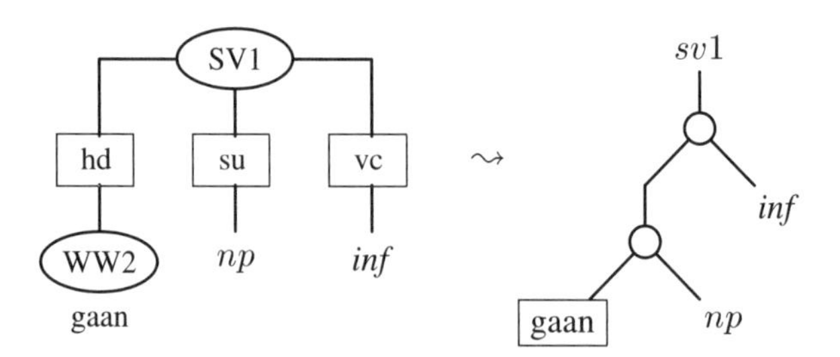

4.4 Multiple Dependencies

Because the auxiliary links for lexical proof structures have more than one parent, it seems evident we can use auxiliary links to encode the multiple dependencies which are possible in the CGN annotation graphs.

The multiple dependency in our example, schematically repeated as Figure 6 fo convenience, will be converted as follows, indicating that the question word 'wat' (what) produces an expression of type whq if it finds a constituent of type $sv1$

to its right with a hypothetical subconstituent of type np in it. For some readers it may be helpful to picture this hypothesis as the 'trace' bound by the question word.

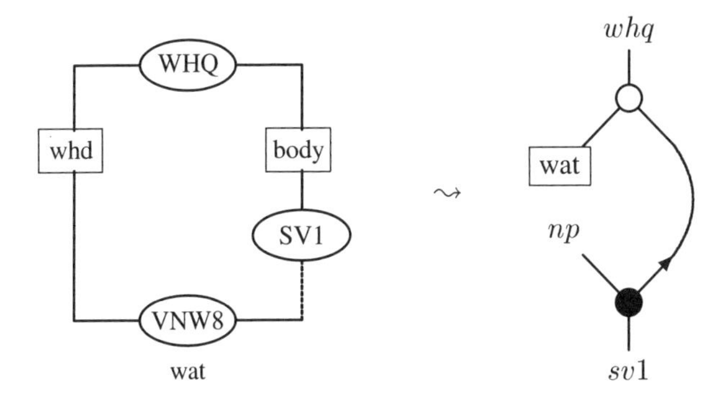

Figure 6: The multiple dependency from Figure 1

The introduction of an auxiliary constructor in the lexical graph commits us to contract this constructor, thus withdrawing the np hypothesis. Creating the appropriate configuration for contraction may require the use of structural conversions. We will return to the topic of structural conversions in §5, where they allow us to derive discontinuous constituents.

4.5 Edge Labels

So far, we have treated the edge labels as only providing us with the information we need to determine which structures are functors and which structures are modifiers. We now want to refine the translation function to also take the information about the dependency relations into account.

In the example below, 'doen' (to do) selects an np which functions as a direct object [obj1]. One possibility is to encode this information into the mode of composition, assigning 'doen' the type $np\backslash_{\mathrm{obj1}} inf$, as in the graph below. Note that the [hd] syntactic relation is implicit in this encoding, in the sense that functors and heads are identified. Note also, that in a language (like Dutch) with both head-initial and head-final phrases, one would have to take the head position into account. This can be done by distinguishing, say, *l(M)* versus *r(M)* for left- versus right-headed structures, assigning the dependency role M to the nonhead component. In the case of our head-final transitive infinitive, this yields the type $np\backslash_{\mathrm{r(obj1)}} inf$.

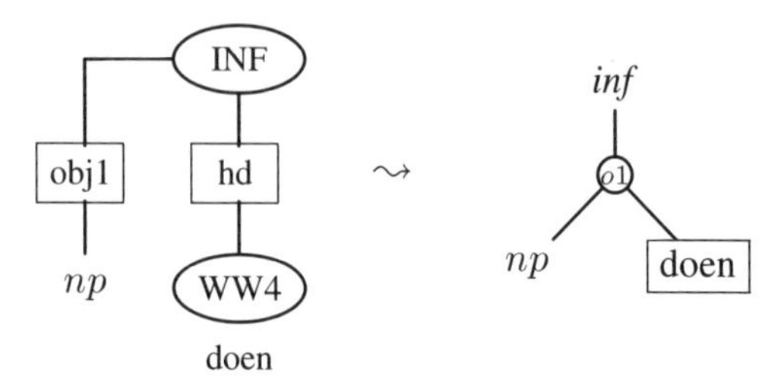

An alternative solution would be to encode the grammatical relations as *unary* branches in the lexical graph. This allows us to code also the [hd] edge label explicitly, as in the graph below. In the remainder, we go for the first option, because we want to reserve the unary connectives for another purpose — they will act as control features for structural reasoning.

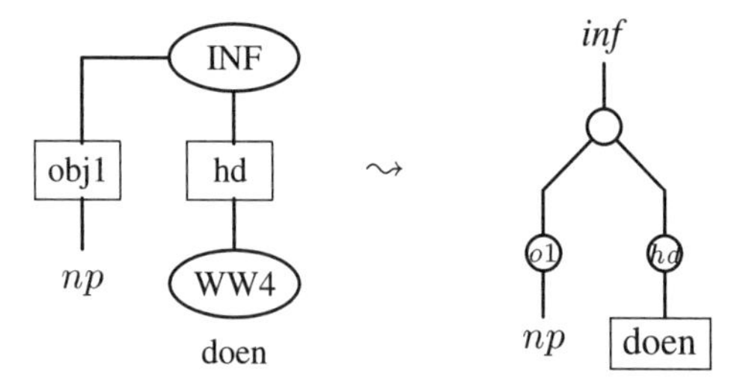

4.6 Implementation

As already suggested by the previous sections, the translation from the CGN annotation graphs to the TLG framework can be fully automated. The implementation of the conversion, given in Figure 7 proceeds on the assumption, which does not necessarily hold of general DAGs, but which is true of the DAGs we use for the CGN annotation, namely that every connected component of the DAG has a unique root vertex.

An implementation of the conversion utility is available through ftp at the following URL.

`ftp://ftp.let.uu.nl/pub/users/moot/cgn.tar.gz`

5 Discontinuous dependencies and structural reasoning

As remarked above, the dependency relations coded in the CGN annotation graphs can be at odds with surface order and constituency. In our example of Figure 1, we already see an illustration of such a discontinuous dependency: the secondary edge linking the question word 'wat' to the direct object role within the infinitival complement headed by 'doen' crosses the finite verb and subject edges.

To make the lexical type-assignments compatible with surface order, we have to combine the categorial base logic with some form of structural reasoning. Earlier versions of categorial grammar were ill equipped to deal with the combination

```
BEGIN
FOR EVERY component c of C
    LOOK UP the formula F corresponding the the unique root vertex v
    TRANSL(v,F)
END FOR
END

PROC TRANSL(v,F)
    IF v is a leaf corresponding to word w
        add w with formula F to the lexicon
    ELSE
        FOR EVERY daughter d with edge label e of v
            IF d is a modifier
                TRANSL(d,F\F)
            ELSE IF d is a complement
                LOOK UP the formula D corresponding to d
                TRANSL(d,f1\r(e1) ... fi\r(ei) D)
                WHERE f1 ... fi are the formulas corresponding to
                    secondary edges of descendants of d
            ELSE IF d is a head
                TRANSL(d,(f1\r(e1) ... fi\r(ei) F)/l(ej) fj ... /l(ej) fm)
                WHERE f1 ... fi are the formulas corresponding to
                    complements occurring to the left of d
                WHERE fj ... fm are the formulas corresponding to
                    complements occurring to the right of d
            END IF
        END FOR
    END IF
END PROC
```

Figure 7: The translation algorithm

of logical and structural inference, because they were operating from an essentially one-dimensional perspective on grammatical composition. If there is only one composition operation around in the grammar, attributing structural properties to this operation (such as associativity, or commutativity) has a *global* effect, destroying structural discrimination (for constituency or linear order) throughout the grammar. What is needed instead of such global choices, is lexically controlled, local options for structural reasoning.

The multimodal architecture of TLG provides for this form of structural control. In the presence of multiple modes of composition, one can differentially treat the structural behavior of individual modes and of their interaction. A constituent bearing the [obj1] dependency role, for example, could have a different structural behavior from a subject constituent. The unary type-forming connectives ($\Diamond$ and the residual $\Box$ in the type language) in this respect act as *licensing* features, providing controlled access to structural inferences.

The expressive power of the unary constants is by now well understood. The embedding results of (Kurtonina and Moortgat 1997) show that every corner of the categorial landscape is in effect reachable by means of the unary control features. (If one goes beyond resource-sensitive composition modes, the unary operators even allow an embedding of Intuitionistic Logic, as shown in (Lambek 1993).) Where exactly in this landscape the natural languages have to be localized, is a big open research question in TLG. An annotated corpus such as CGN provides a valuable tree bank to address this question from a data-oriented perspective.

5.1 The structural package

We are currently experimenting with the structural package below (from (Moortgat 1999)) that seems to have a pleasant balance between expressivity and structural constraint. We first discuss the postulates in schematic form — further fine-tuning in terms of mode distinctions for the $\bullet$ and $\Diamond$ operations is straightforward.

$$\begin{array}{lcll} \Diamond A \bullet (B \bullet C) & \dashv\vdash & (\Diamond A \bullet B) \bullet C & (Pl1) \\ \Diamond A \bullet (B \bullet C) & \dashv\vdash & B \bullet (\Diamond A \bullet C) & (Pl2) \\ & & & \\ (A \bullet B) \bullet \Diamond C & \dashv\vdash & (A \bullet \Diamond C) \bullet B & (Pr2) \\ (A \bullet B) \bullet \Diamond C & \dashv\vdash & A \bullet (B \bullet \Diamond C) & (Pr1) \end{array}$$

The postulates can be read in two directions. In the *Output* $\vdash$ *Input* direction, they have the effect of *revealing* a $\Diamond$ marked constituent, by promoting it from an embedded position to a dominating position where it is visible for the logical rules. In the *Input* $\dashv$ *Output* direction, they *hide* a marked constituent, pushing it from a visible position to an embedded position. Apart from the $\dashv\vdash$ asymmetry, there is a left-right asymmetry: the *Pl* postulates have a bias for left branches; for the *Pr* postulates only right branches are accessible.

We highlight some properties of this package.

Control The postulates operate under $\Diamond$ control. Because the logic doesn't allow the control features to enter a derivation out of the blue, this means they have to be lexically anchored.

Linearity The postulates rearrange a structural configuration; they cannot duplicate or waste grammatical material.

Locality The window for structural reasoning is strictly local: postulates can only see two products in construction with each other (with one of the factors bearing the licensing feature).

Recursion Non-local effects arise through recursion.

5.2 Calibrating the lexicon/syntax interface

In order to give the lexical type assignments of §4 access to structural reasoning, we have to systematically refine them with the licensing control features. We follow the 'key and lock' strategy of (Moortgat 1999), which consists in decorating positive subtypes with a $\Diamond\Box$ prefix. For a constituent of type $\Diamond\Box A$, the $\Diamond$ component provides access to the structural postulates discussed above. At the point where such a marked constituent has found the structural position where it can be used by the logical rules, the control feature can be cancelled through the basic law $\Diamond\Box A \vdash A$ — the $\Diamond$ key unlocking the $\Box$ lock.

We illustrate the effect of the $\Diamond\Box$ decoration on the lexical type assignments for our running example of Figure 1. Note that the positive subtype np in the type assignment to the question word 'wat' (the 'gap' hypothesis) gains access to structural reasoning by means of its *se* decoration (for secondary edge).

doen : $\Diamond_{hd}\Box_{hd}(np\backslash_{r(obj1)}inf)$
gaan : $\Diamond_{hd}\Box_{hd}((s1/_{l(vc)}inf)/_{l(su)}np)$
het : $\Diamond_{det}\Box_{det}(\Diamond_{mod}\Box_{mod}(s1\backslash s1)/_{l(hd)}np)$
komend : $\Diamond_{mod}\Box_{mod}(\Diamond_{mod}\Box_{mod}(s1\backslash s1)/\Diamond_{mod}\Box_{mod}(s1\backslash s1))$
uur : np
wat : $\Diamond_{whd}\Box_{whd}(whq/_{l(body)}(\Diamond_{se}\Box_{se}np\backslash_{r(obj1)}s1))$
we : np

For reasons of space, we shorten the example to 'Wat gaan we doen?' ('what shall we do') — this provides enough information to see how the discontinuous dependency is established, and step through the proof net derivation of the simplified sentence. Figure 8 shows the net with the right connections on the left. Note that the two occurrences of x correspond to the same vertex in the graph. For a successful contraction as required by Definition (4), the direct object hypothesis labeled x has to be moved upward. For this we need the following mode-instantiated version of postulate $Pl2$.

$$\Diamond_{se}A \bullet_{r(obj1)} (B \bullet_{l(vc)} C) \vdash B \bullet_{l(vc)} (\Diamond_{se}A \bullet_{r(obj1)} C) \quad (Pl2)$$

After the $Pl2$ structural rewriting, the unary and binary redexes are all in the right configuration for contraction, as shown in Figure 8 on the right. The resulting tree is displayed in Figure 9.

Note that in this derivation, only the licensing feature on the hypothesis np subtype for 'wat' played an active role — the inert control features in that type assignment could be simplified away. We can anticipate that the *mod* feature for the sentential modifier 'het komend uur' ('the next hour') will be active too, if we want to derive our running example and the variant 'wat willen we het komend uur gaan doen' from the same type assignments. In this variant the modifier separates the infinitival complement from its head — a structural conversion that can be accomplished by $Pr2$ (in the 'hiding' $\dashv$ direction).

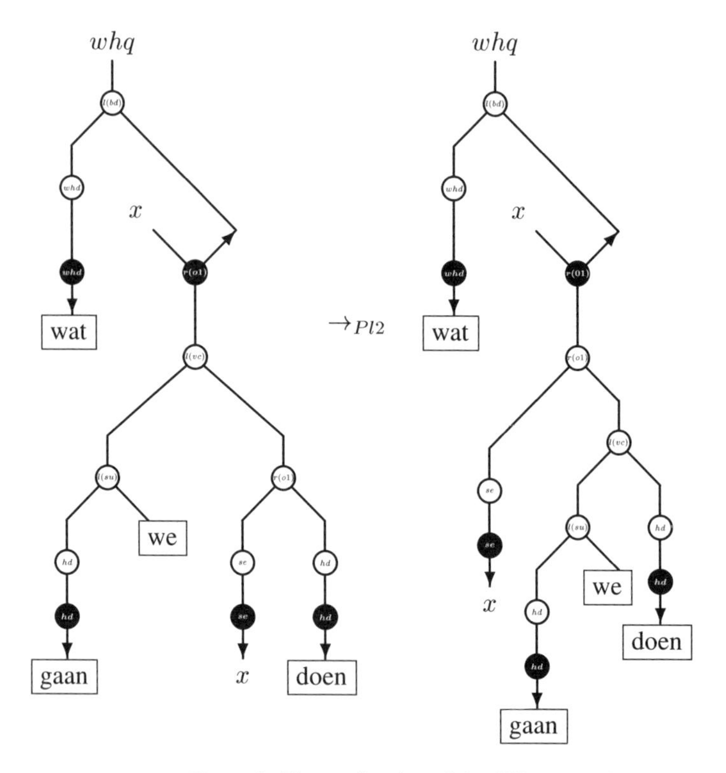

Figure 8: The application of the $Pl2$ conversion

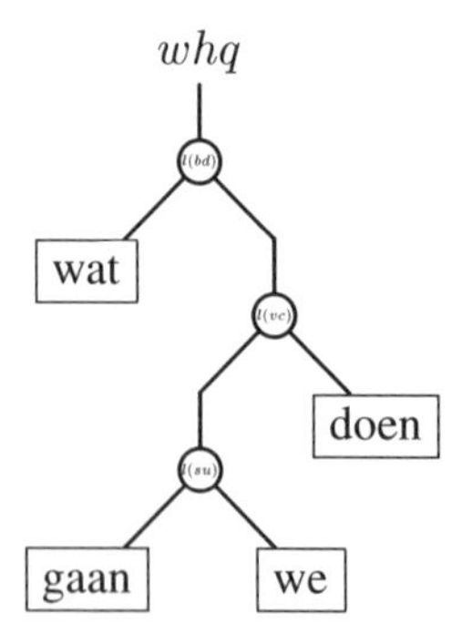

Figure 9: The resulting tree

6 Concluding Remarks

We have shown that the theory neutral annotation format used by CGN contains enough information to construct a type logical lexicon from it. The translation we have proposed is parametric in a number of respects. Our general strategy now is to use the growing CGN tree bank to determine which dependency modes should have access to which structural postulates, and to find out what the proper balance is between storage (the tolerated amount of lexical ambiguity) and computation (the complementary amount of on-line structural reasoning needed).

References

Carpenter, B.(1998), *Type-logical Semantics*, MIT Press.

Hoekstra, H., Moortgat, M., Schuurman, I. and van der Wouden, T.(2001), Syntactic annotation for the spoken Dutch corpus project (CGN), *in* W. Daelemans (ed.), *Proceedings of CLIN2000*.

Kurtonina, N. and Moortgat, M.(1997), Structural control, *in* P. Blackburn and M. de Rijke (eds), *Specifying Syntactic Structures*, CSLI, Stanford, pp. 75–113.

Lambek, J.(1993), From categorial grammar to bilinear logic, *in* K. Došen and P. Schröder-Heister (eds), *Substructural Logics*, Oxford University Press, Oxford, pp. 207–237.

Moortgat, M.(1997), Categorial type logics, *in* J. van Benthem and A. ter Meulen (eds), *Handbook of Logic and Language*, Elsevier/MIT Press, chapter 2.

Moortgat, M.(1999), Constants of grammatical reasoning, *in* G. Bouma, E. Hinrichs, G.-J. Kruijff and R. Oehrle (eds), *Constraints and Resources in Natural Language Syntax and Semantics*, CSLI, Stanford, pp. 195–219.

Moot, R.(1999), Grail: an interactive parser for categorial grammars, *in* R. Delmonte (ed.), *Proceedings of VEXTAL'99*, University Cá Foscari, Venice, pp. 255–261.

Moot, R.(2000), Proof nets and their relation to LTAGs, Manuscript.

Moot, R.(2001), Grail. `http://www.let.uu.nl/~Richard.Moot/personal/grail.html`.

Moot, R. and Puite, Q.(2001), Proof nets for the multimodal Lambek calculus, *in* W. Buszkowski and M. Moortgat (eds), *Studia Logica*, Kluwer. Special Issue Dedicated to Joachim Lambek.

Morrill, G.(1994), *Type Logical Grammar*, Kluwer Academic Publishers.

Plähn, O.(2000), Annotate. `http://www.coli.uni-sb.de/sfb378/negra-corpus/annotate.html`.

Sarkar, A.(2001), Xtag. `http://www.cis.upenn.edu/~xtag`.

Stabler, E.(1997), Derivational minimalism, *in* A. Lecomte (ed.), *LACL97*, Vol. 1582 of *Lecture Notes in Computer Science*, Springer.

Vermaat, W.(1999), *Controlling movement. minimalism in a deductive perspective*, Master's thesis, Utrecht University.

930204

Proper Name Extraction from Non-Journalistic Texts

Thierry Poibeau and Leila Kosseim***

*Laboratoire Central de Recherches, Thales/LCR, and
Laboratoire d'Informatique de Paris-Nord, Institut Galilée, Université Paris-Nord.
**RALI, Université de Montréal

Abstract

This paper discusses the influence of the corpus on the automatic identification of proper names in texts. Techniques developed for the news-wire genre are generally not sufficient to deal with larger corpora containing texts that do not follow strict writing constraints (for example, e-mail messages, transcriptions of oral conversations, etc). After a brief review of the research performed on news texts, we present some of the problems involved in the analysis of two different corpora: e-mails and hand-transcribed telephone conversations. Once the sources of errors have been presented, we then describe an approach to adapt a proper name extraction system developed for newspaper texts to the analysis of e-mail messages.

Key-words: Proper Name Extraction, Information Extraction, Corpus Analysis

1 Introduction

The identification of proper nouns in written or oral documents is an important task in natural language processing. This type of expression holds an important place in many corpora (newspapers, corporate documents, e-mails ...). It is therefore important to be able to identify these expressions either for specific applications (eg. to index documents by proper names or to build mailing lists) or for general research purposes (eg. to improve the syntactic analysis of a text).

Many research projects have addressed the issue of proper name identification in newspaper texts; in particular, the Message Understanding Conferences (MUC) (MUC4 1992, MUC5 1993, MUC6 1995). In these conferences, the first task to achieve is to identify named entities: proper names and also temporal and numerical expressions. This task is generally viewed as being *generic*, in the sense that all texts use such expressions and their identification seems a priori independent of the discourse domain or textual genre. However, the experiments performed within the MUC framework have all used homogeneous corpora constituted primarily of newspaper articles. This type of text respects strict writing guidelines which facilitates the identification task. For example, sequences like *Mr.* or *Ms.* precedes proper names rather systematically. However, these strategies are insufficient to analyse other types of texts such as electronic mail or minutes from a meeting because writing guidelines are either different or are much less strict. With the explosion of documents in electronic format, it is precisely these types of documents that need to be processed automatically.

This paper tries to determine, through two experiments on non-journalistic corpora, the weaknesses of rule-based systems and what modifications are necessary in order to achieve acceptable performance. After a brief overview of the literature on named entity extraction on newspaper texts, we evaluate the performances of some systems developed for the newspaper genre on 2 types of informal texts (e-mails and manual transcriptions of dialogs). We will then present the difficulties associated with these types of texts and propose strategies to adapt rule-based system initially trained on journalistic texts so that they maintain reasonable performances on non-journalistic texts. Finally, a typology of existing errors will be presented.

2 Previous Work

Influenced by the MUC conferences, work on named-entity extraction has traditionally been performed on news texts. This task tries to identify 3 types of expressions:

ENAMEX: Proper names, including names of persons, locations and organizations.

TIMEX: Temporal expressions such as dates and time.

NUMEX: Numerical expressions such as money and percentages.

In this work, we have concentrated our efforts on the first type of expressions: ENAMEX. Two main approaches are generally followed for their identification: a surface linguistic approach or a probabilistic approach. The probabilistic approach uses a language model trained on large pre-tagged corpora to learn patterns of identification (Dekan 1998). The IdentiFinder system (Kubala, Schwartz, Stone and Weischedel 1998)(Miller, Schwartz, Weischedel and Stone 1999), for example, uses such an approach. Studies have shown that this type of method yields good results if the training corpora are large enough. The Hub evaluation series on speech recognition includes a named-entity extraction task from automatic transcripts of news bulletins (HUB 1998, HUB 1999). These transcripts, generated from speech recognition systems, contain properties that render extraction difficult: the texts are in one case, they lack punctuation marks and the word-error rate is significant. For these reasons, most systems that work on transcripts of oral adopt a probabilistic approach[1].

The linguistic approach is based on a syntactic and lexical description of the expressions that are sought. Here, the text is tokenised and tagged with grammatical tags. A full syntactic analysis of the sentences is usually not performed as it is both expensive and unnecessary; only chunking is usually performed. The linguistic approach typically uses several resources:

[1]This is why most research in this area is dedicated not so much to linguistic aspects but to voice recognition aspects such as the effect of word error rate on entity extraction (Miller et al. 1999), the use of prosody to increase recognition scores (Hakkani-Tür, Gökhan, Stolcke and Shriberg 1999) or the effect of the size of the training corpus (Kubala et al. 1998).

1. Lists of markers (titles and trigger words) – eg. *Mr.* for *Mister* or *inc.* for *incorporated*
2. Gazetteers – large dictionaries of known proper names
3. Dictionaries of the general language, essentially to identify unknown words

Grammar rules are then applied to combine the information form these sources to tag the expressions that are identified with the most appropriate semantic tag. Alembic (Aberdeen, Burger, Day, Hirschman, Robinson and Vilain 1995), Proteus (Grishman 1995), and TextPro (Appelt and Martin 1999) (a descendant of Fastus (Appelt, Hobbs, Bear, Israel, Kameyana and Tyson 1993, Appelt, Hobbs, Bear, Israel, Kameyana, Kehler, Martin, Myers and Tyson 1995)) are examples of systems that use this approach.

This paper will only analyse rule-based systems. Each author had developed their own rule-based named-entity extractor (Exibum and Lexis) and wanted to see how these systems performed on texts for which they were not developed (ie. non-journalistic texts). Exibum (Kosseim and Lapalme 1998) is a system developed as part of an bilingual English-French information extraction system; while Lexis (Poibeau 1999) was developed as part of a technology watch system.

Regardless of the approach used, named-entity extraction from written documents is currently the most successful task in information extraction. Combined scores of precision and recall are comparable to human scores (in the order of 0.9 P&R[2] on news texts). The high performances obtained with written documents from newspaper genre demonstrates that the technology is ripe to attract commercial attention, to serve as basis to higher-level NLP tools or to be tested on other types of texts.

3 The use of information extraction system on non-journalistic corpora

The recognition of named entities from journalistic corpora is a task in which systems achieve very good performances. However, companies as well as individuals are facing a huge amount of electronic texts such as e-mails and news messages that do not follow the strict writing constraints of journalistic texts: the vocabulary and the syntax is variable and much more relaxed. This observation has been validated through two experiments.

3.1 Description of the corpora

Two corpora were used for the experiments. We shall call these corpora: the Valcartier and the Communication corpora. The Valcartier corpus is made of manual

[2]Precision measures the ratio of correct answer over all answers given by the system. Recall measures the ration of correct answers given by the system over all correct answers. The F-score combines precision and recall into one single measure using this formula: $F = \frac{(\beta^2+1.0)\times P\times R}{\beta^2\times P+R}$. When $\beta = 1$, precision and recall have the same relative importance and the F-score is called P&R.

transcriptions of telephone conversations in English provided by the Search and Rescue Division of the Canadian Armed Forces[3]. This corpus will be used in the future to develop an Information Extraction system. Even if these transcriptions are made from oral conversations, their quality is very closed to that of written texts. These transcriptions are in mixed cases, they contain very few word recognition errors[4] and they contain punctuation marks that were added by the transcription agents from prosody. Consequently, the corpus can be considered as a highly accurate transcription of oral conversations and lets us focus on the textual content. The Valcartier corpus contains about 25 000 tokens and 2 200 token types.

The Communication corpus is made of e-mails written in English. This corpus has been established by experts in the field of technological survey, who had to elaborate a report on telecommunications. This kind of corpus is often made of heterogeneous pieces: technical documents, product announcements, messages from concerned newsgroups and e-mails. The recognition of named entities, especially person and company names, is a major added-value for analysts facing these texts. Corpus processing can be boosted by such techniques: decisions on document relevance go faster and experts can focus on the analysis of the sole relevant documents. For formatting reasons, we chose to study only the part of the corpus made of electronic mails (technical documents are often in the PDF format and thus, are not directly manageable). The corpus is in mixed cases, is written in an informal manner: incomplete sentences and telegraphic style. Finally, the number of typos in the corpus is limited compared to other experiments on electronic informal corpora.

The corpus is made of 300 000 tokens, that approximately correspond to 50 000 token types. The reference corpus, which is distinct from the training corpus is made of 85 000 tokens that correspond to 12 000 types. The reference was established by a human annotator and corrected by an expert in the fields of telecommunications.

3.2 A drop in performance

The use of extraction rules developed for journalistic texts leads to an important drop of performances when applied to other textual genres. Systems analyzing correctly about 90% of the sequences from a journalistic corpus can have a decrease of performance of up to 50% on more informal texts. Journalistic writing constraints often impose the introduction of person names with the use of titles (*President Chirac*) or trigger words (*Mister Chirac*) (Senellart 1998). This writing style is not systematic in informal texts. Performance largely decreases if one analyses various texts with a too normative grammar. Incomplete sentences and telegraphic style, very frequent in informal texts, hinder syntactic analysis and an

[3]Typically, the dialogs involve controller from a coordination center who is performing an inquiry on the disappearance of a person or an airplane. The controller discusses by telephone with an investigator on location or anyone able to help in the inquiry.

[4]Contrary to texts coming from automatic transcriptions that contain a 30 to 40% error rate. The errors in the corpus are mainly typos or homonymic confusions.

accurate tagging of proper names. This fact has been established independently by the two authors through two different experiments. A first experiment evaluated the results of Exibum on the Valcartier corpus as compared to the MUC-6 corpus. The performances dropped from 0.69 P&R on the MUC-6 corpus to 0.44 P&R on the Valcartier corpus. The second experiment involved Lexis that droped from 0.90 P&R on the MUC-6 corpus to 0.50–0.70 on various subsets of the Communication corpus. Once this decrease of performance was established, we tried to identify if it was specific to our systems or if it also occurred with other systems that have already been tested in larger evaluation campaigns.

3.3 Validation of the initial results

To verify that the poor performances achieved by our system on various corpora were not due to the systems themselves, the evaluation has been enlarged to two systems that participated to the MUC conferences. We analyzed the results from Alembic (Aberdeen et al. 1995) and TextPro (Appelt and Martin 1999): two system that were publicly available. The Valcartier corpus has been given as input to these two systems, and the results have been evaluated using the MUC methodology. Finally we classified the extraction errors to try to identify characteristic features belonging specifically to the change of domain. Alembic (Aberdeen et al. 1995), developed at Mitre Corporation, is one of the pioneer systems in information extraction. It was initially developed to participate to the MUC-4 conference in 1992 and has regularly participated to subsequent competitions, taking advantage of constant improvements. TextPro from SRI (Appelt and Martin 1999) takes its origin in the Fastus system (Appelt et al. 1993) that is also a pioneer in information extraction. TextPro is a light version of Fastus, developed for the Hub-4 conference (HUB 1999). Alembic and TextPro were among the highest performing systems at the MUC conferences.

For the evaluation, three kinds of proper names were taken into account: person names, location names and organization names. Two human annotators independently developed the key templates[5]. Disagreements between annotators were solved by joint decision. Individual results of the human annotators were evaluated with the MUC protocol and achieved 0.97 and 0.96 P&R. Table 2 illustrates the results from the two human annotators and the three systems over the different corpora used. Two different measures are given for Alembic because two specific words were systematically wrongly tagged. These were being especially frequent in our two corpora; therefore the system was unfairly disadvantaged. To obtain a a more accurate measure of the results, we give a first measure on the original corpus and a second one that does not take into account these two specific words.

The results in Table 2 clearly show that human annotators do not seem to be influenced by the change of corpus; while automatic systems obtain systematically much lower results that certainly do not compete with the results of human annotators. It thus becomes interesting to study why these systems drop in performance. Is it due to the dictionaries that are not tuned to the discourse domain or

[5]For the Valcartier corpus, one of the annotators is the second author of this paper.

System	P&R MUC-6	P&R Valcartier	P&R Communication
Human annotators	0.97[6]	0.97	0.90[7]
Alembic[8](Mitre)	0.86	0.50 - 0.57	-[9]
TextPro (SRI)	0.86	0.41	-
Exibum	0.69	0.44	-
Lexis	0.90	-	0.50

Table 1: Extraction of proper names without adaptation of systems

the informal features appearing in the syntax of proper names ?

3.4 A grammar made of variants

The variable syntax of proper nouns is responsible for most cases of silence (i.e. non-detected proper nouns). In journalistic texts, person names are generally preceded by titles and trigger words (*Mr.*, *Mrs.*) whereas it is rarely the case in the two corpora that we are studying here. Proper names, and especially person names, belong to open classes; markers are thus very effective indicators of proper names. This explains why automatic systems achieve good performance on journalistic texts.

The grammar of person names is therefore not stable over corpora but depends on the corpus. Rules that apply to informal texts are sometimes different than the ones dedicated to journalistic texts. A rule that applies very frequently in a journalistic text will be very rare in a corpus made of electronic mails, and vice-versa. Even inside one newspaper, writting constraints do not apply uniformly. A person name can be first introduced by a title (*Prime Minister Edouard Balladur*) and then, simply introduced by a trigger word (*Mr. Balladur*). Some specific sections of a news-paper like the society or art sections can name a person by his or her name, without any trigger word.

The grammar designed to recognize organization and company names in informal texts must include more informal ways of naming entities than the one dedicated to pure journalistic texts. Trigger words like *inc.* or *Ltd.* are not mentioned most of the time. For example, the name of the organization *Transportation Safety Board* includes the trigger word *Board*, which denotes that the preceding sequence designates an organization. In the Valcartier corpus, this organization is

[6] Extraction of all named entities

[7] The MUC-6 score is the official one; while the score with the Valcartier corpus has been calculated using the public version of Alembic Workbench 4.12 (URL: http://www.mitre.org/resources/centers/it/g063/workbench.html)

[8] This score is an estimation. For the Communication corpus, there was one annotator and a manual validation by an expert in the domain. The contrast between the expert and the non expert explains the good quality of the final result for an audio transcription (.97). It also shows that knowledge of the domain is necessary to accurately tag the text.

[9] Alembic performed strangely bad on the Communication corpus.

often abbreviated to *Transportation Safety* without any trigger word. As in the case of person names, reduced organization names are frequently not recognized by the different systems. Lastly, location names are also identified by means of keywords (for example the preposition *in* or the words *lake* or *city*). The absence of trigger words or of the preposition before the location name frequently causes errors (silence or wrong categorization of the sequence). The system must then deal with previously unknown names. The only operational techniques in this circumstance are to dynamically type unknown entities by a local analysis of the context.

4 Towards adaptive systems

After an analysis of the types of errors made by the named entity recognition over different corpora, a set of strategies based on a dynamic mechanism has been defined and evaluated on the Communication corpus. We will provide measures related to our initial experiment, but our results have been validated on other corpora as well.

The fact that expressions are introduced without any marker leads to many isolated unknown words. To solve this problem, it is necessary to improve the coverage of the dictionaries and to add processes of dynamic resource acquisition.

4.1 Improving the dictionary coverage

On the person name recognition task, Lexis achieves a success rate of 0.90 P&R on the MUC-6 corpus, but only 0.50 on the Communication corpus (see section 3.1). Regardless of the corpus on which the system was tested, the grammar remains relatively stable and the sequence `First_Name Last_Name` is generally the most frequent one. The variant of this structure consists in an isolated person name sometimes introduced by the initials of the first name (one or two letters, generally in upper case, and followed by a dot or a space). These sequences introduced by a trigger word are, unfortunately, very rare in the electronic mails of the Communication corpus. A very frequent rule in the Herald Tribune can be very rare in an electronic mail corpus, and vice-versa for other rules. To improve the performance of the system, it is essential to have a good coverage of known proper names of the concerned language, especially first names and toponyms. Lexis currently uses over 24,000 person names. In parallel, unknown words feed in a significant way the dictionaries of proper names. Thus, it is possible to quickly reach a coverage of about 0.60 P&R for person names on the Communication corpus, only by the addition to the dictionary of some of the previously unknown words. The performance is comparable for the recognition of location names that crucially requires exhaustive geographical denomination lists that have to be acquired from existing resources or from a training corpus.

4.2 Dynamically recognizing new entities by machine learning techniques

A limit of the Lexis system is that it does not include any dynamic mechanism to automatically adapt its resources and rules to the corpus. This point is particularly significant for the analysis of texts like electronic mails, which are made of a significant number of person names appearing without being introduced by a marker. Part of these names can however be correctly analyzed if the system can find elsewhere a discriminating context making it possible to correctly identify the named entity. We propose a learning method that uses the previously found elements and the recognition rules of the proper names grammar to extend the coverage of the initial system. It is then a case of EBL, explanation based learning (Mitchell 1997).

The mechanism is based on the registration of the grammatical rules that have been applied with success to tag previously unknown words. For example, the grammar can recognize the sequence *Mr. Kassianov* as being a person name even if *Kassianov* is an unknown word. The isolated occurrences of this word can consequently be tagged as person name. The machine learning process can be seen as an inductive mechanism using the knowledge of the system (grammatical rules) and the entities found previously (the positive set of examples) to improve the overall performances. With this technique, the global gain in performance is about 10 to 15% in function of text, that is to say 0.66 to 0.70 P&R.

4.3 Using discourse structures

Discourse structures are another source for knowledge acquisition. In the terminological field, (Daille, Habert, Jacquemin and Royaute 1996) showed that new terms could be extracted from the analysis of particular sequences of texts. The same principle can be used for the automatic acquisition of new entities. We are particularly interested in enumeration that can be easily localized by the presence of person names, separated by connectors (commas, subordinating conjunction, etc). For example, in the following sequence:

<PERSON_NAME> Kassianov </PERSON_NAME> ,
<UNKNOWN> Kostine </UNKNOWN> **and**
<PERSON_NAME> Primakov </PERSON_NAME>

Kostine is initially tagged as an unknown word because this name is isolated (no marker) and could not be accurately tagged by a gazetteer lookup or from other occurrences in the text. However, the system can infer from the context that it refers to a person name because it appears in an enumeration of other names tagged as person names. Using this strategy, the score of Lexis on the Communication corpus reached 0.84 P&R.

4.4 Resolving tagging conflicts

The learning mechanism can lead to tagging conflicts. For example, dynamic typing can assign a tag to a word that is in contradiction with the tag contained in the dictionary or identified by another dynamic strategy. This is often the case when a word registered as a location name in the dictionary is used as person name in a non-ambiguous text sequence. Must isolated occurrences be assigned the tag that was dynamically identified by the context analysis (person name) or by the tag previously stored in the dictionary (location name)? To illustrate this, let us consider the following excerpt from a MUC-6 text:

```
@  Washington, an Exchange Ally, Seems
@  To Be Strong Candidate to Head SEC
@  ----
<SO> WALL STREET JOURNAL (J), PAGE A2 </SO>
<DATELINE> WASHINGTON </DATELINE>
<TXT>
<p>
   Consuela Washington, a longtime House staffer and
an expert in securities laws, is a leading candidate to be
chairwoman of the Securities and Exchange Commission in the
Clinton administration.
</p>
```

It is clear that in this text *Consuela Washington* corresponds to a person name. The first occurrence of the word *Washington* is more problematic, because the only information in the sentence that makes it possible to disambiguate the tag necessitates world-knowledge, namely that it is generally a person who manages an organization. But it is necessary not to rely too much on this type of world-knowledge, because a metaphorical use of the word cannot be excluded. For example, in the sentence *France wants to continue to manage the IMF*, *France* should be tagged as a location, not a person. In fact, a proper analysis of pronoun references allows humans to perfectly disambiguate the text. An automatic system has very few chances to properly analyze such a text, especially if we take into account the fact that a completely isolated occurrence of *Washington* must be analyzed as a location name, between two other occurrences where *Washington* stands for a person name (the reader infers from the context that *Washington* is certainly the place where the journalist who emitted the news is located).

To circumscribe this kind of problem and to avoid propagation of errors[10], we propose two strategies: to limit the scope of the dynamic tagging mechanism and to let the end-user decide which discourse and linguistic structures to activate during the acquisition process.

The first way to control tagging conflicts is to limit the scope of the dynamic tagging mechanism to single texts rather than to an entire corpus. For example, in the previous text, the system will tag all isolated occurrences of *Washington* as person name, but in a subsequent text, if an isolated occurrence of the word *Washington* appears, the system will tag it as location name, according to the dictionary. When more than one tag is found by the dynamic mechanism from the same text, an arbitrary choice is then taken.

The second way to control tagging conflicts is to let the end-user free to activate the discourse and linguistic structures during the acquisition process. Indeed, it appears that this choice largely depends on the corpus to be analyzed.

[10]That is to say, when a word received from the context a tag which is in conflict with a tag previously recorded in the dictionary. It is the case of *Washington* in the above example.

For example, the structure:

<PERSON_NAME>X</PERSON_NAME> (<PERSON_NAME>Y</PERSON_NAME>)

is very frequently used in the cinema sections of newspapers to designate, between brackets, the name of the actor playing a character (in the above example, X and Y indicate variables; the first occurrence of <PERSON_NAME> often corresponds to a first name). But things will be different in other sections, where we can find, for example, the following structures:

<PERSON_NAME>X</PERSON_NAME> (<POLITIC_ORG>Y</POLITIC_ORG>)
<PERSON_NAME>X</PERSON_NAME> (<COUNTRY>Y</COUNTRY>).

In these cases, even if the system can solve certain ambiguities, contextual rules can introduce too much noise. It is then the end-user who has to choose to activate or not such rules, according to the expected performances and to his own expertise in the field.

Regardless of the training corpus used (the MUC-6 corpus and the Communication corpus for English and The newspaper *Le Monde* and the AFP news-wire for French), and in spite of errors introduced by the learning mechanism (extension of an incorrect tag over the text), the profit remains always positive (P&R measure). We estimate a 12% gain for recall that compensates a 3% precision decrease on the Communication corpus[11].

These experiments show an increase of the overall results. This fact has been validated on the Communication corpus, on the MUC-6 corpus, but also, on various corpora pertaining (e.g. financial corpus) and different languages (English and French, e.g. on stories from the French news-wire agency AFP).

5 Analysis of the remaining errors

The three strategies presented earlier have allowed the Lexis system to go from a score of 0.50 to 0.84 P&R on the Communication corpus. Although the improvement is significant, these performances are still inferior to the average MUC-6 performances. The remaining extraction errors can be divided into 2 classes:

Unsolved errors: Errors that should have been taken into account with the above strategies.

Unaddressed errors: Errors that were not taken into account; whether they arise from a general problem such as spelling mistakes or they arise from the specificity of a particular corpus such as those found in the Valcartier corpus.

[11] In this experiment, the system was just tagging isolated unknown words from the knowledge acquired during the first pass. No discourse structures nor enumeration were used to tag unknown entities.

5.1 Unsolved Errors

Among the unsolved errors, we have identified:

Incompletion of the grammar or the gazetteers: Person names such as *Lloyd Bentsen* or *Strobe Talbott* are difficult to recognize if the first names (*Lloyd, Strobe*), or the last names (*Bentsen, Talbott*) are not present in the gazetteers.

Unrecognized transformations: The names *Robert S. Miller* extended as *Robert S. "Steve" Miller* to explicitly present the meaning of the *S.* are difficult to recognize. This type of sequence is both too complex and too specific for the analyzer. Extending the grammar to account for this type of sequence would introduce more noise (false recognitions) than reduce silence (false non-recognitions).

Ambiguous words: This is the case with words such as *Sun* in *Sun Tzu*, which designates a person. If *Tzu* is an unknown word and if there is no clear context to disambiguate the sequence (lack of trigger word for example), then such a sequence is difficult to tag correctly.

Ambiguous sequences: This is often the case when distinguishing the name of an organization from the name of a person. Names like *Mary Kay* are recognized as person names, while they should be been tagged as organization names. When using the evaluation protocol of MUC, this result is considered wrong because the semantic tag is wrong. Without any information from the context to disambiguate (eg. *Ms. Mary Kay* versus *Mary Kay inc.*) the only solution is to include a priori these sequences in a gazetteer.

5.2 Non-addressed errors

A certain number of problem have not been taken into account. Indeed, we have concentrated our efforts on the absence of linguistic markers. Although named-entity extraction is currently the most reusable information extraction task over different corpora; the fact remains that when applied to specific types of texts (with different discourse domains, genres or modes of communications) different types of phenomena should be taken into account.

Discourse-Specific Terminology: The Valcartier corpus, taken form a military context, includes specific abbreviations and terminology of the military domain (eg. *Alpha, Bravo, Charlie*) that, in this domain, either do not constitute proper names or at least, should tagged with a different semantic tag. Here, the use of a domain-dependent dictionary and anti-dictionary seems to be necessary.

Genre-Specific Grammar: Different genres using different writing guidelines can create extraction errors. In particular spelling mistakes in informal documents can occur frequently and thus cause significantly extraction errors. A first though may be to pre-process the document through a speller; however, because proper names include many unknown words (because proper names are open-class words) a speller will have difficulty recognizing them and may try to correct them. The use of a speller may thus not be such an interesting solution. In addition, in the analysis of languages using diacritics, the lack of such markers in informal documents certainly causes recognition problems. In the case of e-mails, many research have performed descriptive analysis of writing habits used in e-mails and other informal computer-mediated communications (Murray 1988, Yates 1996, Herring 1996, Collot and Belmore 1996). These observations should be used as an aid in developing grammars for proper name extraction in these texts.

Genre-Specific Terminology: Terminology present in texts from informal sources, but considered inappropriate in contexts where writing guidelines are more strict, bring about their share of errors. In the Valcartier corpus, for examples, interjections that also appear in proper names gazetteers are tagged wrongly. This is the case with *Ok* and *Ha*, which, without a discriminating context can be wrongly tagged as location as they are abbreviations of *Oklahoma* and *Hawaï*.

Mode-Specific Grammar: Finally the mode of communication influences the grammar for proper name extraction. In the Valcartier corpus, for example, proper name restarts can cause errors. For example, *Hal ... Halifax* may be tagged twice. This phenomenon is specific to transcripts of spontaneous communications (oral or computer chat) and require the use of specific annotation scheme (cf. (HUB 1998, HUB 1999)).

6 Conclusion

The work presented here allowed us to identify the problems associated with proper name extraction developed for a specific type of text when applied to different types of texts.

While in journalistic texts, the use of grammar rules in the identification of proper names is a well-mastered task that yields results that are comparable to human ones; the same task on documents from informal exchanges has received much less attention and yields less impressive results. Two independent experiences on corpora from *real applications* have shown that systems yielding acceptable results in journalistic texts have yielded much lower scores (from around 0.90 P&R to around 0.50).

By analysing the errors that were committed on two types of informal documents, we have identified the sources of errors that currently lower scores on rule-based approaches. Following these observations, we have proposed strategies to adapt rule-based systems developed for journalistic text to non-journalistic texts. The implementation of these strategies in the Lexis system has increased the extraction scores on the Communication corpus from 0.50 to 0.84 P&R. The analysis of the remaining errors has allowed us to highlight certain types of errors that are dependent on the discourse domain, the textual genre and the mode of communication. Named-entity extraction, although the most re-usable task in information extraction needs, nonetheless, to take into account specific characteristics of the corpus in order to achieve human-level scores regardless of the corpus.

Acknowledgments

The authors wish to thank Luc Lamontagne of DREV and the anonymous referees whose constructive comments greatly improved the paper.

References

Aberdeen, J., Burger, J., Day, D., Hirschman, L., Robinson, P. and Vilain, M.(1995), MITRE: Description of the Alembic System as Used for MUC6,

Appelt, D. and Martin, D.(1999), Named Entity Recognition in Speech: Approach and results using the TextPro System,

Appelt, D., Hobbs, J., Bear, J., Israel, D., Kameyana, M. and Tyson, M.(1993), FASTUS: a Finite-state Processor for Information Extraction from Real-world Text, *Proceedings of the International Joint Conference on Artificial Intelligence (IJCAI'93)*.

Appelt, D., Hobbs, J., Bear, J., Israel, D., Kameyana, M., Kehler, A., Martin, D., Myers, K. and Tyson, M.(1995), SRI International FASTUS system: MUC-6 test results and analysis,

Collot, M. and Belmore, N.(1996), Electronic Language: A New Variety of English, *in* S. Herring (ed.), *Computer-Mediated Communications: Linguistic, Social and Cross-Cultural Perspectives*, John Benjamins, Amsterdam/Philadelphia, pp. 13–28.

Daille, B., Habert, B., Jacquemin, C. and Royaute, J.(1996), Empirical observation of term variations and principles for their description, *Terminology* **3**(2), 197–258.

Dekan, L.(1998), Using Collocation Statistics in Information Extraction, *Proceedings of the Seventh Message Understanding Conference*, San Francisco. http://www.muc.saic.com.

Grishman, R.(1995), Where's the Syntax? The NYU MUC-6 System,

Hakkani-Tür, D., Gökhan, T., Stolcke, A. and Shriberg, E.(1999), Combining Words and Prosody for Information Extraction From Speech, *Proceedings of Eurospeech-99*, Budapest, Hongrie.

Herring, S.(1996), Introduction, *in* S. Herring (ed.), *Computer-Mediated Communications: Linguistic, Social and Corss-Cultural Perspertives*, John Benjamins, Amsterdam/Philadelphia, pp. 1–10.

HUB(1998), Proceedings of the DARPA Broadcast Transcription and Understanding Workshop, Lansdowne, Virginia.

HUB(1999), Proceedings of the DARPA Broadcast News Workshop, Herndon, Virginia.

Kosseim, L. and Lapalme, G.(1998), Exibum: Un système expérimental d'extraction d'information bilingue, *Actes de la Rencontre Internationale sur l'extraction, le Filtrage et le Résumé Automatique (RIFRA-98)*, Sfax, Tunisia, pp. 129–140.

Kubala, F., Schwartz, R., Stone, R. and Weischedel, R.(1998), Named Entity Extraction from Speech,

Miller, D., Schwartz, R., Weischedel, R. and Stone, R.(1999), Named Entity Extraction from Broadcast News,

Mitchell, T.(1997), *Machine Learning*, McGraw-Hill, New York.

MUC4(1992), Proceedings of the fourth message understanding conference, Morgan Kaufmann Publishers, San Francisco.

MUC5(1993), Proceedings of the fifth message understanding conference, Morgan Kaufmann Publishers, San Francisco.

MUC6(1995), Proceedings of the sixth message understanding conference, Morgan Kaufmann Publishers, San Francisco.

Murray, D.(1988), The context of oral and written language: A framework for mode and medium switching, *Language in Society* **17**, 351–373.

Poibeau, T.(1999), Le repérage des entités nommées: un enjeu pour les systèmes de veille, *Terminologies Nouvelles (Actes du colloque Terminologie et Intelligence Artificielle – TIA'99)*, number 19, Nantes, France, pp. 43–51.

Senellart, J.(1998), Locating noun phrases with finite state transducers, *Proceedings of the 17th International Conference on Computational Linguistics (COLING'98)*, Montréal, Canada.

Yates, S.(1996), Oral and Written Linguistic Aspects of Computer Conferencing: A Corpus Based Study, *in* S. Herring (ed.), *Computer-Mediated Communications: Linguistic, Social and Corss-Cultural Perspertives*, John Benjamins, Amsterdam/Philadelphia, pp. 29–46.

Generating Referring Expressions in a Multimodal Context

An empirically oriented approach

Ielka van der Sluis and Emiel Krahmer

Computational Linguistics, Tilburg University
IPO, Center for User-System Interaction, Eindhoven University of Technology

Abstract

In this paper an algorithm for the generation of referring expressions in a multimodal setting is presented. The algorithm is based on empirical studies of how humans refer to objects in a shared workspace. The main ingredients of the algorithm are the following. First, the addition of deictic pointing gestures, where the decision to point is determined by two factors: the effort of pointing (measured in terms of the distance to and size of the target object) as well as the effort required for a full linguistic description (measured in terms of number of required properties and relations). Second, the algorithm explicitly keeps track of the current focus of attention, in such a way that objects which are closely related to the object which was most recently referred to are more prominent than objects which are farther away. To decide which object are 'closely related' we make use of the concept of perceptual grouping. Finally, each object in the domain is assigned a three-dimensional salience weight indicating whether it is linguistically and/or inherently salient and whether it is part of the current focus of attention. The resulting algorithm is capable of generating a variety of referring expressions, where the kind of NP is co-determined by the accessibility of the target object (in terms of salience), the presence or absence of a relatum as well as the possible inclusion of a pointing gesture.

1 Introduction

The generation of referring expressions is one of the most common tasks in natural language generation. It is arguably also one of the most clearly defined ones: given a target object r and its properties, decide what is the best way to refer to r in the current context. In the past decade a number of algorithms for deciding on the form and/or content of a referring expression have been proposed (each given its own interpretation of what "the best way" is; computationally efficient, minimal, brief, etc.). Of these algorithms, the Incremental Algorithm of Dale & Reiter (1995) is generally accepted as the state of the art. The Incremental Algorithm is aimed at determining the content of a *distinguishing description*, that is: a definite description which is an accurate description of the target object r but not of any other object in the current domain of conversation. According to Dale & Reiter, the Incremental Algorithm has at least two important properties: (*i*) it is computationally attractive, because it has a polynomial complexity and is fast, and (*ii*) it is psychologically realistic, because it appears that humans produce distinguishing descriptions in a similar way as the Incremental Algorithm.

In recent years, various extensions of the Incremental Algorithm have been proposed. Horacek (1997) discusses a version which directly incorporates linguistic realization in the algorithm. Van Deemter (2001) presents a number of formal extensions to the Incremental Algorithm, concerned with, for instance, the generation of "vague" descriptions ('the large mouse') and the interaction with plurals ('the large mice'). Krahmer & Theune (1998, 1999) (see also Theune 2000) offer an account of the role of context for the generation of referring expressions, and address a number of extensions required for the embedding of the Incremental Algorithm in a full fledged (spoken) natural language generation system. Most of these extensions explicitly aim at keeping the attractive properties of the Incremental Algorithm (in particular, speed, complexity and psychological plausibility).

In this paper, we discuss a further extension of the Incremental Algorithm, namely the generation of *multimodal* referring expressions: natural language referring expression which may include deictic, pointing gestures. There are at least two motivations for such an extension. First of all, in various situations a purely linguistic description can simply be too complex, for instance because the domain contains many highly similar objects. In that case, including a deictic, pointing gesture may be the most efficient way of singling out the target referent. The second reason is that when looking at human communication it soon becomes clear that referring expressions which include pointing gestures are very common (assuming, of course, that speaker and hearer can both directly perceive the domain of communication). Since our aim is to generate descriptions in a realistic way, it seems expedient to include such pointing gestures.

As the foundation of our enterprise we use the extended version of the Incremental Algorithm by Krahmer & Theune (1999). The multimodal extensions to this algorithm which we propose are based on empirical studies of how human speakers refer to objects in a shared work-space (Piwek et al. 1995, Cremers 1996, Beun & Cremers 1998). The main ingredients of our algorithm are the following. To begin with, we define a function which determines whether a pointing gesture is felicitous given the current context. This decision is based on two factors: the effort required for producing a pointing gesture and the effort required for a full linguistic description. Second, the algorithm explicitly tracks the focus of attention. Objects which are 'closely related' (in a way which we make precise below) to the most recent target object are taken to be more *salient* than objects which are not in the current focus space. Finally, we distinguish various reasons for which a particular object might be more salient than others. To do so, we define a three-dimensional notion of salience, combining focus space salience with linguistic salience and inherent salience. The last form of salience applies to objects which stand out perceptually with respect to the rest of the domain.[1]

[1]Various other algorithms for the generation of referring expressions in a multimodal setting have been proposed (for instance, Reithinger 1992, Claassen 1992, Huls et al. 1995, Cohen 1984, Salmon-Alt & Romary 2000). Of these, Salmon-Alt & Romary (2000) is closest in spirit to the current paper. Salmon-Alt & Romary also take the Incremental Algorithm as their starting point, and argue for an empirical, corpus-based approach. However, they concentrate on using information from different sources (discourse, perception, gestures) to restrict the context set of the Incremental Algorithm (in a similar way as done by Krahmer & Theune 1998, 1999). Contrary to the current paper, they do not address the question how the integration of such sources of information may be used for the actual *generation* of multimodal descriptions which combine language and gesture. Of the other cited works,

The outline of this paper is as follows. In section 2 we describe the Incremental Algorithm. In section 3 we summarize the main empirical findings regarding object reference in a multimodal environment and discuss the repercussions these have for the generation of multimodal descriptions. Then, in section 4 we show how the empirical rules can be captured in a formal and computational manner. Section 5 contains a sketch of the full algorithm, illustrated with a worked example.

2 The Incremental Algorithm of Dale & Reiter

The aim of Dale & Reiter's Incremental Algorithm (henceforth referred to as the D & R algorithm) is to efficiently generate a *distinguishing* description; a description that is applicable to the current object and not to any other object in the domain of conversation. Objects in a domain can be characterized in terms of a set of attribute-value pairs corresponding to their properties. For example, the objects in Figure 1 can be characterized as follows:

d_1 ⟨ *type, block* ⟩ ⟨ *color, white* ⟩ ⟨ *shape, square* ⟩ ⟨ *size, small* ⟩
d_2 ⟨ *type, block* ⟩ ⟨ *color, black* ⟩ ⟨ *shape, square* ⟩ ⟨ *size, small* ⟩
d_3 ⟨ *type, block* ⟩ ⟨ *color, black* ⟩ ⟨ *shape, square* ⟩ ⟨ *size, large* ⟩

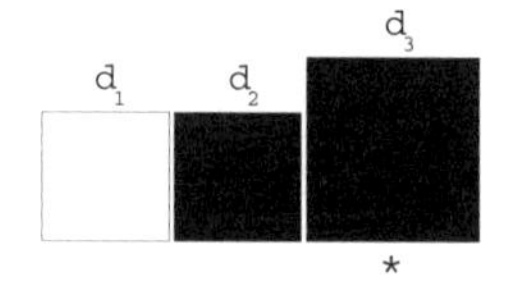

Figure 1: "the large black block"

One of the distinguishing properties of the Dale & Reiter algorithm is its use of a list of *preferred attributes*. In this list the properties relevant for the domain are ordered according to the preference that human speakers and hearers have when discussing objects in that particular domain. The exact ordering of properties for a particular domain is an empirical matter. However, some general trends exists. For instance, speakers have a general preference for *absolute* properties such as *color* and *shape*, over *relative* properties such as *size*. This may be explained by the fact that relative properties are less easily observed and always require inspection of other objects in the domain.[2]

The input of the D & R algorithm consists of the *target object* r and a *distractor set*, where r is the object to be described and where the distractor set contains all the objects in the domain except r itself. The D & R algorithm essentially iterates through the list of preferred attributes, adding a property to the description for r

---

the approach advocated here agrees most with Reithinger in that it focusses on multimodal generation in a way which models human behavior.

[2]For empirical evidence see e.g., Pechmann (1989) and Beun & Cremers (1998).

only if it rules out one or more of the objects in the distractor set not previously ruled out. Moreover, Dale & Reiter make the assumption that the property *type* should always be included in a distinguishing description even if it has no discriminating power (i.e., even if it did not rule out distractors). The D & R algorithm terminates when the distractor set is empty (success) or when all the properties of r have been checked (failure).

As an example reconsider Figure 1, and suppose that we apply the D & R algorithm to the object marked with a $*$ (d_3). This implies that the distractor set contains the other two objects in this particular domain, d_1 and d_2. For the time being, let us assume that the list of preferred attributes is ⟨ *type, color, shape, size* ⟩. First, the algorithm finds that the property *type* is not alone sufficient to distinguish $*$ (it rules out no distractors). Second, by including the property ⟨ *color, black* ⟩ in the set of selected properties, the algorithm can remove the white block d_1 from the distractor set. Still the set of remaining distractors is not empty. Third, the attribute *shape* has no effect on the set of remaining distractors (since d_2 and d_3 have the same shape). Fourth, the algorithm can use the relative attribute *size* to empty the distractor set. Finally, the D & R algorithm checks whether the *type* property was included, and since this was not the case, it is added to the set of distinguishing properties of $*$ after all. The set of selected properties can now linguistically be realized by the distinguishing description "the large black block". Note that the D & R algorithm does not itself output this linguistic description, rather it feeds the selected properties to a linguistic realizer.

Krahmer & Theune (1998, 1999) provide a number of extensions to the basic D & R algorithm. To begin with, they introduce a notion of linguistic context. The idea is that once an object has been mentioned, it is linguistically salient and re-referring to this object can be done using a reduced, anaphoric description. Linguistic salience is modelled using a *salience weight function*, according to which a salience weight is added to each object in the domain of conversation. With these additional salience weights the distractor set can be specified as the set that contains all the objects in the domain having a salience weight *higher than or equal to* the target object. This implies that when the target object is somehow salient, the search space is reduced. Hence, generally fewer properties will be required to empty the distractor set. Moreover Krahmer & Theune (1999) extend the D & R algorithm with the possibility of including relations, so that an object can be described in terms of its relations to other objects in the domain. Finally, following Horacek (1997), the algorithm directly produces linguistic descriptions. Only properties that rule out distractors *and* which can be realized within the constraints of the grammar are included in the final description. Here we take this extended version of the incremental D & R algorithm as our starting point.

The two main advantages of the D & R algorithm (which are essentially kept in the extensions of Krahmer & Theune) are its efficiency and its psychological realism. The efficiency of the algorithm is illustrated by its complexity, which is polynomial in time (Dale & Reiter 1995:247). Within the D & R algorithm there is no backtracking: once a property p has been selected, it will be realised in the final description, even if a property which is added later would render the inclusion of

p redundant. This is partly responsible for the efficiency, but Dale & Reiter claim that this is psychologically realistic because human speakers also often include redundant modifiers in their referring expressions (where they refer to Pechmann 1989).

On the other hand, the D & R algorithm also has its limitations. See for example Figure 2, where we want to single out one particular object in a domain where all the objects have most properties in common. A distinguishing description by means of specifying the exact location of the object ("The fourth block from the left in the third row") or in terms of coordinates ("the block on position (4,3)") is respectively very inefficient or awkward to use in natural communication. Moreover such descriptions contradict the principle of Minimal Cooperative Effort (Clark & Wilkes-Gibbs, 1986) stating that both the speaker's effort in producing the description and the hearer's effort in interpreting it should be minimal. Correspondingly, the most natural way to denote a particular object in Figure 2 is to add a pointing act to its description ("this block"). In the remainder of this paper, we describe the modifications and extensions required for the generation of such multimodal referring expressions.

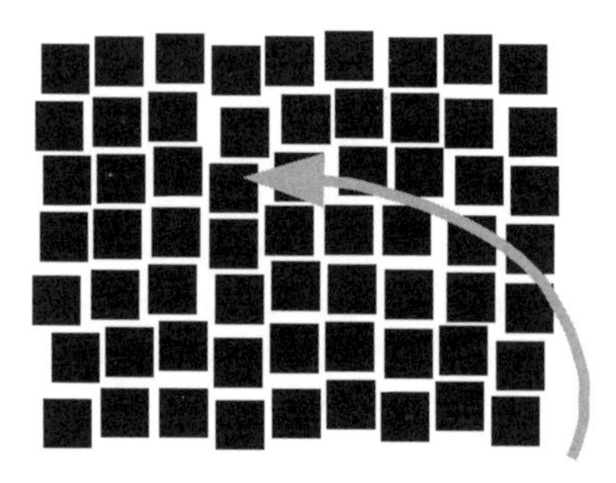

Figure 2: Disadvantage of the D & R algorithm

3 Empirical observations on multimodal object descriptions

In this section we discuss five rules for referring to objects in a multimodal setting, derived from the empirical results reported by Beun & Cremers (1998) and Cremers (1996). Beun & Cremers performed several experiments with Dutch subjects in which one participant (*the instructor*) had to instruct another participant (*the builder*) to make certain changes in a block building that was located in a shared workspace. This implied that participants could both talk about and point to the blocks in front of them. Below each of the rules is introduced and illustrated with an example. The first rule is concerned with *inherently salient objects*. Beun & Cremers assume that an object is inherently salient if it is the *only* object in the domain which has a particular property. They claim that inherently salient objects are referred to by *reduced* descriptions; i.e., descriptions which contain less properties than are strictly speaking required to generate a fully distinguishing description.

Rule 1 If the target object is inherently salient within the domain of conversation, use reduced information.

According to Beun & Cremers' definition, the object labeled $*$ in Figure 3 is inherently salient, because it differs from the other objects by its color. Following rule 1, $*$ can therefore be referred to as "the block", even though this description is by itself not a distinguishing description since it is applicable to all the blocks.

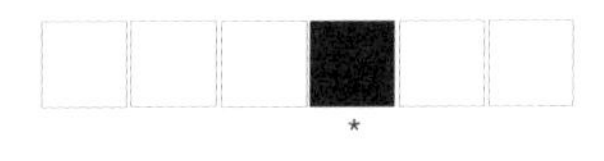

Figure 3: "the block"

It is worth stressing that this is the only rule for which Beun & Cremers found no significant evidence (due perhaps to the relatively small size of their corpus and the sparseness of inherently salient objects within a given domain). Interestingly, rule 1 is probably also the most controversial rule. Horacek (1997), for instance, argues for the exact opposite: one should use the property that makes the object inherently salient, even if it does not rule out distractors. For example: a single pink elephant should be referred to as "the pink elephant" even when the contrast set entirely consists of flamingos. Arguably, world knowledge (that elephants are typically grey) plays an important role in this case, but not for the examples that Beun & Cremers discuss. This suggests that the respective positions of Beun & Cremers and Horacek do not really contradict each other, but apply to different cases. However, more research is required to test this hypothesis.

Rule 2 If the target object is located in the current focus area use only information that distinguishes the object from other objects in the focus area.

This rule can be illustrated by Figure 4. Assume that speaker and hearer are currently focussed on the two left most blocks in Figure 4. Within such a focus space, participants in the experiments of Beun & Cremers typically would describe the block marked with a $*$ simply as "the white block", even though there is another white block in the domain (but outside the current focus space).[3]

Rule 3 Use only information that distinguishes the target object from other objects that would be suitable for use in carrying out the current action.

This rule concerns functional expressions like "put the white block in between" in a situation in which there is only one object that fits in the intended space between two black objects (see $*$ in Figure 5). Notice that the referring expression crucially

[3]In fact, subjects typically produce *de witte* (English: 'the white (one)'). For the sake of simplicity, we follow Dale (1992) here in assuming that "one" is used instead of a full head noun N when the context of a description contains another NP whose head is also N.

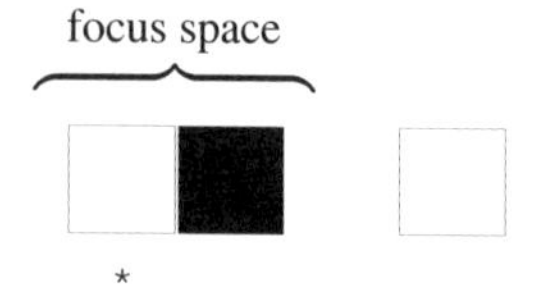

Figure 4: “the white block”

exploits the functional information expressed in the rest of the utterance. Only by considering the action, a hearer can decide which white block the speaker is referring to. Since the algorithm we propose in this paper is solely aimed at producing referring expressions and has no direct access to functional information expressed by the entire utterance, this problem will not be dealt with here.

Figure 5: “put the white block in between”

Rule 4 Use absolute features as much as possible and use relative features only as necessary.

This rule is already implicit in the ordering of preferred attributes argued for by Dale and Reiter (see section 2). In the situation of Figure 6, the D & R algorithm would describe $*$ as “the black black” (not including *size*), but $**$ would be referred to as “the large white block”, since the inclusion of *white* (an absolute property) is not sufficient to rule out all distractors. For this, the relative property *large* is required.

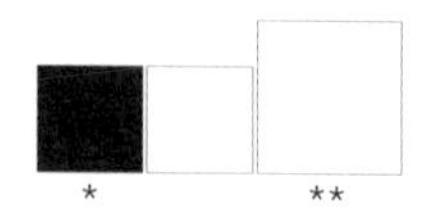

Figure 6: $*$ “the black block”; $**$ “the large white block”

Rule 5 If an explicit relatum is needed for referring to the target object, choose as a relatum an object that is salient.[4]

[4]This rule is a slight generalization of Beun & Cremers, who do not discuss linguistic salience and only mention relata which are inherently salient and/or in the focus of attention.

In other words, if another object is needed to describe the target object, then select one which is salient. An object can be salient for a number of reasons, for instance because it has just been talked about (linguistic salience, see Krahmer & Theune, 1999). Suppose that the black block in Figure 7 has just been talked about and the grey block has not been mentioned. In that context, $*$ is typically referred to as "the white block next to the black one".

Figure 7: "the white block next to the black one"

4 Main ingredients of the multimodal algorithm

In this section we describe the main novelties of our multimodal extension of the D&R algorithm, based on the empirically motivated rules discussed above.

4.1 When to point?

According to the principle of Minimal Cooperative Effort (Clark & Wilkes-Gibbs, 1986), a balance should be found between on the one hand the speaker's effort to produce a description and on the other hand the effort necessary for interpretation of this description by the hearer. Hence we assume that the decision to use a pointing act for distinguishing an object is determined by two factors: the effort of pointing and the effort required for a full, linguistic description.

We assume that the effort of pointing is determined by two factors: the distance to and the size of the target object. The trade-off between these factors has been captured in Fitts' law, the index of difficulty ID (Fitts, 1954). The index is computed from the size of the target object and the distance between the object and the position of the pointing device used, in our case the speaker's hand. If this index is below a certain (task and domain dependent) threshold (i.e., it is easy to point), the algorithm includes a pointing act in the output.[5]

DEFINITION 1 (Index of Difficulty (ID))

$$\mathrm{ID} = \log_2\left(\frac{2d}{w}\right)$$

[5]Piwek et al. (1995:13) contains some suggestive evidence supporting this idea. They found that builders are more likely to point than instructors. This might be explained by the fact that builders, by the very nature of their task, are forced to touch the blocks anyway, implying that the distance between their hands and the blocks is much smaller for builders than for instructors. Interestingly, there is also a certain amount of individual variation in that some subjects point very frequently while others never do. This suggests that the threshold is not only task and domain dependent, but also subjective.

where w is the width (or 'size') of the object and d is the distance from the pointing device to the object.

The second factor that contributes to the decision to point is the effort required for a purely linguistic description. Arguably, this effort is proportional to the number of attributes and relations needed to generate a distinguishing description. When the complexity of the linguistic description is above a certain threshold, the linguistic description generated so far is discarded and a pointing act is generated instead.[6]

Once a pointing act is included in a referring expression, we assume that the distractor set is immediately emptied and the target object is uniquely identified (it will be clear for the hearer which object is being referred to).[7] Finally, if an object cannot be uniquely identified in terms of a purely linguistic description, then the algorithm similarly provides for a pointing act accompanied by a short and general linguistic expression.

4.2 Computing the focus space

The second rule of Beun & Cremers described in section 3 concerns the objects in the current focus space from which the target object should be distinguished. The notion of a focus space is not only psychologically plausible, but is also beneficial from a computational point of view. By defining the focus space as a subset of the objects in the whole domain, the search space of the algorithm is reduced. In this section we will first give an insight in how we define the current focus space using an example, before we present a formal definition.

The focus space consists of the last mentioned object o and the set of objects directly related to o (such as to o's left or right, below o etc.). An object d is standing in a direct relation to an object o if d is the closest object to o for which that particular relation holds. The set of objects related to o can be illustrated with Figure 8. If the object last mentioned is the black block, the focus space contains three blocks as shown in the picture (the black block itself plus the two white ones). The grey block to the right of the black block is excluded because there is a closer block which is also to the right of the black block. Once the algorithm has generated a referring expression for $*$, the focus space needs to be updated. The updated focus space contains $*$ and the set of objects that are directly related to

[6]We have our doubt whether the approach which first tries to generate a complex description only to discard it later in favor of a pointing act is psychologically realistic. In a sense, this problem is a specific instance of the general problem of finding a solution which requires minimal effort (Zipf 1949). Arguably, one needs to calculate the effort required for *each* solution to be able to determine which one is minimal. And this process certainly is not minimal.

[7]Mariët Theune (p.c.) notes that less precise (i.e., non distinguishing) gestures could also be useful. In particular, if all distractors close to the target object have been ruled out by the properties selected so far, then adding such a less precise gesture pointing to the region which contains the target object would also suffice. Such a gesture could typically also be used when the hand is relatively far away. Rather then postulating an absolute threshold, it would be interesting to assign a "denotation" to pointing gestures: if the hand is close, the denotation will consist of few objects, if it is father away, the denotation will consist of more objects.

Figure 8: "the white block to the right of the black one"

$*$, which would be the black and the grey block. However, on a second note the grey block seems rather far apart from the current focus. To be able to take into account the relative distance between the objects in the domain of discourse, we use *perceptual grouping* (Thorisson, 1994). Thorrison defines a proximity score for the distance of each object in the domain to a particular object o. The proximity score between the object o and an object d in the domain D is defined as follows:

$$F = \frac{\text{distance}(o, d)}{\max\limits_{y \in D} (\text{distance}(o, y))}$$

By setting a threshold to this fraction, we can exclude far away objects from the focus space of o. For example, consider Figure 8 again, and suppose, for the sake of illustration, that we set the threshold to 0.5. In Figure 8, the distance between $*$ and the black block is 1cm, the distance between $*$ and the white block to the left of the black block is 1.5cm and the distance between $*$ and the grey block is 6cm. Then the maximal distance in this domain is 6cm. By perceptual grouping with a threshold of 0.5 this will result in the following fractions (for $o = *$): $1/6 = 0.17$ (d = black block), $1.5/6 = 0.25$ (d = leftmost white block) and $6/6 = 1$ (d = grey block). Hence we can exclude the grey block from the focus space of $*$.

Summarizing, the new, updated focus space contains $*$ (the last mentioned object) and the black block. In definition 2, the focus space of an object o is formally defined as the union of the object o itself with the set of objects in the domain that are closest to o for any relation of a given type (with *type* $\in$ { left_of, below, ... }) and which are not 'too far away' in terms of perceptual grouping (with F as defined above).

DEFINITION 2 (Focus space)
focus_space(o) = $\{o\} \cup \{d \in D \mid$ relation(*type*, o, d) $\wedge \neg \exists d'$ (relation(*type*, o, d') $\wedge$ (distance(o, d') $\leq$ distance(o, d))) $\wedge F \leq 0.5$ }

Notice that the target object r need not be an element of the current focus space around object o. When it is not, we speak of a *focus shift*.

4.3 A three-dimensional notion of salience

As mentioned in section 2, Krahmer & Theune (1998, 1999) extended the D & R algorithm with a linguistic notion of salience. As we have seen in the previous section, other forms of salience are also relevant for the generation of referring expressions. In particular, objects can be inherently salient and/or they can be salient because they are in the current focus space. To model these differences, we define a three-dimensional notion of salience. More precisely, each object in the domain receives three salience weights, one indicating whether or not the object is linguistically salient, one indicating whether it is inherently salient and one indicating its focus space salience. The total salience weight of an object is determined by taking the sum of the three separate salience weights (which is in line with the observation of Beun & Cremers (1998:141) that an inherently salient object in the current focus space is more salient than an inherently salient object outside the focus space). Arguably, some forms of salience are more important than others. We assume that linguistic context salience is primary, for instance, in the sense that an object r which was just described is more salient than an object which is in the current focus space (i.e., close to r) but has not itself been mentioned so far. In a similar vein, we take it that an object which is in focus is somewhat more salient than an object which is inherently salient but falls outside of the current focus space.

The first two rules of Beun & Cremers are immediately satisfied, when (following Krahmer & Theune 1998, 1999) we restrict the distractor set to objects which are at least as salient as the target object. This implies that if the target object is inherently salient and/or part of the focus space, this will generally lead to a reduction of the distractor set (assuming that not all objects are equally salient) and consequently fewer properties should suffice for emptying the distractor set. Thus, when an object is inherently salient we can use reduced information. When the target object is part of the current focus space (and is not linguistically salient), the distractor set will typically consist of the other objects that are in the current focus space, together with the objects that are linguistically salient. According to the fifth rule, when a relatum is needed the algorithm will select the most salient one.

Within the algorithm presented here, linguistic salience (L-salience) is modelled as it is done by Krahmer & Theune (1999), who determine linguistic salience on the basis of the ranking of forward looking centers according to centering theory (Grosz et al, 1995) augmented with a notion of recency. Linguistic salience weights range from 0 to 10 (maximum salience). In the initial state, every object is assigned an L-salience weight 0. There are various ways to determine inherent salience (I-salience); see Cremers (1996:24) for references and discussion. Here we opt for a strong criterion, where an object is inherently salient only if for some attribute it has a particular value V_1 while the other objects in the domain all have a different value V_2 for that particular attribute. If an object is inherently salient, it has a constant I-salience weight of 1. Finally, focus space salience (FS-salience) is easily determined given definition 2. An object has an FS-salience weight of 2 iff it is part of the current focus space.

Definition 3 calculates the salience weight of each object d in a state s_i as the sum of the three kinds of salience associated with d in that state. In the initial state s_0 (the beginning of the discourse) no object has been described and we assume that there is no focus space. Thus, initially each object in the domain has an L-salience and an FS-salience weight of zero. In this definition, $C_f(U_i)$ is the ordering of the forward looking centers of U_i (the sentence uttered at time i) according to Centering Theory (Grosz et al. 1995). This ordering is such that the syntactic subject of U_i is the most salient object (mapped to salience weight 10) followed by the indirect object (mapped to 9) and the other objects (mapped to 8). Thus, more formally, $\mathsf{level}(d_i, \langle d_1, \ldots, d_n \rangle) = \mathsf{max}(0, 11 - i)$, where $\langle d_1, \ldots, d_n \rangle$ is the ordered set of forward looking centers of the relevant utterance. If an object is not mentioned in U_i its salience weight is reduced with 1, unless it is already 0. The FS-salience weight 2 is assigned to every object d in the focus space of object o, where o is the most recently described object (or, slightly more general, the object with the highest L-salience).

DEFINITION 3 (Three-dimensional Salience)
For each object $d \in D$, the salience weight of d in state s_i is

$$\text{salience\_weight}(d, s_i) = \text{I-salience}(d, s_i) + \text{L-salience}(d, s_i) + \text{FS-salience}(d, s_i)$$

where:

Linguistic Salience

$$\text{L-salience}(d, s_0) = 0$$

$$\text{L-salience}(d, s_{i+1}) = \begin{cases} \mathsf{level}(d, C_f(U_i)) & \text{if } d \in C_f(U_i) \\ \mathsf{max}(0, \text{L-salience}(d, s_i) - 1) & \text{otherwise} \end{cases}$$

Focus Space Salience

$$\text{FS-salience}(d, s_0) = 0$$

$$\text{FS-salience}(d, s_{i+1}) = \begin{cases} 2 & \text{if } d \in \text{focus\_space}(o) \wedge o = \underset{d'}{\mathsf{max}}\ \text{L-salience}(d', s_i)) \\ 0 & \text{otherwise} \end{cases}$$

Inherent Salience

$$\text{I-salience}(d, s_i) = \begin{cases} 1 & \text{if object } d \text{ is inherently salient} \\ 0 & \text{otherwise} \end{cases}$$

4.4 Linguistic Realization

So far we have not said much about the actual linguistic realization; here we make up for this lack. To determine the form of the multimodal referring expressions we inspected the corpus collected by Beun & Cremers. For starters, we can decide on the list of preferred attributes for the block domain used in their experiments. Table 1 contains the distribution of the attributes in 141 initial, distinguishing descriptions from the corpus of Beun & Cremers. It is clear that *color* is by far the most

attribute	+ *Point*	− *Point*	total
Color	38	42	80
Location	4	19	23
Shape	3	10	13
Type	5	8	13
None	11	1	12

Table 1: Selected attributes as a function of pointing acts.

preferred attribute in this domain. The attribute *type* is the least preferred attribute in this domain. This is not surprising since all objects in this domain are of the block type, which makes this is very uninformative property. However, the D & R algorithm stipulates that *type* should always be included in the final description, even if it is not discriminating. Table 1 clearly contradicts this. We conjecture that it should not be the *type* attribute which is always included, but rather the most preferred attribute for a particular domain.

In the (Dutch) corpus used in the various studies of Cremers, Beun and Piwek, demonstrative determiners are preferred over articles. Piwek & Cremers (1996) claim that Dutch proximate demonstratives (deze/dit; 'this') are preferred when referring to objects which are relatively hard to access. The use of distal demonstratives (die/dat; 'that') is equally distributed over more and less accessible referents.[8] Piwek & Cremers' notion of accessibility can be defined for the purposes of the current paper as follows:

DEFINITION 4 (Accessibility)

$$\text{accessible}(r, s_i) = \begin{cases} \text{False} \quad \text{if} & \text{I-salience}(r, s_i) = 0 \vee \\ & \text{L-salience}(r, s_i) \leq 8 \vee \\ & \text{FS-salience}(r, s_i) = 0 \\ \text{True} \quad \text{otherwise} & \end{cases}$$

The choice of determiner does not solely depend on the accessibility of the object, also the occurence of a relatum or a pointing act is important. In the data from Beun & Cremers' corpus, proximate demonstratives are never used in combination with a relatum, contrary to distal demonstratives. For the relatum itself a definite article is used. On the other hand, the data from the experiments by Beun & Cremers show that in all cases in which a proximate demonstrative is used it is accompanied by a pointing act. A distal demonstrative in combination with a pointing act occurs only in 35% of the cases in which a distal demonstrative is used. Piwek & Cremers

[8]We are aware of the fact that there are certain differences between English and Dutch where determiners are concerned. Our algorithm, primarily based on Dutch data, formalizes the findings of Piwek & Cremers for Dutch demonstratives. For the generation of English referring expressions, some minor changes in the selection of determiners are required.

(1996) conclude that distal demonstratives are preferred without a pointing act in case they are used to refer to accessible entities.

In sum, the resulting algorithm generates a variety of 'multimodal' NPs where the kind of NP is determined by the occurence of a pointing act, the presence or absence of a relatum and the accessibility of the target object described in terms of salience. In contrast to including the *type* of the target object (as the D&R algorithm stipulates) we include the most preferred attribute, which is in the block domain the property *color*.

5 Outline of the multimodal algorithm

In this section we present our expanded, multimodal version of the algorithms of Dale & Reiter and Krahmer & Theune, simply called *make_referring_expression*, and illustrate it with two examples.[9]

5.1 Sketch of the algorithm

Before *make_referring_expression* is actually called, certain variables are initialised using the procedure *initialise*. This procedure takes as input three arguments, namely the target object R for which a referring expression should be generated, the current focus space FS and the current state S. The first variable which is initialised is *SW_list*. This is a list of all the objects in the domain, ordered with respect to their salience weights. *PA_list* is a list with the attribute-value pairs of the object *R*, ordered according to human preference. In *PR_list* all the relations of *R* with other objects in the domain are listed (*next to*, *on top of*, *below*, etc.), ordered by the salience weights of the relata. *Access* is a boolean variable depending on the three kinds of salience of *R*. *RemDist* is the set of objects from which *R* has to be distinguished, containing all the objects with a salience weight higher than or equal to the salience weight of *R*. Finally *make_referring_expression* is called to generate a distinguishing expression for the target object *R* with the relevant, initialized parameters. Notice that the state S is also passed on as a parameter. This is required for the generation of relata, where all the relevant parameters need to be re-initialised for the generation of the relatum. We assume that the parameters *S* and the *FS* are both updated by the main generation algorithm (hosting *make_referring_expression)* as soon as it has produced a complete utterance.

```
initialise(R,FS,S)
SW_list = generate_salience_weights(R,FS,S)
PA_list = preferred_properties(R)
PR_list = preferred_relations(R,SW_list)
Access = accessible(R,SW_list)
RemDist =dist(R,SW_list)
make_referring_expression(R,FS,PA_list,PR_list,RemDist,Access,S)
```

[9]Krahmer & Theune's modified version of the D & R algorithm has been implemented. We are currently working on extending this implementation to include the multimodal additions described in this section.

In *make_referring_expression* it is first determined whether pointing to R does not require too much effort. For this the function *index_of_difficulty* is used (see definition 1), and if this index is below a certain threshold, a pointing act is included. If this is the case, the *RemDist* list is emptied, and an accompanying linguistic expression is put together by including the most preferred property of *R*. Finally, the appropriate determiner is inserted and the resulting tree is returned. If the effort of pointing is too high (the boolean variable *Point* is *False*), the algorithm first tries to find properties that rule out objects in the *RemDist* list; calling *find_properties* results in *Tree1*. If all the properties of *R* are considered and the *RemDist* still contains objects from which *R* is not distinguished, the algorithm selects the first relation on the *PR_list* which rules out distractors. If a relation between the target object R and a (salient) relatum R' is selected, then the algorithm also has to generate a referring expression for R'. For this purpose the main algorithm is called again, but now with R' as input (*initialise* (R', FS, S)). The resulting description for R' is stored in *Tree2*, after which *Tree1* and *Tree2* are combined resulting in *Tree* and the boolean *Relatum* (indicating whether or not a relatum was needed for the generation of R) is set to *True*. If no relation was needed to empty the *RemDist* list, only *Tree1* is stored in *Tree*. As argued in section 4.1, two factors contribute to the decision to point, namely the effort of pointing and the effort of a linguistic description. The second factor is modelled in the algorithm by counting the required properties and attributes included in the description of R under construction. If this number is above a certain Threshold, the algorihm classifies the linguistic description (stored in *Tree*) as too complex and discards it in favour of a pointing act. Finally, with *include_most_preferred_property*, *Tree* is enriched with the most preferred property of *R* if this property was not already present in *Tree*. (Notice that this marks a difference from the Incremental Algorithm for those domains where *Type* is not the most preferred attribute.) Finally, with *insert_det* (see below) a determiner is added to *Tree* and the complete description is returned.

```
make_referring_expression(R,FS,PA_list,PR_list,RemDist,Access,S)
Point = index_of_difficulty(R)
if (Point == true) RemDist = [ ]
if (Point == false)
        Tree1 = find_properties(R,PA_list,RemDist)
        if (RemDist ≠ [ ])
                Tree2 = find_relations(R,FS,PR_list,RemDist,S)
                if (Tree2 ≠ nil)
                        Tree = add_tree(Tree1,Tree2)
                        Relatum = True
                else Tree = Tree1
        if (Threshold ≤ determine_efficiency(Tree)) || (RemDist ≠ [ ])
                        Point = True
                        Relatum = False
                        Tree = nil
Tree = include_most_preferred_property(Tree,R)
```

Tree = insert_det(R,Tree,Access,Point,Relatum)
return Tree

The functions *find_properties* and *find_relations* are (minimal variants of) functions found in Dale & Reiter (1995) and Krahmer & Theune (1999) respectively. The function *find_properties* determines which properties of the *PA_list* rule out any of the remaining distractors and should therefore be included in the referring expression of *R*, essentially as it is done in the Incremental Algorithm. The function *find_relations* looks for relations of R to be included in the referring expression, in essentially the same way as for properties. The function *insert_det* determines which determiner to add to the tree generated by the algorithm according to the Dutch data of Beun & Cremers (1998) and the rules for Dutch proposed by Piwek & Cremers (1996). When the referring expression for *R* contains no relatum, a pointing act is included and the object is inaccessible (it has a low salience weight), then a proximate demonstrative is inserted. A distal is used when the referring expression includes a pointing gesture or when the referent is accessible. In all other cases a definite article is selected.

5.2 Worked example

We end our presentation of the multimodal algorithm by discussing an example in which a sequence of two generated referring acts is considered. In the initial situation in Figure 9 below, there is no focus space, no inherently salient object and no linguistic salience. The salience weights of all the objects in the domain of conversation are zero. The task is to refer to $*$. The algorithm includes a pointing act because the index of difficulty for pointing to this object is below the threshold *C*. At this point, all distractors are ruled out. Next, the relevant value of the most preferred attribute is added (*color*). A proximate demonstrative determiner is chosen on the basis of the values of three boolean variables: *Point* = *True*, *Access* = *False* (since all objects are equally non-salient) and *Relatum* = *False*. The algorithm outputs a pointing act accompanied by the referring expression "this black block".

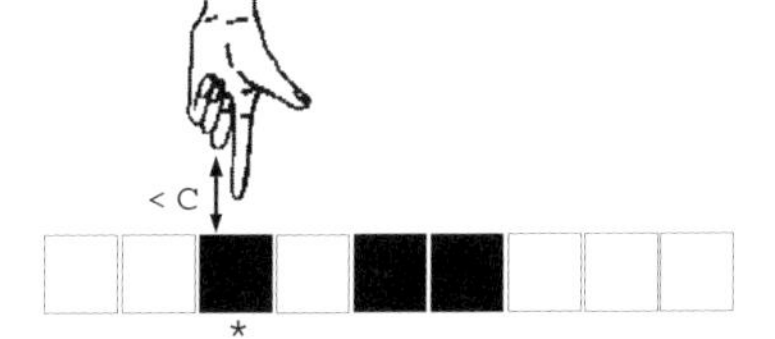

Figure 9: "this black block"

In the follow-up situation, presented in Figure 10, the focus space is updated (in the way defined above) and indicated by the curly bracket. Now the previously described object (the black one) is the only object in the domain with a non-zero linguistic salience weight. Within the focus space the black block has a total salience weight of 12 (10 for maximal linguistic salience plus 2 for focus space salience) and both the white blocks have a salience weight of 2. The task is to refer to $*$, and the distractor set contains all the objects with a salience weight higher than or equal to the target object (in this particular example, the distractor set coincides with the focus space). Because the hand is too far away from $*$, the index of difficulty is above the threshold and no pointing act is generated. Instead, the algorithm enters the *find_properties* routine. The algorithm adds the preferred property (*color*) to distinguish $*$ from the black block in the focus space. No other properties can be used to rule out the other white block. So, next the function *find_relations* is called. The function first tries the relation with the most salient relatum (the first element of the *PR_list*: the left-of relation between $*$ and the black block. Including this relation does empty the distractor set: the remaining white block in the distractor set does stand in the left-of relation to a black block, but that one falls outside the focus space and thus has a zero salience weight. The algorithm generates a description for the relatum: "the black one". This description is inserted in the description for $*$. Finally, a distal demonstrative determiner is inserted since the referent is accessible.[10]

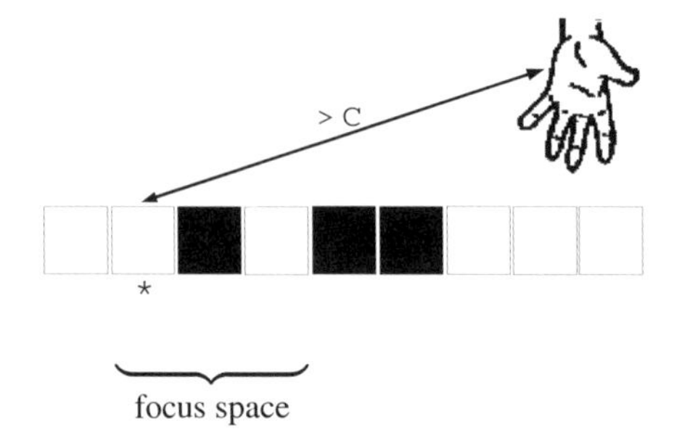

Figure 10: "that white block to the left of the black one"

6 Concluding remarks

As noted in section 2, Dale & Reiter's Incremental Algorithm has two attractive properties: it is computionally attractive and psychologically realistic. To what extent has our proposed algorithm inherited these properties? Given that our extensions are to a large extent motivated by empirical research, the current algorithm can be claimed to model the way humans refer to objects in a multimodal setting. In this respect, the multimodal algorithm presented here is as psychologically realistic as Dale & Reiter's. It arguably also captures more of the variety found in human object references than the Incremental Algorithm does. The original Incremental Algorithm is efficient (polynomial) because there is no possibility of back-

[10] Recall that the algorithm is currently aimed at generating Dutch descriptions (*die witte links van de zwarte*). The use of a distal demonstrative determiner is probably less natural for English. See Piwek & Cremers 1996 for discussion.

tracking, there can be no 'wrong' decisions. Unfortunately, as soon as we include relations, this property cannot be kept: the generation of relational descriptions is NP complete (see e.g., Krahmer et al. 2001). In general, there is no guarantee that we always immediately select the right relatum, so either backtracking or multiple embeddings may be required. However, two factors should be noted. First, the use of salience guides the search for a relatum. In particular, following the empirical findings of Beun & Cremers, only salient relata are chosen, which in most cases offers a substantial reduction of the search space. Second, we define an upper bound to the number of properties and relations which can be included in the final description. When this maximum value is reached, the tree under construction is discarded and a pointing act is included. Fortunately, as soon as such an upper bound is defined, we regain polynomial complexity (see e.g., van Deemter 2001).

Acknowledgements

We would like to thank Paul Piwek, Mariët Theune and Harry Bunt for discussions and comments on an earlier version of this paper.

References

Beun, R.J. & A. Cremers (1998), Object reference in a shared domain of conversation, *Pragmatics & Cognition* **6**(1/2):121-152.

Cohen, P. (1984), The pragmatics of referring and the modality of communication, *Computational Linguistics* **10**(2):97-125.

Claassen, W. (1992), Generating referring expressions in a multimodal environment, in: *Aspects of Automated Natural Language Generation*, R. Dale et al. (eds.), Springer Verlag, Berlin.

Cremers, A. (1996), *Reference to objects: An empirically based study of task-oriented dialogues*, Ph.D. dissertation, Eindhoven University of Technology.

Clark, H. & D. Wilkes-Gibbs (1986), Referring as a collaborative process, *Cognition* **22**:1-39.

Dale, R. & E. Reiter (1995), Computational interpretations of the Gricean maxims in the generation of referring expressions, *Cognitive Science* **18**:233-263.

Deemter, K. van (2001), Generating referring expressions: Beyond the Incremental Algorithm, *Proceedings of the 4th International Workshop on Computational Semantics*, Tilburg, The Netherlands.

Fitts, P. (1954), The information capacity of the human motor system in controlling amplitude of movement, *Journal of Experimental Psychology* **47**:381-391.

Grosz, B., A. Joshi & S. Weinstein (1995), Centering: A framework for modeling the local coherence of discourse, *Computational Linguistics* **21**(2):203-225.

Horacek, H. (1997), An algorithm for generating referential descriptions with flexible interfaces, *Proceedings of the 35th ACL/EACL*, 206-213, Mardrid, Spain.

Huls, C. E. Bos & W. Claassen (1995), Automatic referent resolution of deictic and anaphoric expressions, *Computational Linguistics* **21**(1):59-79.

Krahmer, E. & M. Theune (1998), Context sensitive generation of referring expressions. *Proceedings of the 5th International Conference on Spoken Language Processing (ICSLP'98)*, 1151-1154. Sydney, Australia.

Krahmer, E. & M. Theune (1999). Efficient generation of Descriptions in Context, *Proceedings of the ESSLLI Workshop on the Generation of Nominals*, R. Kibble and K. van Deemter (eds.), Utrecht, The Netherlands.

Krahmer, E. S. van Erk & A. Verleg (2001). A meta-algorithm for the generation of referring expressions, *Proceedings of the Eight European Workshop on Natural Language Generation*, Toulouse, France.

Pechmann, T. (1989), Incremental speech production and referential overspecification, *Linguistics* **27**:98-110.

Piwek, P., R.J. Beun & A. Cremers (1995), *Demonstratives in Dutch cooperative task dialogues.*, IPO manuscript 1134, Eindhoven University of Technology.

Piwek, P. & A. Cremers (1996), Dutch and English demonstratives: A comparison, *Language Sciences* **18**(3-4):835-851.

Reithinger, N. (1992), The performance of an incremental generation component for multi-modal dialog contributions, in: *Aspects of Automated Natural Language Generation*, R. Dale et al. (eds.), Springer Verlag, Berlin.

Salmon-Alt, S. & L. Romary (2000), Generating referring expressions in multimodal contexts, *Proceedings of the INLG 2000 workshop on Coherence in Generated Multimedia*, Mitzpe Ramon, Israel.

Theune, M. (2000), *From data to speech: Language generation in context*, Ph.D. dissertation, Eindhoven University of Technology.

Thorisson, K. (1994), Simulated perceptual grouping: An application to human computer interaction, *Proceedings of the 16th Annual Conference of Cognitive Science Society*, 876-881, Atlanta GA.

Zipf, G.K. (1949), *Human behavior and the principle of least effort: An introduction to human ecology*, Addison-Wesley, Cambridge.

Transforming a Chunker to a Parser

Erik F. Tjong Kim Sang

CNTS - Language Technology Group, University of Antwerp

Abstract

Ever since the landmark paper Ramshaw and Marcus (1995), machine learning systems have been used successfully for identifying base phrases (chunks), the bottom constituents of a parse tree. We expand a state-of-the-art chunking algorithm to a bottom-up parser by recursively applying the chunker to its own output. After testing different training configurations we obtain a reasonable parser which is tested against a standard data set. Its performance falls behind that of current state-of-the-art parsers. We give some suggestions for modifications of the parser which may lead to future performance improvements.

1 Introduction

Ramshaw and Marcus (1995) have proposed approaching base phrase identification by regarding it as a tagging task. Phrases in a text can be represented by word-related phrase chunk tags, like I (inside chunk) and O (outside chunk). The advantage of this approach is that arbitrary simple machine learning algorithms, for example classifiers, can be used for performing this task. This paper has initiated a lot of follow-up research, both regarding base noun phrase identification and finding arbitrary base chunks.

A group of chunkers can build a complete parse tree if each of them identifies syntactic chunks at a different level of the tree. The first chunker finds base chunks and send these to the second chunker which identifies syntactic constituents one level above the base level. This chunker sends its output to another one which identifies constituents at the next level and so on. The chunkers can be implemented with any classification algorithm which enables researchers from different segments of the machine learning field to build a parser.

The idea of using chunkers in a parser is not new. Ejerhed and Church (1983) describe a grammar for Swedish which includes noun phrase chunk rules. Abney (1991) built a chunk parser which first finds base chunks and then attaches them with a separate attachment process. Brants (1999) used a cascade of Markov model chunkers for obtaining parsing results for the German NEGRA corpus.

In this paper, we expand a state-of-the art chunking algorithm to an algorithm for full parsing. Our approach is most similar to Brants (1999) : we use a chunker for retrieving all parse tree levels. However, we apply the chunk parser to a standard data set for English in order to allow a comparison with earlier parser results. We describe the chunker-parser transformation process in detail and examine different training configurations of the chunk parser. After this we test the parser and compare its performance with a state-of-the-art statistical parser.

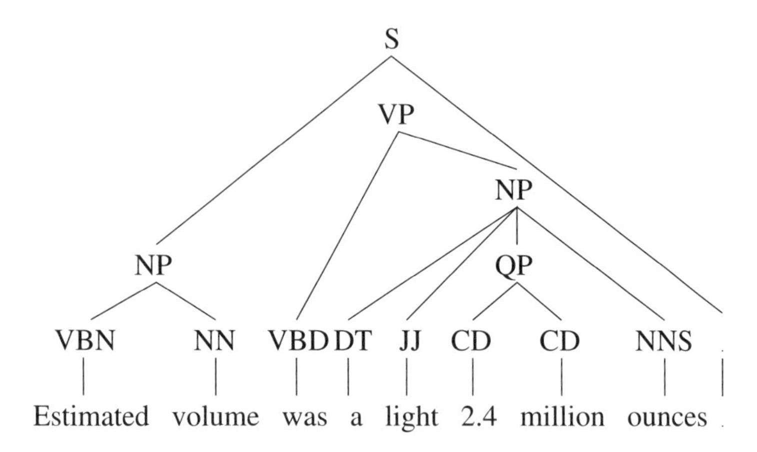

Figure 1: Example parse tree from the Penn Treebank. The bottom row contains the words (*Estimated...*), the row above that one contains the part-of-speech tags (VBN...) and the next the chunk tags (NP QP).

2 Chunking

Identifying the phrases at the bottom part of the tree is called chunking. For example, the tree in figure 1 contains two base phrases, a noun phrase and a quantifier phrase:

> (NP Estimated volume) was
> a light (QP 2.4 million) ounces .

The first report on applying statistical methods to this task dates back to 1988 (Church 1988). The most influential work in this area is Ramshaw and Marcus (1995). They showed that this task can be approached as a tagging task by replacing the common bracket notation for chunks with a tagging representation:

> Estimated/B-NP volume/I-NP was/O
> a/O light/O 2.4/B-QP million/I-QP ounces/O ./O

Their tagging scheme contains three types of tags: B-XX for the first word of a chunk of type XX, I-XX for non-initial words in such chunks and O for words outside of any chunk.[1] The tagging representation has an advantages over the bracket representation: while the latter may suffer from bracket-pairing problems, the tagging representation requires almost no consistency checks. Furthermore it allows existing tagging technology to be used for deriving chunks in text.

[1]The original Ramshaw and Marcus (1995) chunk format was slightly different from the one shown here. It included an extra punctuation chunk type (P) and the tags did not contain hyphens.

	IOB1	IOB2	IOE1	IOE2	O+C	
Estimated	I-NP	B-NP	I-NP	I-NP	[-NP	O
volume	I-NP	I-NP	I-NP	E-NP	O	]-NP
was	O	O	O	O	O	O
a	O	O	O	O	O	O
light	O	O	O	O	O	O
2.4	I-QP	B-QP	I-QP	I-QP	[-QP	O
million	I-QP	I-QP	I-QP	E-QP	O	]-QP
ounces	O	O	O	O	O	O
.	O	O	O	O	O	O

Table 1: Five representations of the chunk structure of the sentence *Estimated volume was a light 2.4 million ounces* . IOB1 and IOE1 only use a B-XX or an E-XX tag at the boundaries of adjacent chunks of the same type (not present in this sentence). IOB2 and IOE2 use B-XX and E-XX tags at boundaries of all chunks. O+C is the bracket representation.

Recent work has shown that with a good method for repairing bracket problems, a noun phrase chunking system using the bracket representation performs better than one that uses the tagging representation (Muñoz, Punyakanok, Roth and Zimak 1999). Even more promising is the approach that combines the output of chunkers that use different data representations (Tjong Kim Sang 2000a). The idea is build five chunking systems, one which uses the bracket representation and four which use variants of the tagging representation (see table 1). Because of the different formats of the data, the five systems will make different errors. After converting their output to the bracket representation, one can extract a new chunk segmentation by only accepting brackets which have been predicted by the majority of the systems. The new chunk segmentation proves to be better than any generated by the individual systems (Tjong Kim Sang 2000a).

We have used the combination of representations chunking method of Tjong Kim Sang (2000b). This means training five classifiers with each of the data representations shown in table 1. Each of the classifiers performs four passes over the data. First they determine the chunk boundaries regardless of the type (two passes for the bracket representation). After this the four systems that use the tagging representation use the chunk structure found as extra information for producing an improved segmentation. Next all data is converted to the bracket representation and each system performs two passes for determining the types of the open and close brackets, respectively. This process with four passes over the data was chosen after a comparative chunking study (Tjong Kim Sang 2000b). An example of the features used in the four passes can be found in figure 2. When the output of the five systems is available, the five open bracket and five close bracket data streams are combined with majority voting. Finally, the resulting open and close brackets are made consistent by throwing away all brackets that cannot be matched with an adjacent bracket of the same chunk type.

Est JJ vol NN was VBD a DT lig JJ 2.4 CD mil CD oun NNS . .
vol NN I was VBD O a DT O lig JJ 2.4 CD B mil CD I oun NNS O

Figure 2: Features used for classifying *light* in the sentence *Estimated volume was a light 2.4 million ounces* . Word length has been limited three characters to make the lines fit in this figure. The first row contains the features used in the first, third and the fourth pass: the word and its part-of-speech (POS) tag with the four previous and four next words with their POS tags. The second row shows the features used in the second pass of the system that worked with the IOB2 tagging representation: the word, its POS tag and the three previous and three next words with their POS tag and the chunk tag found in pass one.

Various machine learning methods can be used for the basic task of determining the most appropriate chunk tag sequences for a text. We use the memory-based learning algorithm IB1-IG which is part of TiMBL package (Daelemans, Zavrel, van der Sloot and van den Bosch 1999). In memory-based learning the training data is stored and a new item is classified by the most frequent classification among training items which are closest to this new item. Data items are represented as sets of feature-value pairs. In IB1-IG each feature receives a weight which is based on the amount of information which it provides for computing the classification of the items in the training data. These feature weights are used for computing the distance between a pair of data items (Daelemans et al. 1999). IB1-IG has been used successfully on a large variety of natural language processing tasks.

The overall results of the chunking process are measured with labeled precision and recall, respectively the percentage of detected phrases that are correct and the percentage of phrases in the data that were found by the parser. We have combined these two in the $F_{\beta=1}$ rate which is equal to (2*precision*recall)/(precision+recall).

3 Parsing

In this paper we will perform parsing, generating syntactic analyses for sentences, with a chunking algorithm. Most parsing work describes a process for finding base chunks which are combined by another process to trees (for example Ejerhed and Church (1983) and Abney (1991)). However, like Brants (1999), we want to build a parser in which constituents et all levels of the parse tree are produced by a chunking algorithm. This is a natural follow-up of our earlier work (Tjong Kim Sang 2000a, Tjong Kim Sang 2000b) in which we build a noun phrase chunker, a noun phrase parser and a general chunker. Our general parser performs the following actions:

w	Estimated	volume	was	a	light	2.4	million	ounces	.
p	VBN	NN	VBD	DT	JJ	CD	CD	NNS	.
0	(NP	NP)				(QP	QP)		
0w		volume	was	a	light		million	ounces	.
0p		NP	VBD	DT	JJ		QP	NNS	.
1				(NP				NP)	
1w		volume	was					ounces	.
1p		NP	VBD					NP	.
2			(VP					VP)	
2w		volume	was						.
2p		NP	VP						.
3		(S							S)

Figure 3: An example of the parsing process: first the base chunks are identified (row 0). The chunks are compressed and replaced by their heads (0w) and labels (0p). Then the next level of phrases is identified (1) and compressed to head words (1w) and labels (1p). This is followed by two more levels of phrase identification (2 and 3) and another compression (2w and 2p).

1. use a tagger for finding a part-of-speech tag for each word,
2. use a chunker for identifying base phrases,
3. replace all identified phrases with their head and their label,
4. find 'base' phrases in the new data stream
5. if the previous step discovered new phrases then repeat steps 3-5.

In this set-up only step 4 requires a training phase. The other actions are either fixed (3 and 5) or depend on parser-external processes (1 and 2). Ideally steps 2 and 4 would be the same but unfortunately we have discovered that the combination of representations chunking approach does not work well for non-base phrases. The systems which use the tagging representation perform much worse than the one that uses the bracket representation. The reason for this is that, based on a limited context, it is hard to determine if a word should be included in a chunk at level *n* or at level *n+1*. With the bracket representation, incorrect brackets will be generated but these will be eliminated in the bracket combination process. However, the systems that use the tagging representation produce incorrect B and I tags which cause errors in their output. A combination of the five systems performs worse than the system that uses the bracket representation and therefore we have decided to use only the latter for step 4 of the chunk parser.

In order to be able to compare our results with earlier work like Collins (1999), we have used the Maximum Entropy tagger described in Ratnaparkhi (1996) for assigning part-of-speech tags to our data. The words in the data have been combined to base chunks by the chunking approach described in the previous section. After finding the base phrases, each of them will be replaced by their head (the

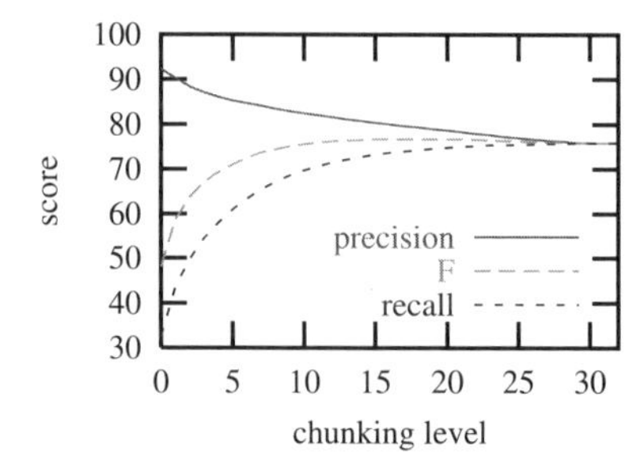

Figure 4: Precision, recall and $F_{\beta=1}$ rates for one run of the parser applied to the parameter tuning data set. The precision decreases when the chunking level increases, the recall increases at higher levels and the F rate increases until about level 19 and drops slightly afterwards (not noticeable in this graph).

most important word in the phrase) and their type, conform figure 3. The head word of each phrase is generated by a list of rules put forward by Magerman (1995) and modified by Collins (1999). [2] It chooses a head word of a phrase based on the type of the phrase, the types/POS tags of the phrases/words immediately under the phrase and the order of the latter. The approach of compressing identified phrases provides us with a standard data format. At all levels of the bottom-up process, sentences are represented by a sequence of lexical items (usually words) with associated syntactic tags (POS tags or phrase type tags).

The parsing process generates a unique tree for each sentence. The tree can be interpreted as a set of phrases. The output of the parser are evaluated with the same measures as the chunking results: labeled precision, labeled recall and $F_{\beta=1}$ rate, all applied to phrases. Additionally we have used the crossing brackets measure (CB) for indicating the average number of identified phrases per sentence that cross phrases in the original data.

4 Results

We have used two segment pairs of the Wall Street Journal (WSJ) part of the Penn Treebank (Marcus, Santorini and Marcinkiewicz 1993) for training and testing. First we used sections 15-18 (8,936 sentences) as training material and section 20 (2012 sentences) as test material for determining the optimal parameters of the parser (tuning data). The best configuration for that data was used for processing section 23 (2416 sentences) after training with sections 02-21 (39,832 sentences). The results for that data set have been used for a comparison with performance of other parsers.

In our first experiment we tested the influence of varying context size and

[2]Available on http://www.research.att.com/~mcollins/papers/heads

	k=1	k=3
c=1	74.13 (18)	70.20 (13)
c=2	77.17 (19)	75.13 (15)
c=3	77.05 (16)	76.02 (16)
c=4	76.33 (15)	75.33 (14)

Table 2: $F_{\beta=1}$ rates for four context sizes combined with two sizes of nearest neighborhood. The parser was tested on the tuning data. The numbers between brackets are the optimal levels at which processing was stopped. We obtained the best $F_{\beta=1}$ rate for context size 2 combined with nearest neighborhood size 1.

neighborhood size in step 4 of the parser, the non-base chunking process. The context size is the number of words and syntactic tags that are used as features, for example context size 2 means that the classification of a word is determined while using the word, the two previous words, the next two words and the syntactic tags of all these words. The size of the neighborhood size determines the number of nearest neighbor regions that the memory-based learner uses to determine the class of the current data item. We have performed experiments with the tuning data with four different symmetric context sizes (1, 2, 3 and 4) and two neighborhood sizes (1 and 3).

Our parsing process works bottom-up, level by level. At each level it finds new phrases and therefore the number of detected phrases is expected to increase which means that the recall rate increases. Unfortunately, since we use one level of training data at a time (like Brants (1999)), the amount of available training data decreases at higher levels and therefore the precision of the recognition process decreases at higher levels (figure 4). Our goal is to optimize the $F_{\beta=1}$ rate of the results. In our experiments with the tuning data set, we have found that this rate reaches an optimum after about 15 levels of phrase recognition. At that point the parser is still finding new phrases but the improved recall rate cannot compensate for the drop in precision rate. For this reason we have decided to stop the cascaded phrase recognition processes in the tuning experiments when the F rate was optimal. We have added a post-processing stage which adds a top S node to trees which do not contain such a node. The results of the eight experiments, F rates and halting levels, can be found in table 2. The configuration with context size 2 and nearest neighborhood size 1 performed best. The best context size found here is the same as used by Ratnaparkhi (1998).

In the next series of experiments, we tested the influence of training data segmentation on parsing performance. In our previous experiments, we only used training data from one level at a time. For example, during identification of phrases at level 1, the ones immediately above the base chunks, we only used training data from level 1. This causes problems at higher levels, for which there are fewer examples available. Ideally, we should be able to use one body of training data for all levels. We have performed two extra experiments with context size 2 and

	$F_{\beta=1}$
using current training level only	77.17 (19)
using current, previous and next	77.13 (17)
using all training data	67.69 (20)
disregarding open bracket types	72.33 (24)
disregarding close bracket types	76.06 (29)

Table 3: The performance of five training variants. In these experiments we used the same context size (2) and nearest neighborhood size (1) but varied the amount of training material used at each chunk level or disregarded the types of the open brackets or close brackets during the bracket combination process. We obtained the best performance when using training data from the current chunking level.

nearest neighborhood size 1: one using all training data apart from the base chunk level (levels 1-31) and another which uses the previous, current and next level. The results can be found in table 3. Neither of the two set-ups performed better than the configuration which uses one level of training data at a time.

Our bracket combination algorithm is very strict: it only uses adjacent brackets if they have the same type and appear next to each other in the correct order (first open and then close) without intervening brackets. Chunkers which use this approach obtain high precision rates and low recall rates because they generate phrases which are likely to be correct and disregard all other phrases (Tjong Kim Sang 2000a). We have tested two alternative approaches: one which uses the type of the close brackets and disregards the type of the open brackets and another which uses the type of the open brackets and ignores close bracket types. The second approach performed better than the first but neither of them improved on the standard method we used for bracket combination (see table 3).

We have applied the best training configuration (context size 2, neighborhood size 1, train with current level and use 19 iterations plus post-processing stage) to the large data set. After training we obtained an $F_{\beta=1}$ rate of 80.49 on arbitrary sentences of the test data (precision 82.34%, recall 78.72% and crossing bracket rate 1.69). Figure 5 contains an overview of the progression of precision, recall and $F_{\beta=1}$ rate measured at different levels. The performance of the chunk parser is reasonable but it does worse than state-of-the-art statistical parsing systems (Collins 1999, Charniak 2000) which achieve $F_{\beta=1}$ rates close to 90 and CB rates under 1.10.[3]

[3]Obviously the parser has problems with deeply embedded sentences, because of the maximum parsing depth (19). However, its performance on short sentence (10 words or shorter) is not perfect either ($F_{\beta=1}$ = 89.5). We have not spotted systematic errors in the parsing output yet.

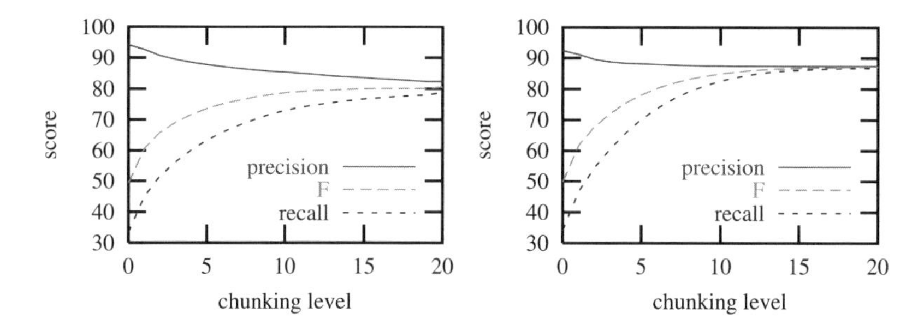

Figure 5: Per-level precision, recall and $F_{\beta=1}$ rates for sentences shorter than 100 words obtained by our chunk parser applied to section 23 of the Penn Treebank (left) compared with the parser of Collins (1999) (right). The parsers have generated 20 levels of chunk tags (0-19). An extra post-processing step (20) has added top S nodes to incomplete parse trees. The precision of the chunk parser drops faster and the recall grows slower than that of the Collins parser. The final F rates are respectively 80.49 and 87.08.

5 Related work

A lot of work has been done on natural language parsing. In this section we mention some of the work which uses machine learning methods for building parsers rather than hand-crafted grammars. Black et.al. (1992) introduce history-based grammars: a statistical parsing model which obtains probabilistic clues of the optimal parses from training data. It is hard to compare their performance with other work because they used different test data and different evaluation methods. Magerman (1995) built SPATTER, a statistical parser which uses decision trees. It obtained an F rate of 86.0 on sentences shorter than 40 words of section 00 of the Penn Treebank.

The parsing method used by Ratnaparkhi (1998) is closely related to our approach. He uses a classification algorithm, maximum entropy models, for building parse trees in a bottom-up, left-to-right fashion. The parser performs better than the previous two and obtains F=86.9 on Penn Treebank section 23. Collins (1999) describes different statistical parsing models. They use complex statistical predicates for deriving optimal parse trees. His best model obtains F=88.2 on section 23. Charniak (2000) combines earlier work by Ratnaparkhi, Collins and himself and creates a parser which obtains an F rate of 89.5 on section 23 of the Penn Treebank. Finally Bod (2000) mentions a parser which performs slightly better by using a big database of stored subtrees of limited depth.

Regarding parsing with chunking techniques, three more papers need to be mentioned. Ejerhed and Church (1983) approach parsing of Swedish by starting with identifying noun phrase chunks. Their approach requires a partial order the non-terminal symbols which limits the format of the trees that can be produced. Abney (1991) describes a parser which starts with identifying base phrases which are combined to a complete tree by an attachment process. Brants (1999) built a bottom-up parser which identifies chunks in German text with Markov models. An interesting feature of his parser is that it is capable of correcting errors made at earlier stages.

6 Discussion

The parsing method described here leaves open many options for future work. An important difference between statistical parsers and our approach is the information that is available to the parser. For example, our chunk parser does not have access to the internal structure of a chunk apart from its type and its head word. If we compare it performance with a study of Charniak (1997) , we note that our parser performs better than a standard probabilistic context-free grammar ($F_{\beta=1}$=73.7) but worse than than the Minimal extension of this grammar ($F_{\beta=1}$=82.8). However, even this Minimal extension is provided with more information than our parser: the rule probabilities depend on the head and the type of the phrase and the type of the parent. The bottom-up parser described in this paper does not have access to information about the parents. The availability of this information would probably improve the parser's performance although it would also complicate the chunk identification processes.

The parser would also benefit from using a less greedy method of bracket prediction which would enable it to backtrack from earlier phrase structures choices at later processing levels. At this moment, it attempts to find the best bracket structure at each level and sticks with that. This is different from most other parsers, like for example the one of Ratnaparkhi (1998) which is capable of storing up to 20 intermediate trees and examines structural extensions of all of them.

Another opportunity for performance enhancement lies in using a different bracket estimation algorithm. At this moment, we feel that we do not have used the best method for finding chunks at the non-base level. We have achieved a reasonable improvement by using combinations of classifiers for chunking rather than a single classifier (Tjong Kim Sang 2000a). Something similar should be possible while identifying higher level chunks, possibly by using a variety of machine learning algorithms. It would also be interesting to examine the process which combines open with close brackets. At this moment combinations are made without regarding more than two brackets. A combination method which examines the complete sentence before creating a bracket pair, like the one of Muñoz, Punyakanok, Roth and Zimak (1999), might improve performance.

Extra improvements of this parser will undoubtfully make it slower and increase its memory requirements. The present process already requires a lot of computational resources: close to 100 megabytes of internal memory for generating base chunks with the small training data at a processing speed of more than a second per word. This is orders of magnitude slower than for example Ratnaparkhi's parser which in 1998 achieved a processing speed of 0.14 seconds per sentence which achieving a higher performance rate (Ratnaparkhi 1998). It is doubtful whether extension of the work reported on here is worth the trouble.

7 Concluding remarks

We have presented a method for transforming a chunker to a full parser. It consists of using a cascade of phrase recognition algorithms for building parse trees in a bottom-up fashion. The advantage of this approach is that it enables building a parser by using the same simple machine learning algorithms (classifiers) which have successfully been used for base phrase recognition. We have tested this approach by converting a chunking algorithm to a parsing algorithm and evaluated the resulting chunk parser on a standard data set. The parser performed reasonably (F=80) but it did not reach the performances of the state-of-art statistical parsers (F=90).

References

Abney, S.(1991), Parsing by chunks, *Principle-Based Parsing*, Kluwer Academic Publishers.

Black, E., Jelinek, F., Lafferty, J., Magerman, D. M., Mercer, R. and Roukos, S.(1992), Towards history-based grammars: Using richer models for probabilistic parsing, *Proceedings DARPA Speech and Natural Language Workshop*, Morgan Kaufmann.

Bod, R.(2000), Parsing with the shortest derivation, *Proceedings of COLING 2000*, Saarbruecken, Germany.

Brants, T.(1999), Cascaded markov models, *Proceedings of EACL'99*, Bergen, Norway.

Charniak, E.(1997), Statistical parsing with a context-free grammar and word statistics, *Fourteenth National Conference on Artificial Intelligence*, MIT Press.

Charniak, E.(2000), A maximum-entropy-inspired parser, *Proceedings of the ANLP-NAACL 2000*, Seattle, WA, USA. Morgan Kaufman Publishers.

Church, K. W.(1988), A stochastic parts program and noun phrase parser for unrestricted text, *Second Conference on Applied Natural Language Processing*, Austin, Texas.

Collins, M.(1999), *Head-Driven Statistical Models for Natural Language Processing*, PhD thesis, University of Pennsylvania.

Daelemans, W., Zavrel, J., van der Sloot, K. and van den Bosch, A.(1999), *TiMBL: Tilburg Memory Based Learner, version 2.0, Reference Guide*, ILK Technical Report 99-01. http://ilk.kub.nl/.

Ejerhed, E. and Church, K. W.(1983), Finite state parsing, *Papers from the Seventh Scandinavian Conference of Linguistics*, University of Helsinki, Finland.

Magerman, D. M.(1995), Statistical decision-tree models for parsing, *Proceedings of the 33rd Annual Meeting of the Association for Computational Linguistics (ACL'95)*, Cambridge, MA, USA.

Marcus, M. P., Santorini, B. and Marcinkiewicz, M. A.(1993), Building a large annotated corpus of english: the penn treebank, *Computational Linguistics*.

Muñoz, M., Punyakanok, V., Roth, D. and Zimak, D.(1999), A learning approach to shallow parsing, *Proceedings of EMNLP-WVLC'99*, Association for Computational Linguistics.

Ramshaw, L. A. and Marcus, M. P.(1995), Text chunking using transformation-based learning, *Proceedings of the Third ACL Workshop on Very Large Corpora*, Cambridge, MA, USA.

Ratnaparkhi, A.(1996), A maximum entropy model for part-of-speech tagging, *Proceedings of EMNLP-1*, University of Pennsylvania, PA, USA.

Ratnaparkhi, A.(1998), *Maximum Entropy Models for Natural Language Ambiguity Resolution*, PhD thesis Computer and Information Science, University of Pennsylvania.

Tjong Kim Sang, E. F.(2000a), Noun phrase recognition by system combination, *Proceedings of the ANLP-NAACL 2000*, Seattle, Washington, USA. Morgan Kaufman Publishers.

Tjong Kim Sang, E. F.(2000b), Text chunking by system combination, *Proceedings of CoNLL-2000 and LLL-2000*, Lisbon, Portugal.

Automatic detection of problematic turns in human-machine interactions

Antal van den Bosch, Emiel Krahmer† and Marc Swerts†,‡*

∗ *ILK Research Group / Computational Linguistics, Tilburg University*
† *IPO, Center for User-System Interaction, Eindhoven University of Technology*
‡ *CNTS, Center for Dutch Language and Speech, University of Antwerp, UIA*

Abstract

This paper addresses the issue of on-line detection of communication problems in spoken dialogue systems. In particular, the usefulness is investigated of the sequence of system question types and the word graphs corresponding to the respective user utterances. By applying both rule-induction and memory-based learning techniques to data obtained with a Dutch train time-table information system, the current paper demonstrates that the aforementioned features indeed lead to a method for problem detection that performs significantly above baseline. The results are interesting from a dialogue perspective since they employ features that are present in the majority of spoken dialogue systems and can be obtained with little or no computational overhead. The results are also interesting from a machine learning perspective, since they show that the rule-based method performs significantly better than the memory-based method, because the former is better capable of representing interactions between features.

1 Introduction

Given the state of the art of current language and speech technology, communication problems are unavoidable in present-day spoken dialogue systems. The main source of these problems lies in the imperfections of automatic speech recognition, but also incorrect interpretations by the natural language understanding module or wrong default assumptions by the dialogue manager are likely to lead to confusion. If a spoken dialogue system had the ability to detect communication problems on-line and with high accuracy, it might be able to correct certain errors or it could interact with the user to solve them.

Recently there has been an increased interest in developing automatic methods to detect problematic dialogue situations using machine learning techniques. For instance, Litman et al. (1999) and Walker et al. (2000a) use RIPPER (Cohen 1996) to classify problematic and unproblematic dialogues. Following up on this, Walker et al. (2000b) aim at detecting problems *at the utterance level*, based on data obtained with AT&Ts *How May I Help You* (HMIHY) system (Gorin et al., 1997). Walker and co-workers apply RIPPER to 43 features which are automatically generated by three modules of the HMIHY system, namely the speech recognizer (ASR), the natural language understanding module (NLU) and the dialogue manager (DM). The best result is obtained using all features: communication problems are detected with an accuracy of 86%, a precision of 83% and a recall of 75%. It should be noted that the NLU features play first fiddle among the set of all features. In fact, using only the NLU features performs comparable to using all features. Walker et al. (2000b) also briefly compare the performance of RIPPER with some other machine learning approaches, and show that it performs comparable to a memory-based (instance-based) learning algorithm (IB, see Aha et al. 1991).

The results which Walker and co-workers describe show that it is possible to automatically detect communication problems in the HMIHY system, using machine learning techniques. Their approach also raises a number of interesting follow-up questions, some concerned with problem detection, others with the use of machine learning techniques. (1) Walker et al. train their classifier on a large set of features, and show that the set of features produced by the NLU module are the most important ones. However, this leaves an important general question unanswered, namely which particular features contribute to what extent? (2) Moreover, the set of features which the NLU module produces are highly specific to the HMIHY system and indicate things like the percentage of the input covered by the relevant grammar fragment, the presence or absence of context shifts, and the semantic diversity of subsequent utterances. Many current day spoken dialogue systems do not have such a sophisticated NLU module, and consequently it is unlikely that they have access to these kinds of features. In sum, it is uncertain whether other spoken dialogue systems can benefit from the findings described by Walker et al. (2000b), since it is unclear which features are important and to what extent these features are available in other spoken dialogue systems. Finally, (3) we agree with Walker et al. (and the machine learning community at large) that it is important to compare different machine learning techniques to find out which techniques perform well for which kinds of tasks. Walker et al. found that RIPPER does not perform significantly better or worse than a memory-based learning technique. Is this incidental or does it reflect a general property of the problem detection task?

The current paper uses a similar methodology for on-line problem detection as Walker et al. (2000b), but (1) we take a *bottom-up* approach, focussing on a small number of features and investigating their usefulness on a per-feature basis and (2) the features which we study are automatically available in the majority of current spoken dialogue system, namely the sequence of system question types and the word graphs corresponding to the respective user utterances. A word graph consists of a lattice of word hypotheses, and we assume that various features which have been shown to cue communication problems (prosodic, linguistic and ASR features, see e.g., Hirschberg et al., 1999, Krahmer et al. 1999 and Swerts et al., 2000) may have some correlate in the word graph. The sequence of system question types is taken to model the dialogue history. Finally, (3) to gain further insight into the adequacy of various machine learning techniques for problem detection we use both RIPPER and the memory-based IB1-IG algorithm (Aha et al., 1991, Daelemans et al., 1997).

baseline	acc (%)	prec (%)	rec (%)	$F_{\beta=1}$
majority-class	58.2±0.4	—	0.0	—
system-knows	85.6±0.4	100	65.5	79.1

Table 1: Baselines

We shall see that on the basis of the previous and the current word graph and the six most recent system question types communication problems can be determined with an accuracy of 91%, which is a significant improvement of the relevant baseline. This shows that spoken dialogue systems may use these features to better predict whether the ongoing dialogue is problematic. These features are present in many spoken dialogue system and do not require additional computation, which makes this a very cheap method to detect problems. In addition, the current work is interesting from a machine learning perspective; we shall describe some interesting differences between IB1-IG and RIPPER.

2 Approach

2.1. Data and Labelling The corpus we used consisted of 3739 question-answer pairs, taken from 444 complete dialogues. The dialogues consist of users interacting with a Dutch spoken dialogue system which provides information about train time tables. The system prompts the user for unknown slots, such as departure station, arrival station, date, etc., in a series of questions. The system uses a combination of implicit and explicit verification strategies.

The data were annotated with a highly limited set of features. In particular, the kind of system question and whether the reply of the user gave rise to communication problems or not. The latter feature is the one to be predicted. The following labels are used for the system questions.

O open questions ("From where to where do you want to travel?")

I implicit verification ("When do you want to travel from Tilburg to Schiphol Airport?")

E explicit verification ("So you want to travel from Tilburg to Schiphol Airport?")

Y yes/no question ("Do you want me to repeat the connection?")

M Meta-questions ("Can you please correct me?")

The difference between an explicit verification and a yes/no question is that the former but not the latter is aimed at checking whether what the system understood or assumed corresponds with what the user wants. If the current system question is a repetition of the previous question it asked, this is indicated by the suffix R. A question only counts as a repetition when it has the same *contents* as the previous system question. Of the user inputs, we only labelled whether they gave rise to a communication problem or not. A communication problem arises when the value which the system assigns to a particular slot does not coincide with the value given by the user in his or her most recent contribution to the dialogue or when the system makes an incorrect default assumption (e.g., the dialogue manager assumes that the user wants to travel today). Communication problems are generally easy to determine since the spoken dialogue system under consideration here always provides direct feedback (*via* verification questions) about what it believes the user intends. Consider the following exchange.

> U: I want to go to Amsterdam.
> S: So you want to go to Rotterdam?

As soon as the user hears the explicit verification question of the system, it will be clear that his or her last turn was misunderstood. The problem-feature was labelled by two of the authors to avoid labelling errors. Differences between the two annotators were infrequent and could always easily be resolved.

2.2 Baselines Of the 3739 user utterances 1564 gave rise to communication problems (an error rate of 41.8%). The majority class is thus formed by the unproblematic user utterances, which form 58.2% of all user utterances. This suggests that the baseline for predicting communication problems is obtained by always predicting that there are no communication problems. This strategy has an accuracy of 58.2%, and a recall of 0% (all problems are missed). The precision is undefined,[1] and consequently neither is the $F_{\beta=1}$.[2] This baseline is misleading, however, when we are interested in predicting whether the previous user utterance gave rise to communication strategies. There are cases when the dialogue system is itself clearly aware of communication problems. This is in particular the case when the system repeats the question (labelled with the suffix R) or when it asks a meta-question (M). In the corpus under investigation here this happens 1024 times. It would not be very illuminating to develop an automatic error detector which detects only those problems that the system was already aware of. Therefore we take the following as our base-line strategy for predicting whether the previous user utterance gave rise to problems, henceforth referred to as the system-knows-baseline:

if the Q(t) is repetition or meta-question,
then predict user utterance t-1 caused problems,
else predict user utterance t-1 caused no problems.

This 'strategy' predicts problems with an accuracy of 85.6% (1024 of the 1564 problems are predicted, thus 540 of the 3739 decisions are wrong), a pre-

[1] Since 0 cases are selected, one would have to divide by 0 to determine precision for this baseline.
[2] Throughout this paper we use the $F_{\beta=1}$ measure (van Rijsbergen 1979:174) to combine precision and recall in a single measure. By setting β equal to 1, precision and recall are given an equal weight, and the F measure simplifies to $2PR/(P+R)$ (P = precision, R = recall).

cision of 100% (of the 1024 predicted problems 1024 were indeed problematic), a recall of 65.5% (1024 of the 1564 problems are predicted to be problematic) and thus an $F_{\beta=1}$ of 79.1. This is a sharp baseline, but for predicting whether the previous user utterance caused problems or not the system-knows-baseline is much more informative and relevant than the majority-class-baseline. Table 1 summarizes the baselines.

2.3 Feature representations Question-answer pairs were represented as feature vectors (or patterns) of the following form. Six features were reserved for the history of system questions asked so far in the current dialogue (6Q). Of course, if the system only asked 3 questions so far, only 3 types of system questions are stored in memory and the remaining three features for system question are not assigned a value. The representation of the user's answer is derived from the word graph produced by the ASR module. It should be kept in mind that in general the word graph is much more complex than the recognized string. The latter typically is the most plausible path (e.g., on the basis of acoustic confidence scores) in the word graph, which itself may contain many other paths. Different systems determine the plausibility of paths in the word graph in different ways. Here, for the sake of generality, we abstract over such differences and simply represent a word graph as a Bag of Words (BoW), collecting all words that occur in one of the paths, irrespective of the associated acoustic confidence score. A lexicon was derived of all the words and phrases (such as "dank je wel", *thank you*) that occurred in the corpus. Each word graph is represented as a sequence of bits, where the i-th bit is set to 1 if the i-th word in the pre-derived lexicon occurred at least once in the word graph corresponding to the current user utterance and 0 otherwise. Finally, for each user utterance, a feature is reserved for indicating whether it gave rise to communication problems or not. This latter feature is the one to be predicted.

There are generally two approaches for detecting communication problems. One is to try to decide on the basis of the *current* user utterance whether it will be recognized and interpreted correctly or not. The other approach uses the current user utterance to determine whether the processing of the previous user utterance gave rise to communication problems. This approach is based on the assumption that users give feedback on communication problems when they notice that the system misunderstood their previous input. In this study, eight prediction tasks have been defined: the first three are concerned with predicting whether the current user input will cause problems, and naturally, for these three tasks, the majority-class-baseline is the relevant one; the last five tasks are concerned with predicting whether the previous user utterance caused problems, and for these five tasks the sharp, system-knows-baseline is the appropriate one. The eight tasks are: (1) predict on the basis of the (representation of the) current word graph BoW t whether the current user utterance (at time t) will cause a communication problem, (2) predict on the basis of the six most recent system question up to t (6Q t), whether the current user utterance will cause a communication problem, (3) predict on the basis of both BoW t and 6Q t, whether the current user utterance will cause a problem, (4) predict on the basis of the current word graph BoW t, whether the previous user utterance, uttered at time t-1, caused a problem, (5) predict on the basis of the six most recent system questions, whether the previous user utterance caused a problem, (6) predict on the basis of BoW t and 6Q t, whether the previous user utterance caused a problem, (7) predict on the basis of the two most recent word graphs, BoW t-1 and BoW t, whether the previous user utterance caused a problem, and finally (8) predict on the basis of the two most recent word graphs, BoW t-1 and BoW t, and the six most recent system question types 6Q t, whether the previous user utterance caused a problem.

2.4 Learning techniques For the experiments we used the rule-induction algorithm RIPPER (Cohen 1996) and the memory-based IB1-IG algorithm (Aha et al. 1991, Daelemans et al., 1997).[3]

RIPPER is a fast rule induction algorithm. It starts with splitting the training set in two. On the basis of one half, it induces rules in a straightforward way (roughly, by trying to maximize coverage for each rule), with potential overfitting. When the induced rules classify instances in the other half below a certain threshold, they are not stored. Rules are induced per class. By default the ordering is from low-frequency classes to high frequency ones, leaving the most frequent class as the default rule, which is generally beneficial for the size of the rule set.

The memory-based IB1-IG algorithm is one of the primary memory-based learning algorithms. Memory-based learning techniques can be characterized by the fact that they store a representation of some set of training data in memory, and classify new instances by looking for the most similar instances in memory. The most basic distance function between two features is the *overlap metric* in (1), where $\Delta(X, Y)$ is the distance between patterns X and Y (both consisting of n features) and δ is the distance between the features. If X is the test-case, the Δ measure determines which group k of cases Y in memory is the most similar to X. The most frequent value for the relevant category in k is the predicted value for X. Usually, k is set to 1. Since some features are more important than others, a weighting function w_i is used. Here w_i is the gain ratio measure. In sum, the weighted distance between vectors X and Y of length n is determined by the following equation where $\delta(x_i, y_i)$ gives a point-wise distance between features which is 1 if $x_i \neq y_i$ and 0 otherwise.

$$\Delta(X, Y) = \sum_{i=1}^{n} \delta(x_i, y_i) \qquad (1)$$

Both learning techniques were used for the same 8 prediction tasks, and received exactly the same feature vectors as input. All experiments were performed using ten-fold cross-validation, which also yields errors margins in the prediction accuracy.

[3]We used the TiMBL software package, version 3 (Daelemans et al., 2000) to run the IB1-IG experiments.

input features	problem at	acc (%)	prec (%)	rec (%)	$F_{\beta=1}$
BoW t	t	63.2±4.1[a]	57.1±5.0	49.6±3.8	53.0±3.8
6Q t	t	63.7±2.3[a]	56.1±3.4	60.8±5.0	58.3±3.6
BoW t + 6Q t	t	63.5±2.0[a]	57.5±2.8	49.1±3.3	52.8±1.9
BoW t	t-1	61.9±2.3	55.1±2.6	48.8±1.9	51.7±1.2
6Q t	t-1	82.4±2.0	85.6±3.8	69.6±3.7	76.6±3.5
BoW t + 6Q t	t-1	87.3±1.1[b]	85.5±2.8	83.9±1.3	84.7±1.3
BoW t-1 + BoW t	t-1	73.5±1.7	69.8±3.8	64.6±2.3	67.0±2.3
BoW t-1 + BoW t + 6Q t	t-1	88.1±1.1[b]	91.1±2.4	79.3±3.1	84.8±2.0

Table 2: IB1-IG results (accuracy, precision, recall, and $F_{\beta=1}$, with standard deviations) on the eight prediction tasks. [a]: this accuracy significantly improves the majority-class-baseline ($p < .001$). [b]: this accuracy significantly improves the system-knows-baseline ($p < .001$).

input	problem at	acc (%)	prec (%)	rec (%)	$F_{\beta=1}$
BoW t	t	65.1±2.4[a]	58.3±3.4	59.8±4.2	58.9±2.0
6Q t	t	65.9±2.1[a,*]	58.9±3.5	60.7±4.8	59.7±3.2
BoW t + 6Q t	t	66.0±2.3[a,‡]	64.8±2.6	50.3±3.1	56.5±1.1
BoW t	t-1	63.2±2.5	60.3±5.5	36.1±5.5	44.8±4.6
6Q t	t-1	83.4±1.6	99.8±0.4	60.4±3.1	75.2±2.4
BoW t + 6Q t	t-1	90.0±2.1[b,†]	93.2±1.7	82.5±4.5	87.5±2.6
BoW t-1 + BoW t	t-1	76.7±2.6[†]	74.7±3.6	66.0±5.7	69.9±3.8
BoW t-1 + BoW t + 6Q t	t-1	91.1±1.1[b,†]	92.6±2.0	85.7±2.9	89.0±1.5

Table 3: RIPPER results (accuracy, precision, recall, and $F_{\beta=1}$, with standard deviations) on the eight prediction tasks. [a]: this accuracy significantly improves the majority-class-baseline ($p < .001$). [b]: this accuracy significantly improves the system-knows-baseline ($p < .001$). [*]: this accuracy result is significantly better than the IB1-IG result given in Table 2 for this particular task, with $p < .05$. [†]: this accuracy result is significantly better than the IB1-IG result given in Table 2 for this particular task, with $p < .001$. [‡]: this accuracy result is significantly better than the IB1-IG result given in Table 2 for this particular task, with $p < .01$.

3 Results

We first describe the results obtained with the IB1-IG algorithm and displayed in Table 2. Consider the problem of predicting whether the current user utterance will cause problems. Either looking at the current word graph (BoW t), at the six most recent system questions (6Q t) or at both, leads to a significant improvement with respect to the majority-class-baseline.[4] The best results are obtained with only the six system question types (although the difference with the results for the other two tasks is not significant): a 63.7% accuracy and an $F_{\beta=1}$ of 58.3. However, even though this is a significant improvement over the majority-class-baseline, the accuracy is improved with only 5.5%.[5]

Next consider the problem of predicting whether the *previous* user utterance caused communication problems (these are the five remaining tasks). The best result is obtained by taking the two most recent word graphs and the six most recent system question types as input. This yields an accuracy of 88.1%, which is a significant improvement with respect to the sharp, system-knows-baseline. In addition, the $F_{\beta=1}$ of 84.8 is nearly 6 points higher than that of the relevant, majority-class baseline.

The results obtained with RIPPER are shown in Table 3. On the problem of predicting whether the current user utterance will cause a problem, RIPPER obtains the best results by taking as input both the current word graph and the types of the six most recent system question, predicting problems with an accuracy of 66.0%. This is a significant improvement over the majority-class-baseline, but the result is not significantly better than that obtained with either the word graph or the system questions in isolation. Interestingly, the result *is* significantly better than the results for IB1-IG on the same task.

On the problem of predicting whether the previous user utterance caused a problem, RIPPER obtains the best results by taking all features into account (that is: the two most recent bags of words and the six system questions).[6] This results in a 91.1% accuracy, which is a significant improvement over the sharp system-knows-baseline (an error-reduction of more than 38%). Moreover, the $F_{\beta=1}$ is 89, which is 10 points higher than the $F_{\beta=1}$ associated with the system-knows baseline strategy. Notice also that this RIPPER result is significantly better than the IB1-IG results for the same task.

To gain insight into the rules learned by RIPPER for the last task, we applied RIPPER to the complete data set. The rules induced are displayed in Figure 1. RIPPER's first rule is concerned with repeated questions (compare the system-knows-

[4] All checks for significance were performed with a one-tailed t test.

[5] As an aside, we performed one experiment with the words in the actual, transcribed user utterance at time t instead of BoW t, where the task is to predict whether the current user utterance would cause a communication problem. This resulted in an accuracy of 64.2% (with a standard deviation of 1.1%). This is not significantly better than the result obtained with the BoW.

[6] Notice that RIPPER sometimes performs *below* the system-knows-baseline, even though the relevant feature (in particular the type of the last system question) is present. Inspection of the RIPPER rules obtained by training only on 6Q reveals that RIPPER learns a slightly suboptimal ruleset, thereby misclassifying 10 instances on average.

1.	**if** Q (t) = R, **then** *problem.*	(939/2)
2.	**if** Q (t) = I ∧ "naar" ∈ BoW (t-1) ∧ "naar" ∈ BoW(t) ∧ "om" ∉ BoW (t) **then** *problem.*	(135/16)
3.	**if** "uur" ∈ BoW(t-1) ∧ "om" ∈ BoW(t-1) ∧ "uur" ∈ BoW(t) ∧ "om" ∈ BoW(t) **then** *problem.*	(57/4)
4.	**if** Q(t) = I ∧ Q(t-3) = I ∧ "uur" ∈ BoW (t-1) **then** *problem.*	(13/2)
5.	**if** "naar" ∈ BoW(t-1) ∧ "vanuit" ∈ BoW (t) ∧ "van" ∉ BoW(t) **then** *problem.*	(29/4)
6.	**if** Q(t-1) = I ∧ "uur" ∈ BoW (t-1) ∧ "nee" ∈ BoW (t) **then** *problem.*	(28/7)
7.	**if** Q(t) = I ∧ "ik" ∈ BoW(t-1) ∧ "van" ∈ BoW(t-1) ∧ "van" ∈ BoW(t) **then** *problem.*	(22/8)
8.	**if** Q(t) = I ∧ "van" ∈ BoW (t-1) ∧ "om" ∈ BoW(t-1) **then** *problem.*	(16/6)
9.	**if** Q(t) = E ∧ "nee" ∈ BoW (t) **then** *problem.*	(42/10)
10.	**if** Q(t) = M ∧ BoW (t-1) = ∅ **then** *problem.*	(20/0)
11.	**if** Q(t-1) = O ∧ "ik" ∈ BoW (t) ∧ "niet" in BoW(t) **then** *problem.*	(10/2)
12.	**if** Q(t-2) = I ∧ Q(t) = O ∧ "wil" ∈ BoW(t-1) **then** *problem.*	(8/0)
13.	**else** *no problem.*	(2114/245)

Figure 1: RIPPER rule set for predicting whether user utterance t-1 caused communication problems on the basis of the Bags of Words for t and t-1, and the six most recent system questions. Based on the entire training set. The question features are defined in section 2. The word "naar" is Dutch for *to*, "om" for *at*, "uur" for *hour*, "van" for *from*, "vanuit" is slightly archaic variant of "van" (*from*), "ik" is Dutch for *I*, "nee" for *no*, "niet" for *not* and "wil", finally, for *want*. The (n/m) numbers at the end of each line indicate how many correct (n) and incorrect (m) decisions were taken using this particular **if** ... **then** ... statement.

baseline). One important property of many other rules is that they explicitly combine pieces of information from the three main sources of information (the system questions, the current word graph and the previous word graph). Moreover, it is interesting to note that the words which crop up in the RIPPER rules are primarily function words. Another noteworthy feature of the RIPPER rules is that they reflect certain properties which have been claimed to cue communication problems. For instance, Krahmer et al. (1999), in their descriptive analysis of dialogue problems, found that repeated material is often an indication of problems, as is the use of a marked vocabulary. The rules 2, 3 and 7 are examples of the former cue, while the occurrence of the somewhat archaic "vanuit" instead of the ordinary "van" is an example of the latter.

4 Discussion

In this study we have looked at auotmatic methods for problem detection using simple features which are available in the vast majority of spoken dialogue systems, and require little or no computional overhead. We have investigated two approaches to problem detection. The first approach is aimed at testing whether a user utterance, captured in a noisy[7] word graph, and/or the recent history of system utterances, would be predictive of whether the utterance itself would be misrecognised. The results, which basically represents a signal quality test, show that problematic cases could be discerned with an accuracy of about 65%. Although this is somewhat above the baseline of 58% decision accuracy when no problems would be predicted, signalling recognition problems with word graph features and previous system questions as predictors is a hard task; as other studies suggest (e.g., Hirschberg et al., 1999), confidence scores and acoustic/prosodic features could be of help.

The second approach aimed to predict on the basis of word graph for the current user utterance and/or the recent history of system question types could be employed to predict whether the *previous* user utterance caused communication problems. The underlying assumption is that users will signal problems as soon as they become aware of them through the feedback provided by the system. Thus, in a sense, this second approach represents a noisy channel filtering task: the current utterance has to be decoded as signalling a problem or not. As the results show, this task can be performed at a surprisingly high level (about 91% decision accuracy, with an $F_{\beta=1}$ of the problem category of 89), but only when the recent history of system questions is also taken into account as predictive features. Neither the word graph features in isolation nor the system question types in isolation offer enough predictive power to reach above the sharp baseline of 86% accuracy and an $F_{\beta=1}$ on the problem category of 79.

Keeping information sources isolated or combining them influences directly the relative performances of the memory-based IB1-IG algorithm versus the RIPPER rule induction algorithm on the second task. When features are of the same type (i.e., all word graph features, or all system question types), accuracies of the

[7] In the sense that it is not a perfect image of the users input.

memory-based and the rule-induction systems do not differ significantly (with one exception). In contrast, when word graph features are combined with question type features, as is necessary to perform beyond baseline accuracy, RIPPER profits more than IB1-IG does, causing RIPPER to perform significantly more accurately. The feature independence assumption of memory-based learning appears to be the harming cause: by its definition, IB1-IG does not give extra weight to apparently relevant interactions of feature values from different sources. In contrast, in nine out of the twelve rules that RIPPER produces, word graph features and system questions type features are explicitly integrated as joint left-hand side conditions.

On a global level, the results show that for on-line detection of communication problems at the utterance level it is already beneficial to pay attention only to the lexical information in the word graph and the sequence of system question types. These features are present in most spoken dialogue system and can be obtained with little or no computational overhead.

Bibliography

Aha, D., Kibler, D. and Albert, M. (1991), Instance-based Learning Algorithms, *Machine Learning*, **6**:36-66.

Cohen, W. (1996), Learning trees and rules with set-valued features, *Proceedings of the 13th National Conference on Artificial Intelligence* (AAAI).

Daelemans, W., van den Bosch, A. and Weijters, A. (1997), IGTree: using trees for compression and classification in lazy learning algorithms, *Artificial Intelligence Review* **11**, 407–423.

Daelemans, W., Zavrel, J., van der Sloot, K. & van den Bosch, A. (2000), *TiMBL: Tilburg Memory-Based Learner, version 3.0, reference guide*, ILK Technical Report 00-01, http://ilk.kub.nl/~ilk/papers/ilk0001.ps.gz.

Gorin, A., Riccardi, G., Wright, J. (1997), How may I Help You?, *Speech Communication* 23:113-127.

Hirschberg, J., Litman, D. & Swerts, M. (1999), Prosodic cues to recognition errors, in: *Proceedings of the 1999 International Workshop on Automatic Speech Recognition and Understanding* (ASRU), Keystone, CO, December 1999.

Krahmer, E., Swerts, M., Theune, M., Weegels, M., (1999), Error spotting in human-machine interactions, *Proceedings of the European Conference on Speech Communication and Technology* (EUROSPEECH), Budapest, Hungary.

Litman, D., Walker, M.A. & Kearns, M. (1999), Automatic Detection of Poor Speech Recognition at the Dialogue Level. In: *Proceedings of the Annual Meeting of the Association for Computational Linguistics* (ACL'99), pp. 309-316, College Park, MD, June 1999.

van Rijsbergen, C.J. (1979), *Information Retrieval*, London: Buttersworth.

Swerts, M., Litman, D. & Hirschberg, J. (2000), Corrections in spoken dialogue systems, *Proceedings of the International Conference on Spoken Language Processing* (ICSLP 2000), Beijing, China.

Walker, M., Langkilde, I., Wright, J., Gorin, A., Litman, D. (2000a), Learning to predict problematic situations in a spoken dialogue system: Experiment with How May I Help You?, *Proceedings of the First North-American Chapter of the Association for Computational Linguistics* (NAACL), Seattle, WA.

Walker, M., Wright, J. Langkilde, I. (2000b), Using natural language processing and discourse features to identify understanding errors in a spoken dialogue system, *Proceedings of the Interntational Conference on Machine Learning* (ICML), Stanford, CA.

List of Contributors

Julie Carson-Berndsen

Department of Computer Science, University College Dublin
Belfield, Dublin 4, Ireland
Julie.Berndsen@ucd.ie

Lars Borin

Department of Linguistics, Uppsala University
PO Box 527, SE-751 20 Uppsala, Sweden
Lars.Borin@ling.uu.se

Antal van den Bosch

ILK Research Group / Computational Linguistics, Tilburg University
PO Box 90153, NL-5000 LE Tilburg
Antal.vdnBosch@kub.nl

Gosse Bouma

Alfa-informatica, Rijksuniversiteit Groningen
PO Box 716, NL-9700 AS Groningen
gosse@let.rug.nl

Gregory Grefenstette

Clairvoyance Corporation
5301 Fifth Avenue, Pittsburgh, PA 15232, United States of America
grefen@clairvoyancecorp.com

Pius ten Hacken

Abteilung für Geisteswissenschaftliche Informatik, Universität Basel
Petersgraben 51, CH-4051 Basel, Switzerland
pius.tenhacken@unibas.ch

Heleen Hoekstra

UiL-OTS, Utrecht University
Trans 10, NL-3512 JK Utrecht, The Netherlands
Heleen.Hoekstra@let.uu.nl

Gina Joue

Department of Computer Science, University College Dublin
Belfield, Dublin 4, Ireland
Gina.Joue@ucd.ie

André Kempe

Xerox Research Centre Europe, Grenoble Laboratory
6 chemin de Maupertuis, 38240 Meylan, France
andre.kempe@xrce.xerox.com

Leila Kosseim

RALI, Universit de Montral
Pavillon Andr-Aisenstadt, 2920 chemin de la Tour,
Local 2194, Montral, Qubec, H3T 1J8, Canada
kosseim@iro.umontreal.ca

Wessel Kraaij

TNO TPD
PO Box 155, 2600 AD Delft, The Netherlands
kraaij@tpd.tno.nl

Emiel Krahmer

Computational Linguistics, Tilburg University
PO Box 90153, 5000 LE Tilburg, The Netherlands
e.j.krahmer@kub.nl

Robert Malouf

Alfa-informatica, Rijksuniversiteit Groningen
PO Box 716, NL-9700 AS Groningen, The Netherlands
malouf@let.rug.nl

S. Marcus

Romanian Academy
Calea Victoriei 125, 71103 Bucureşti, Romania
smarcus@imar.ro

C. Martín-Vide

Research Group in Mathematical Linguistics, Rovira i Virgili University
Pl. Imperial Tàrraco 1, 43005 Tarragona, Spain

cmv@astor.urv.es

V. Mitrana

Faculty of Mathematics, University of Bucharest
Str. Academiei 14, 70109, Bucharest, Romania
mitrana@funinf.cs.unibuc.ro

Michael Moortgat

Utrecht institute of Linguistics OTS
Trans 10, 3512 JK Utrecht, The Netherlands
Michael.Moortgat@let.uu.nl

Richard Moot

Utrecht institute of Linguistics OTS
Trans 10, 3512 JK Utrecht, The Netherlands
Richard.Moot@let.uu.nl

Gertjan van Noord

Alfa-informatica, Rijksuniversiteit Groningen
PO Box 716, NL-9700 AS Groningen, The Netherlands
vannoord@let.rug.nl

Gh. Păun

Institute of Mathematics of the Romanian Academy
PO Box 1-764, 70700 Bucureşti, Romania
gpaun@imar.ro

Renée Pohlmann

TNO TPD
PO Box 155, 2600 AD Delft, The Netherlands
pohlmann@tpd.tno.nl

Thierry Poibeau

Laboratoire Central de Recherches, Thales/LCR, and
Laboratoire d'Informatique, Université de Paris-Nord, Institut Galilée,
avenue J.-B. Clément, F-93430 Villetaneuse, France
Thierry.Poibeau@lcr.thomson-csf.com

Klas Prütz

Department of Linguistics, Uppsala University
PO Box 527, SE-751 20 Uppsala, Sweden
Klas.Prytz@ling.uu.se

Ineke Schuurman

Centre for Computational Linguistics, K.U.Leuven
Maria-Theresiastraat 21, B-3000 Leuven, Belgium
Ineke.Schuurman@ccl.kuleuven.ac.be

Ielka van der Sluis

Computational Linguistics, Tilburg University
PO Box 90153, NL-5000 LE Tilburg, The Netherlands
if.vdrsluis@kub.nl

Marc Swerts

CNTS - Language Technology Group, University of Antwerp
Universiteitsplein 1, B-2610 Wilrijk, Belgium
M.G.J.Swerts@tue.nl

Erik F. Tjong Kim Sang

CNTS - Language Technology Group, University of Antwerp
Universiteitsplein 1, B-2610 Wilrijk, Belgium
erikt@uia.ua.ac.be

Michael Walsh

Department of Computer Science, University College Dublin
Belfield, Dublin 4, Ireland
Michael.Walsh@ucd.ie